# WHEN
# WOMEN
# RULED
# THE
# WORLD

ALSO BY MAUREEN QUILLIGAN

*Incest and Agency in Elizabeth's England*

*The Allegory of Female Authority:*
*Christine de Pizan's* Cité des Dames

*Milton's Spenser: The Politics of Reading*

*The Language of Allegory: Defining the Genre*

# WHEN WOMEN RULED THE WORLD

*Making the Renaissance in Europe*

## Maureen Quilligan

LIVERIGHT PUBLISHING CORPORATION

A Division of W. W. Norton & Company

*Independent Publishers Since 1923*

For information about permission to reproduce selections from this book, write to
Permissions, Liveright Publishing Corporation, a division of W. W. Norton & Company, Inc.,
500 Fifth Avenue, New York, NY 10110

For information about special discounts for bulk purchases, please contact
W. W. Norton Special Sales at specialsales@wwnorton.com or 800-233-4830

Manufacturing by Lakeside Book Company
Book design by Beth Steidle
Production manager: Beth Steidle

Library of Congress Cataloging-in-Publication Data

Names: Quilligan, Maureen, 1944– author.
Title: When women ruled the world : making the Renaissance in Europe / Maureen Quilligan.
Description: First edition. | New York : Liveright Publishing Corporation, [2021] |
Includes bibliographical references and index.
Identifiers: LCCN 2021033989 | ISBN 9781631497964 (hardcover) |
ISBN 9781631497971 (epub)
Subjects: LCSH: Queens—Europe—History—16th century. | Women heads of state—
Europe—History—16th century. | Europe—Politics and government—1492–1648. |
Mary I, Queen of England, 1516–1558. | Elizabeth I, Queen of England, 1533–1603. |
Mary, Queen of Scots, 1542–1587. | Catherine de Médicis, Queen, consort of Henry II,
King of France, 1519–1589. | Renaissance.
Classification: LCC D226.7 .Q55 2021 | DDC 321/.60940903—dc23
LC record available at https://lccn.loc.gov/2021033989

Liveright Publishing Corporation, 500 Fifth Avenue, New York, N.Y. 10110
www.wwnorton.com

W. W. Norton & Company Ltd., 15 Carlisle Street, London W1D 3BS

1  2  3  4  5  6  7  8  9  0

*To Maggie Malone and*
*Maisie Malone Shakman.*
*May they rule long and well.*

# CONTENTS

❧

# PART III
## THE MEDICI

# PART IV
## THE HAPSBURGS

# Inalienable Posessions and Female Power

In 1558, when John Knox, the radical Scottish religious reformer, published his misogynist tract, *The First Blast of the Trumpet against the Monstrous Regiment of Women*, he called attention to what was strangely true in the middle of the sixteenth century in Europe: a remarkable number of women had ascended to supreme governmental power. Knox was outraged and argued that "To promote a Woman to bear rule, superiority, domin-ion or empire above any realm, nation or city is: *A. Repugnant to nature. B. Contumely to GOD. C. The subversion of good order, of all equity and justice.*"

Knox was focused on two women then ruling in Britain: Marie de Guise, who was governing as regent for her daughter, Mary, Queen of Scots, and Mary Tudor, who had only five years earlier ascended to the throne to become the first independently ruling queen in England.[1] At the time Knox wrote, Isabella of Castile had already ruled in Spain on her own, her husband Ferdinand of Aragon having no executive power whatsoever in her domain. She had been involved in the martial reconquest of Granada, and of course on her own had funded Columbus's first voyage to the New World. And even though France had outlawed rule by women with the Salic law, many women had exercised supreme power when they were acting as regents for sons or brothers. Many Hapsburg women assumed positions of great authority over the family's far-flung lands, including the Netherlands,

Portugal, and Spain; following his father Charles V's lead, Philip II of Spain in particular continued to use his female relatives to administer a vast family network of European powers. Because his grandmother Isabella of Castile had ruled alone, he seems to have been more amenable to rule by women than other Renaissance royalty.

The Hapsburg dynasty, in fact, provides a paradigmatic example of how the exercise of vast administrative authority on the part of its women enables a family to achieve and maintain supreme political power. Margaret of Austria, Mary of Hungary, and Juana of Austria provided excellent exemplars of the "regiment of women" in Northern Europe. Although Knox ignored them in his tirade, they clearly had an important effect on Philip II of Spain. Related through close marriage ties to three of the ruling queens, and ruling throughout the same decades as they, experiencing the same history, he deserves a place in this history by offering an important gauge by which to judge the overall success of monarchy in the sixteenth century.

Catherine de' Medici came to power two years after Knox's blast, so she escaped his blistering opprobrium; she ruled France for twenty-nine years (1560–89) as *La Reine Mère,* mother of three French kings. Although Knox was using the term "Regiment" primarily to mean "rule," or "governance," in his provocative title he was also playing with a newer use of the term "regiment," as if women were making a warlike attack on male dominance, against which a soldier's trumpet blast had become necessary.

With some nice historical irony, Queen Elizabeth I of England— probably the most famous of the women who ruled in sixteenth-century Europe—came to power only a few short months after Knox published his rant. Although he tried to apologize to her as a *Protestant* queen, saying he only meant to interdict *Catholic* women rulers, she was profoundly offended by his anti-woman diatribe. She was not amused. In consequence, Elizabeth never allowed Knox to travel through her realm again. On the number of trips he took to and from

Scotland and the continent thereafter, he always had to go around England by ship, a far more perilous way to travel.

However daunting Elizabeth's rejection of him might have been, Knox's *First Blast* has done history a real service by calling our attention to the remarkable number of European women who were in positions of premier authority in the sixteenth century and by suggesting that they were rightly to be understood as a regiment. Like fellow soldiers in a sororal troop, they did try to protect and aid each other, keeping each other's backs, as it were, asking each other to aid any one of them who might be in peril. They called each other sisters— in the case of Mary and Elizabeth Tudor, they actually were sisters. Mary, Queen of Scots was also their first cousin once removed. Save for Catherine de' Medici, they were all born royal, and their nearness to monarchal power that had descended to them through generations had given them divinely sanctioned authority to rule over men.

Rather than narrate the experiences of the remarkable number of individual women who exercised executive authority in sixteenth- century Europe, I have chosen to focus on these four, the best known women rulers, because their history has exerted the greatest influence and also because this history has previously been told from a prejudiced point of view.[2] Following the lead of Knox, who argued that women were simply incompetent to govern by reason of their biologically based hysteria and passionate, irrational natures, this misogynist narrative has placed the women rulers in jealous and war- like opposition to each other rather than in the context of their real aim, to make peace together. A reported adolescent slur by Mary, Queen of Scots on Catherine de' Medici's pedigree has provided an undying history about Catherine's "hatred" of her daughter-in-law. Fictional accounts like Friedrich Schiller's *Maria Stuart* (1800), in which Elizabeth stands raging over Mary, who kneels before her pleading desperately for clemency, have made it impossible not to revel in their hostility to each other or to choose one woman over the other. Often in the recent past, summer spectacles of *son et lumière* (sound and light) have offered stereotypic slanders of Catherine de'

Medici howling diabolically over loudspeakers while lurid bloodred lights drip down the façades of Loire Valley chateaux. These special effects were doubtless holdovers from such portraits as nineteenth-century French historian Jules Michelet's, who called Catherine "a maggot that crawled out of Italy's tomb," ignoring her many cultural and political achievements. They are stories that have allured us by their phantasmagoric horror at the power of women who, when not controlled by men, destroy everything and especially each other in monstrously seductive catfights.[3]

It is possible to imagine a far different story for these queens not only because of recent developments in twentieth-century historiography; new scholarship, often by women, has delved into an untouched archive of evidence that Renaissance women's lives were culturally consequential at all levels of society. But a different story may now also be told because of recent (and heretofore underused) new anthropological theory that has rewritten the "rules" of human society. These very different new rules help us to understand the kinds of connections women create among themselves, connections that we have rejected as being beneath notice. In brief, women give each other gifts. The gifts are no mere signals of affection but are massively central agents in the creation of a steep social hierarchy that allows women to assume political authority powerful enough to trump their usually disabling gender. These gifts are "inalienable possessions" handed down the generations of a family, enlarging that family's social prestige, increasing it so much that the women of the family may ascend in time to positions of supreme political authority over men.[4] Unlike the gifts men give each other that are meant to be widely circulated throughout society, gifts between women are meant to be possessed as private treasure forever, accruing vast social powers for the family over succeeding generations.

Such giving among women in the same family, where special objects are created and then kept close and do not circulate outward, contrasts sharply with the traditional understanding of gift exchange among men. We have been taught that a gift from one man or group of men *forces* the reciprocal *return* of another gift. We have for a long time assumed that this was the entire nature of the gift, and while an incomplete view of *all* gift-giving, it has enabled us to understand fundamental features of the creation of society. While all objects of trade in male-to-male gift exchange empower social connection between groups of men, twentieth-century anthropology has argued that the most important gift that can be given between men is a woman. The "exchange of women," whereby some women are thus set aside (by the incest taboo) as a special group, so that they can be given by men as gifts to another group of men, powers the strongest social bonds. In essence, sisters and daughters of one group are exchanged to become wives of another group, and vice versa. It has been assumed by this traditional accounting of the "traffic in women" that women themselves have little to no agency of their own, but instead simply act as the silent conduits of connection between the two groups of males.[5]

The very different nature of the gifts that women give each other, however, reveals that women do not lose their connections to their natal family when they are "traded out" in marriage, but instead keep close ties to that family. Much like the women themselves, the gifts given among them allow a concentration of treasure to be possessed inalienably by the family, increasing its wealth and prestige within society.

Let me offer, as a central example, Princess Elizabeth Tudor's gift of a book to her stepmother Queen Katherine Parr. Eleven-year-old Elizabeth's gift celebrates the queen's help in returning her previously disinherited daughter to her rightful place within the Tudor family and the royal line of succession. The book is no random choice, for Elizabeth made the entire book herself. Having previously translated into English a poem by a French queen, Marguerite de Navarre, she had written out the text in her school-girl printing. Then, exercising a traditional feminine skill with rather more finesse than her printing, the princess also embroidered a cover, in blue, silver, and gold thread. Along with Katherine Parr's initials within an interlaced design, there were prominent embroidered pansies on each of the four corners, a clever young girl's pun on the French

Elizabeth Tudor, *The Glasse of the Synful Soul.*
*MS. Cherry 36, Bodleian Library, Oxford University*

word for thoughts, *pensées.* It is currently one of the most valuable manuscripts housed in the Bodleian Library in Oxford.[6] The text was subsequently printed numerous times throughout Queen Elizabeth's reign, testifying not only to her precocious intellect, but also to her connections with three other queens: her stepmother, her mother, Anne Boleyn, and Queen Marguerite de Navarre, who may have given a copy to her mother.

A second prominent example of a woman-to-woman gift enlarging a family's prestige is Catherine de' Medici's gift or "prestation" (to use the anthropological term) of the Valois tapestries to her granddaughter Christina de Lorraine. The book is quite small and the tapestries are very, very large, but both objects, intended to be kept forever, have the same impact on family identity. Elizabeth celebrates her own repaired social position as princess by her gift of gratitude to her stepmother, the queen. She rejoins and strengthens the Tudor dynasty (and she of course will in time become its most illustrious member). Christina, as Grand Duchess of Tuscany after marrying the Duke, carried to Florence the spectacular record of Catherine de'

Valois tapestry, "Tournament"; unknown atelier, 1576. At left, Catherine stands with her daughter Marguerite de Valois and her daughter's husband, Henri de Navarre (the future Henri IV of France). They face the figures on the right, who include Louise de Vaudément, wife of Catherine's son Henri III of France, and the king himself, behind her and in profile. *Gallerie degli Uffizi, Florence*

Medici's magnificent achievement of royal power in France. Possibly designed from the very beginning to be a gift to her granddaughter, Catherine de Medici's Valois tapestries are an almost textbook demonstration of inalienable possessions: that is, clothworks that increase the status of a woman's natal family, bringing to it increased social power. Housed within the Uffizi Galleries, these artworks in monumental cloth continue to this day to proclaim the value of the Medici dynasty's enduring cultural prestige. They had achieved the royal pinnacle of society when their daughter Catherine de' Medici, as a brilliant queen, governed France for nearly three decades amid an immense efflorescence of renewed Renaissance culture.[7]

Although inalienable possessions given between women are traditionally items of cloth—such as Elizabeth's embroidered book and Catherine's tapestries—there is one significant gift given by Catherine de' Medici to Queen Elizabeth I that, while not exactly made out of cloth, expresses a quintessential bond between the two queens. It is, like Elizabeth's gift to her stepmother, a book.

Pierre de Ronsard's *Elegies, Mascarades et Bergerie* (Paris, 1565) was a book of poetry, commissioned by Catherine de' Medici, and sent to Elizabeth as part of her attempt to court the English queen as a bride for her son King Charles IX. In part made of paper (itself made of rags), the book's real and profound importance is the central argument Ronsard makes: that women are entirely worthy of rule and often do a much better job than men. Celebrating Catherine and Elizabeth's signing of the Treaty of Troyes, seven years after Knox's *Blast*, Ronsard sings the praises of women as peacemakers who achieved what no kings had managed to do: peace between England and France. Said to have been long in love with Mary, Queen of Scots, the daughter of Marie de Guise, whom Knox directly attacked in the *First Blast* of his misogynist horn, Ronsard counters Knox with a full-throated defense of rule by women. Both he and his patroness Catherine de' Medici understood, supported, and celebrated the regiment of women.

Poetry has seldom been taken as a reliable guide to historical fact. However, especially in the Renaissance, art can offer acute political glimpses into a culture that itself spoke of politics in terms of architecture, theater, painting, literature, and dance. Ronsard's collection of poems, dedicated to Elizabeth, Mary, Queen of Scots, Catherine de' Medici, Robert Dudley, William Cecil, and others, offers heretofore unrecognized insights into Catherine's assessment of the dangers the ruling women of the sixteenth century all faced together, as queens confronting a political attack on monarchy itself.[8] In particular, Ronsard and Catherine pointed to Elizabeth's pivotal counselor, William Cecil, later Lord Burghley (a supporter and friend of Knox's), as potentially one of the most dangerous figures in the challenge to monarchy launched by the growing power of the Protestant Reformation.[9] In the end, Cecil managed to force Elizabeth's execution of Mary, Queen of Scots in 1587.[10] It was an act Elizabeth abhorred and called an "accident" she had never intended. The official state-sanctioned death of an anointed monarch changed the nature of English monarchy for all time, making possible the overthrow of a king a mere sixty years later. It has taken almost three and a half centuries for modern scholarship to drop the narrative of personal jealousy and rancor among the three queens and to discover what Catherine and Ronsard already seemed to know quite clearly. They knew how threatened all monarchs were by the looming patriarchal power of the Reformation, and how necessary it had become for them, particularly Elizabeth Tudor and Mary Stuart, to assist each other in maintaining their regal powers. Catherine clearly wanted Elizabeth to be warned.

Historians, rightly prizing official documents, have not often cared to scrutinize the information offered by such trivial things as books of poems, embroidery, jewelry, sewing, and drawings about the ways women in the sixteenth century came to power and used the inheritance embodied in those objects to rule their world. Earlier scholars—through many centuries for the most part men—have overlooked or ignored not only the objects but also the shared nature of power, including the crucial acknowledgment by these sixteenth-century rulers that governance was something that they exercised as "sisters" and that they collectively needed to band together to protect their power against the patriarchal assault menacing them all. The brilliance of the monumental culture they achieved together in order to protect their power to rule should compel us to take another—and rather different—look.

# PART ONE

❧

## THE TUDORS

# The Device for Succession

On March 17, 1554, charged with treason and surrounded by armed guards in Whitehall Palace in the royal City of Wesminster, twenty-one-year-old Princess Elizabeth Tudor penned a terrified letter to her older sister Queen Mary Tudor; she was writing to the very first woman ever to rule England entirely in her own right. Elizabeth was panicked because she knew Catholic Mary I feared further violence from Elizabeth's Protestant supporters, who the month before had made an armed attack on London, proclaiming a plan to depose Mary in favor of her younger sister. While Mary's forces had beaten back the rebels, her hold on her throne remained precarious. Elizabeth feared for her life.

The previous July, only nine months earlier, thirty-three-year-old Mary Tudor had succeeded to the throne after her younger brother King Edward VI, son of Henry VIII's third wife, died at age fifteen from tuberculosis. Mary's path to the throne had been made very difficult by her teenaged brother. In January of 1553, Edward had written out, in his own hand, "My Device for Succession," in which he denied *both* of his sisters the royal right to succeed him.[1] In doing so, Edward went against his father's own will, which stipulated that the two sisters should succeed him in proper order, first Mary, then Elizabeth. Edward Tudor was—like his father—someone who did not think it good for women to rule. In the "Device" he specified it should be any *male* child born to Jane Grey, a first cousin to the

Tudor siblings, who should rule. His older sister Queen Mary did not agree; she had indeed never agreed to the burning need for a male ruler, from the start resisting her father's "divorce" from her mother, Catherine of Aragon, because Catherine had produced no living male child to be heir to the throne. Strangely, everyone at court had thought Mary would never protest the takeover attempt by a radical Protestant faction on Edward's Privy Council to follow through on his plan to put a son of Jane Grey's on the throne. The only action she had taken when her brother had cruelly outlawed her private devotions in the Catholic Mass, at which she often found solace by attending four times a day, was to make plans to flee England to Catholic Brussels. She had, however, never followed through on those plans, making many think her timid and fatally irresolute.

When, however, Edward's Protestant Council proclaimed Jane queen in London, Mary—having remained in England doubtless to protect her right—boldly sent out her own proclamation far and wide, claiming that she was, as the eldest daughter of Henry VIII (and sister to Edward), his proper heir. She was therefore the true queen of England. The English public very quickly recognized her right to the throne, and Mary was triumphantly crowned on the first day of October 1553. Not a drop of blood was shed to bring her to the throne, although she did subsequently execute the Earl of Northumberland, the father-in-law of Jane Grey, for his leading role in the attempted Protestant coup.

At the moment that Princess Elizabeth was writing a desperate letter pleading for her life, the burning question she tried to answer was had she, in fact, personally colluded with the rebels? They had recently fought running street battles in London against Mary, who was planning to marry Philip II of Spain, a powerful Catholic king, who, the rebels feared, would force England to return to Catholicism. Although they had been defeated, they had clearly been using Elizabeth's name as heroine of their cause. Was she thus guilty of treason? Would her older sister execute her as she had the rebel leaders?

While Queen Mary's armed guards waited to remove the suspect sister from the Royal City of Westminster and take her three miles downriver to the secure stronghold of the "White Tower" of London, Elizabeth wrote her crucial letter to her sister very deliberately, and also very, very slowly. In it, she pleaded,

> I humbly beseech your majesty to let me answer afore yourself,
> and not suffer me to trust to your counselors, yea, and that afore
> I go to the Tower, if it be possible.[2]

Wishing to avoid the doom-filled Tower, the medieval prison where her own mother Anne Boleyn had been beheaded in 1536, Elizabeth pleaded, beseeching throughout the letter that she be allowed to address her sister in person, to explain that she was no traitor. When she ended her letter, she slashed the last page with eleven sloping lines, from upper left to lower right, taking up all the white space of the paper, before she wrote her last sentence: "I humbly crave but only one word of answer from yourself."

The slashes were self-protective marks, put there to make it impos-

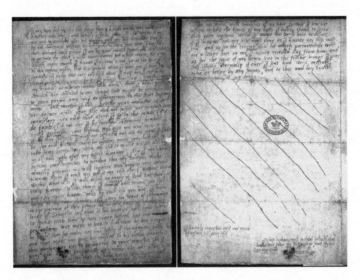

Elizabeth Tudor, the "Tide Letter," March 17, 1554.
© *National Archives, London*

sible for anyone else to write anything more on the page, any words that might incriminate Elizabeth in the current rebellion against Mary's rule. She carefully explained in her letter, and again insisted when interrogated later in the Tower, that she had played absolutely no part in the coup of February 25, 1554, led by the young Protestant nobleman Thomas Wyatt, son of a famous poet who had years earlier written love poetry to her mother Anne.

Now, in the time the young princess had taken to write her famous delaying tactic, the current in the river Thames had turned direction. Roaring torrentially upriver through the narrow passages between the stanchions of London Bridge, the incoming tide had made it impossible to pass downriver safely. To attempt to do so would risk life and limb for all—prisoner, soldiers, and boatmen included. Elizabeth had by this means, as she had intended, delayed by a day a journey to what she feared might well be her death by axe on Tower Green. Perhaps in that one day her sister would relent, and consent to see her in person to hear her pleas.

On the next day, however, Elizabeth was swiftly taken to the Tower on a falling tide. When she ascended into the Tower from the river, she had to pass by the scaffold on Tower Green where the young Guildford Dudley and his equally young sixteen-year-old wife Lady Jane Grey had finally been beheaded only the month before. Postponed for almost a year, the execution of Lady Jane was finally enacted when Mary's mercy could no longer be sustained in the face of Jane's continuing attraction for Protestant rebels. Mary did not personally fault Jane, who had been forced to ascend the English throne for nine days by the cruel manipulation of her parents and her father-in-law, the Earl of Northumberland; but Jane's father and brother had both joined Wyatt, putting an end to Queen Mary's mercy. The recent rebellion had made all Protestant heirs to the throne suspect, including Elizabeth, who had known her cousin Jane well.

Mary had not postponed Northumberland's execution, as she had Jane's; his beheading had been immediate. The Earl had begged

Mary for mercy, explaining that he had only been obediently following Edward VI's orders when he put Jane on the throne. For centuries scholars have assumed that this was a flat-out lie, and that Northumberland was masking his own ambition to continue governing England (he had been regent for Edward). However, it is now thought that Northumberland was telling the simple truth, and that it was in fact Edward's own idea to elevate Jane's son to be king. Even though the fifteen-year-old loved his older sisters (as his father King Henry also had), he did not think either of them, being female, should govern England (an assumption that had led his father to dispose of his first and second wives, hoping to beget a male heir with a third). It was not just Mary's Roman Catholicism to which Edward objected, but the sisters' shared illegitimacy, foisted upon them when Henry VIII divorced both their mothers. But quite clearly, Edward objected to their succeeding him because of their female gender. Perhaps he was hoping to match his father's final (however bloodied) success in providing a male heir for England. Dying before he could provide a male heir himself, Edward concocted a plan that would make sure a male king would rule after he died.

In January of 1553, well before he fell ill, Edward VI had written out in his own hand, "My Device for Succession." Arguing in it that Mary and Elizabeth were, after all, only half-sisters to him, and still bastardized as well, the teenaged king claimed his sisters had no right to succeed him. So he chose for his heirs the males born to his younger cousin, Jane.

In July of that year, Edward had to amend his gendered restrictions to male heirs when it became clear that he would not live long enough for Jane Grey to give birth to a son. So he revised his "device" to name her as direct heir herself. His decision would lead Northumberland, father-in-law of the hastily married sixteen-year-old girl, to push her onto the throne at Edward's death. Jane reigned as "queen" for a mere nine days, until Mary Tudor's clear and obvious right, supported by the presence of an army, compelled the dissolution of Northumberland's Protestant forces. Having postponed it for nearly

Edward VI; the circle of William Scrots, 1550.

a year, Mary finally decided to execute her cousin Jane, even though she had not played a part in any of Wyatt's wrongdoing. In this perilous moment, would Queen Mary also execute another prisoner in the Tower, her half-sister Princess Elizabeth?

This crucial moment, with one female relative in jail and the other deciding whether to execute her, has become something of a hallmark tale of the relations among women rulers in the sixteenth century. No wonder the story of their jealousy and hatred of each other has crystallized into a tale of the failed Bloody Mary and the triumphant Virgin Queen who followed her. In large part, however, these enmities were not of Mary and Elizabeth's making, but thrust upon them by circumstance, mostly the result of machinations by powerful men. Henry VIII's overwhelming desire for a son to reign after him created all the tensions between the sisters, pitting them against each other, one a Catholic and one a Protestant, a conflict in which one had to be a bastard if the other was to be legitimate.

Later, the claims on Elizabeth's throne made in the name of Mary, Queen of Scots, at the time dauphine of France, wedded to François de Valois, the dauphin, would be first voiced by Mary's father-in-law, Henri II, King of France. Mary's own personal refusal to relinquish her place in the English succession was very different from her father-in-law's desire to dethrone Elizabeth and make his son king of England. Mary Stuart's desire was simply to bolster her own royal position as heir—and as equal—to a powerful woman who ruled a separate kingdom on the same island, a question of parity and rightful succession, not violent overthrow. Mary Stuart's claim to be in line to inherit England's throne derived from her Tudor grandmother, Henry VIII's *older* sister Margaret, who had married the Scottish King James IV; similarly, Jane Grey's claim had derived from her grandmother, Henry VIII's *younger* sister Mary. In both cases, these claimants had legitimate positions through Henry VIII's sisters.

The first attempt to deprive Mary Tudor of her rightful place on the throne was due to her younger brother's assumption that a woman could not rule; the second major attempt to usurp Mary's throne was the one led by Thomas Wyatt the Younger, a Protestant nobleman who, along with other Protestant nobles, and joined by a mass of malcontents, marched on London to stop Mary's planned marriage to Philip II of Spain. They wished to forestall what they feared would be a Spanish (and therefore Catholic) takeover of their realm. There were supposed to have been gatherings of rebels in multiple English counties, but at the uprising, only Wyatt himself had managed to collect enough men to make a march into London. Hot-headed and young, he went forward, and along the way his forces won several skirmishes. However, when they arrived in London with a force of four thousand, they faced some two thousand Londoners ready to defend their city. First, Queen Mary had had all the bridges across the Thames destroyed so the rebels had to march elsewhere to find a crossing. Having thereby delayed the rebel army, Mary rode to the Guildhall, a Gothic building that had been the traditional center for city elections since the fourteenth century. Outside her royal city of Westminster, and among the citizenry of the city of London, she gave a rousing speech. Speaking from the platform where candidates for city leadership usually addressed the assembly, she told them, in significantly maternal terms, that she knew they loved her as she loved them.

> I am your Queen, to whom at my coronation . . . I was wedded to the realm and laws of [England]. I cannot tell how naturally the mother loveth the child, for I was never the mother of any; but certainly, if a Prince and Governor may as naturally and earnestly love her subjects as the mother doth love the child, then assure yourselves that I, being your lady and mistress, do as earnestly and tenderly love you.

Profoundly moved by Mary's call, the assembly of Londoners rallied en masse to confront the invaders in the narrow city streets, finally forcing them to retreat. Yet, while Mary had won a decisive victory, Wyatt's rebellion proved how shaky her power still was in the face of Protestant resistance.[3]

When later Elizabeth came to the throne, she often used this same language to her people, understanding that even a virgin queen could claim the power of being "mother" of her nation as Mary had. Although these were not necessarily gifts Mary consciously gave to Elizabeth, as the first independent queen of England it was she who established a powerful rhetoric for female rule, which Elizabeth quite literally inherited. Mary's claims include: (1) the idea that she was the virgin mother of her country; (2) the idea that England's people were her children; (3) the idea that she was a virgin wedded to her kingdom, her coronation ring being, specifically, her wedding ring.

The new queen to whom Elizabeth had written in mortal fear shared with her younger sister more than the red hair and steely will they had both inherited from their father, Henry VIII. They also shared the deep traumas caused by their father's long-term and increasingly cruel quest for a male heir, a ruthless drive in which he destroyed their mothers, banished both daughters from his court as bastards, and hardly knew them as his children at all.

Of all the candidates to succeed him, Mary Tudor had the most illustrious pedigree, and she had a long and affectionate history with the English populace. For seventeen years she was the only living child of Henry VIII and Catherine of Aragon, the first of Henry's six wives, whose marriage had lasted almost twenty-four years. In comparison, Henry was married to his other five wives for a combined total of ten years only: he had two of them beheaded, one died, one's marriage was annulled, and one survived him. He was rather afraid of Catherine of Aragon, the daughter of the warrior queen Isabella of Castile, and doubtless out of respect for Catherine's lineage and her profound loyalty to him, he did not think to execute her. Still, he annulled their marriage and exiled her from court, perhaps hastening her death by the enforced separation from her daughter and the penury in which she lived.

Even before his second marriage (to Anne Boleyn in 1532), when Mary turned sixteen, Henry VIII was the author of a pamphlet, *A glasse of the Truthe,* in which he argued the case for the greater national stability that would be provided by a male heir to his throne. "We ought of our duty . . . [decide] how we might attain the succession of male heirs." The king graciously acknowledged that in his daughter Mary he already had a female heir "endowed with much virtue and grace in gifts." "Yet," his text goes on, "if a male might be attained it were much more sure."[4]

Mary was indeed endowed with gifts. She had been well tutored by the renowned scholar and Renaissance humanist Thomas Linacre, the king's physician, theologian and scholar at both Oxford and Cambridge. As a nine-year-old, Mary had delivered a Latin oration to a visiting dignitary that she'd written herself. She could reliably be called upon to converse or perform publicly with great confidence and ability.

Moreover, she played a number of different musical instruments

Queen Catherine of Aragon, age 35; British School, 1520.
*National Trust Images / National Portrait Gallery, London*

with famed skill and was one of the best dancers at the court. Athletic abilities such as dancing showed off the physical strength of the individual at a time when health was always a major consideration in building family dynasties—the purpose of all aristocratic as well as royal families. Renaissance nobles performed music and danced a great deal at court, often every day, both men and women needing to display their sturdy physical (and thus genetic) makeup and therefore to attract mates. Like Mary, Anne Boleyn was also famous for her dancing skill, as was her daughter Elizabeth.

More personally, Mary shared with her father a genuine talent for music: as queen she spent far more money on music than anyone else in the Tudor family. Yet despite this bond of affection and talents, Henry implacably decided to ignore his oldest child and to divorce her forty-year-old mother, in order to beget a son with a new and younger wife.

Queen Catherine, formerly sweet-faced and elegant but now worn down with multiple pregnancies and problematic births and miscarriages, put up a compelling resistance to Henry's decision to divorce her. She was a woman of impeccable heritage and powerful allies: her parents were King Ferdinand of Aragon and Queen Isabella of Castile—they who had finished reconquering Spain from Islamic rule in battles where the queen rode out in armor against their enemies. Queen Isabella had also famously funded Columbus's voyages to the New World, and then vehemently objected, until the day she died, to the practice of slavery that developed there. Perhaps most crucially, however, Catherine's nephew was at this time the Holy Roman Emperor Charles V, the most powerful ruler in Europe. In Catherine flowed English Plantagenet blood as well, deriving from a royal English and Spanish marriage made two hundred years earlier. She was arguably more royally English than her husband, as he was only the second son of the Henry Tudor who had usurped the throne from Richard III after defeating him in battle.

The ground on which Henry VIII requested the pope to dissolve his marriage to Catherine was incest because she had formerly been married to his older brother Arthur. Notably, Henry VII had named his first son Arthur, hoping to garner some further royal legitimacy from the chivalric myth of the Round Table; to the same end, he married Arthur to Catherine's far better bloodlines. Although the marriage between a brother- and sister-in-law is not considered incest today, it was clearly interdicted by the Roman Catholic Church, and couples who were so related continued to be prosecuted by English courts up through and beyond Elizabeth's reign. An earlier pope had duly granted Catherine and Henry a dispensation for incest that took the stain of sin off the union; but after they were unable to beget a male heir for England in twenty-four years of trying, Henry decided, quite on his own, that God was punishing him for the sin of incest by denying him living male heirs. Henry ultimately went on to argue that the pope had *not* had the power to grant the original dispensation in the first place, and that he and Catherine had all along been living in sin, and that was why they had no sons. Catherine countered that both she and God (and Henry) knew full well that she had been a virgin when she came to him on their wedding night. Henry's older brother Arthur, sickly during his brief five-month union with Catherine, had died young, just as later, Arthur's nephew and Henry's son, King Edward, would die at only fifteen. Catherine argued that since she and Arthur had never consummated their marriage, she had never truly been Arthur's wife, and so her own marriage to Henry had never been incestuous. God Himself had known (as had Henry himself, of course) the intact state of her hymen on the day of their marriage:

> When ye had me at the first, I take God to be my judge, I was a true maid without touch of man; and whether it be true or no, I put it to your conscience.[5]

Her intimate appeal to her husband failed, and she became victim of Henry VIII's irrational displays of cruelty in pursuit of a son, his increasingly tyrannical behavior quite possibly also the result of a brain injury when he fell off his horse, after which he had lain unconscious (and his brain without a normal supply of oxygen) for two hours. A later wound to his leg, which never healed but festered painfully, doubtless added to his irascibility, so unlike the equable temperament he had displayed in his youth.

In 1528, at the time Henry began trying to persuade the pope to annul his marriage to Catherine, the pope was imprisoned in the Castle St. Angelo, a rebuilt Roman stronghold on the Tiber River, surrounded by the emperor's German mercenary troops, who had sacked Rome the year before. The pope had fled to the castle, a massive round tower made of Roman brick, which was now as much his prison as his sanctuary. He clearly could not risk angering Emperor Charles V by assenting to Henry VIII's request to annul his marriage to the emperor's favored aunt, Catherine of Aragon. The sack of Rome was so catastrophic that Rome's population fell from 55,000 to 10,000, and took thirty years to rebound.

Undaunted and with astonishing hypocrisy, Henry then asked this same pope for a dispensation, again because of incest, to marry Anne Boleyn! The reason he asked for this dispensation is that he formerly had taken as his mistress Mary Boleyn, Anne's younger sister. While Mary Boleyn and Henry VIII had never married, Henry knew that their previous carnal relations, when he was twenty-nine and Mary was twenty, made it incest for either of them to have sexual congress with the other's sibling (a sexual relationship between them would thus be, by the rules of the day, the same as the incest in his marriage to Catherine). A papal dispensation would excuse the incest that would necessarily occur when he married Anne, as he was determined to do. With a cynical show of goodwill, the pope granted the king this second dispensation—knowing he could never sanction the dissolution of Henry's first marriage to the emperor's aunt Catherine. The hypocritical pseudo-logic of both king and pope is astonishing and a bit incredible: Henry asked for a second dispensation from incest to allow another marriage at the very same time he was supporting many of the universities in Europe to argue vehemently on his behalf that the Pope *never had any power to grant a dispensation for incest* in the first place. Henry's argument was that God's law against incest was beyond the pope's authority to undo. The king's hypocrisy was only matched by the pope's cynicism, who granted the dispensation for incest to allow Henry's second marriage, knowing that without the unattainable dissolution of the first marriage, any dispensation to marry Anne Boleyn would be useless.

Finally deciding not to wait for the pope's permission, Anne forced the issue by agreeing to succumb to Henry's pleas. After eight years of resisting, she allowed Henry to make love to her and subsequently became pregnant. Worried that unless they married, the baby—of course assumed to be Henry's male heir—would be illegitimate, Henry quickly moved to marry Anne in 1533 despite the lack of papal permission. Accordingly, he secretly began to undo England's ties with the Catholic Church, installing himself as Supreme Head

Anne Boleyn; unknown English artist, late sixteenth century, based on a
work of circa 1533–1536. © *National Portrait Gallery, London*

of the Church of England in place of the pope; he was thus able to
appoint an Archbishop of Canterbury (Thomas Cranmer, chaplain to
the Boleyn family) who would grant the annulment of the marriage
to Catherine, and would then quickly sanctify the marriage to Anne.

While making the country Protestant or "Anglican," Henry did
nothing at all to change the Catholic service of the Mass or any other
church rituals. As his government began taking over the smaller monasteries, directing their money to the crown, he added to his papal
title "Defender of the Faith"—which had been granted to him by the
pope for writing a book against Luther—a second title, calling himself
"Head of the Church." When Elizabeth inherited her father's titles, she
was not allowed to use this one, because Parliament decided the English
Church could not have, as Knox had argued, a female "Head"; instead
she was to be called "Governor" of the Church. Elizabeth responded
by burying the less exalted term, writing her titles thus: "Queen of
England, France, and Ireland, Defender of the Faith, ETC.").

As Head of the Church, Henry also began the largest land grab in the history of England. From 1536 to 1541, he "dissolved" eight hundred Catholic monasteries that had comprised approximately one quarter of the kingdom's wealth in land and that had housed approximately 12,000 religious men and women. He gave much of this wealth to himself and then rewarded his loyal courtiers with the rest. The nation's "one percent" accepted the lands and estates, and also accepted that Anne Boleyn was queen and that England was now Anglican. (A line in a sonnet by Shakespeare laments the lost chantry chapels where monks sang to help along the departed souls working their way through purgatory to heaven: "Bare ruined choirs where late the sweet birds sang." Having rejected the concept of Purgatory, the Protestant church cut off the people from having any direct contact with their departed family members, whom they had formerly been able to aid with their prayers and donations.)

But not long after, in a soon to be catastrophic turn of events for her, Anne delivered not a boy but a girl, Elizabeth Tudor. Even though the birth of his second daughter was yet another major disappointment for Henry, much as Mary's had been earlier, he immediately acknowledged Elizabeth as his heir—something he had long postponed doing for Mary. He cast out his first daughter, whom he had only recently recognized as heir, and abruptly replaced her as his legitimate successor with his second.

So seventeen-year-old Mary Tudor lost her royal title when the infant Elizabeth came into the world. No longer called "Princess" but "Lady Mary," she was made to serve in the baby's entourage (apparently at the vengeful instigation of Anne), and was wholly denied the solace of her discarded mother Catherine's presence. Forced to acknowledge the new infant girl as the sole legitimate child of her father while she herself was declared a bastard, Mary was cut off abruptly from the world in which she had lived all her life—the petted child of a doting young father and mother, denied nothing she wished for, dressed in beautiful clothes, given skilled teachers in the arts, privately provided a superb humanist education that included much Latin if also less Greek.

Most significantly, Mary had from birth been trained by her now exiled mother to see herself as someone who would eventually become queen of England. Then, after her parents' divorce, Mary was thrown aside in favor of the baby Elizabeth; her charmed life shattered, she was seldom allowed even to lay eyes on her mother, who remained far away, essentially under house arrest, banished from court, growing ill.

When she refused to condemn her parents' marriage as incestuous and said bluntly that she would not accept her father as Head of the Church in England, Mary was threatened with similar banishment. In some ways it was not surprising that teenaged Mary stood her ground, resisting her father's command and enduring her stepmother's hostility: she was after all the granddaughter of Isabella of Castile, who had led armies into battle. And Mary's mother, Catherine of Aragon, had also led an army as Regent of England, forming a third line of defense against the Scots in 1513. The great victory against Scotland at Flodden Field happened when Henry was off in France and Catherine was his regent at home, technically in charge of the English army. Descended from such illustrious Spanish royal women forebears, and as someone whose lineage stretched back to the Plantagenet kings of England, Mary refused to give up her title of "Princess."

It seems that Henry had not thought through what would happen to Mary when he married Anne, and so up until Elizabeth's birth, Mary had retained all of her former privileges and titles. Moreover, Henry continued to show the real affection he had felt for her for seventeen years as his first and only living legitimate child. When Mary refused to relinquish her title and her place in the succession to her baby sister, she and her father suffered a catastrophic collision. Her education had come to a halt with her demotion from a princess to a mere ladyship; she suffered all the indignities of a bastardization she would not accept but did not have the power to change. As her biographer sardonically summarizes, Mary Tudor "had the character of her Castilian grandmother but not the armies."[6]

Mary's tragic situation changed very little when, on May 2, 1536, only three short years after her bastardization and only four months after her mother Queen Catherine of Aragon's death, Henry VIII had Anne Boleyn arrested and put to trial for adultery, incest, and treason. He needed to get rid of this second wife—who had, like the first, failed to produce a male baby after a number of miscarriages. He wanted to try for a son with a third wife, the far more docile Jane Seymour. Queen Anne was subjected to a quick trial with corrupt witnesses and testimony from tortured victims, and found guilty on charges of incest and adultery with five partners. That made her and the men guilty of treason against the King. Despite torture, all but one of the men pleaded not guilty, as did Anne. Quite the contrary, she produced solid alibis for most of the occasions on which her adulterous acts had allegedly taken place. But the verdict was pre-determined. Indeed, it appears likely that the French swordsman who would execute the queen had been sent for during, or perhaps even before, the verdict had been reached.

Anne's incest was supposedly committed with her own brother George Boleyn, Lord Rochford (who was also beheaded—along with Anne's other falsely charged "lovers"). It is entirely possible that the incest charge against Anne and her brother actually grew out of Henry's projection onto her of his haunting sense of his own acts of sibling incest: he had married his brother's wife, Catherine, and then kept Mary Boleyn as his mistress before marrying her sister Anne. Executing Anne would have been a way to ease his conscience, especially if the real reason for abjuring her was a stillborn male baby, a haunting reminder of his failure to have a live son with Catherine, who had suffered numerous stillbirths.[7]

After Anne's death, her three-year-old daughter Elizabeth faded from court into the same twilight existence the older Mary had endured, bastardized, motherless, and equally bereft of a father's favor. Elizabeth's claim to royal precedence had lasted only her three short years as her father's favored child—a position Mary herself had occupied for the first seventeen years of her life.

Even though Elizabeth was now a fellow sufferer from their father's tyranny, Mary had every reason to nurture negative feelings about her younger sibling, every cause to look down on the daughter of the usurping Boleyn woman of no royal blood (Anne's great-grandfather had been a London hatter), the adulteress who had stolen Mary's father and broken her mother's heart.

But if "Lady Mary" never doted on Elizabeth—a "princess" until she was three years old—she also never took out on the child the rage she must have felt at her father's treatment. She was consistently kind to her little sister, offering her gifts and treats as she grew, perhaps repeating in these gestures the generosity she had early received at her affectionate parents' hands. When Henry's bastard son—the Duke of Richmond, who had been born out of wedlock and was thus illegitimate from birth—died at the age of seventeen and Henry was disconsolate, Mary wrote to him, "My sister Elizabeth is well and such a [promising] child . . . that I doubt not but your highness shall have cause to rejoice of in time coming." Kind as this is, Mary might also have been making an argument for herself as another "promising" daughter of her father.

Henry VIII became betrothed to Jane Seymour only one day after Anne's execution, and married her a very short ten days later on May 30, 1536. The new queen was (as Anne had also been) resistant to Henry's sexual advances before marriage; unlike the radical reforming Anne, however, Jane was far more conservative in religion and was from the start a great advocate for her Catholic stepdaughter Mary; Queen Jane helped Mary's relations with her estranged father, and although Jane died shortly after giving birth to *the* long-awaited son, she had asked that Mary stand as godmother to her baby, Edward. At the close of the baptismal ceremony, Mary left holding four-year-old Elizabeth's hand, a public statement that the sisters and their younger brother were now united as siblings. Mary and Elizabeth Tudor, bastardized at different times, were placed back

Lady Mary; Hans Holbein the Younger, 1536. *Royal Collection Trust /*
*© Her Majesty Queen Elizabeth II 2020*

in the line of succession simultaneously, now that there was a male heir, the future Edward VI, to precede them.

It should be no surprise then that fifteen years later, at her own triumphant coronation in 1553, Queen Mary I acknowledged her half-sister Elizabeth to be her heir, at least at that moment. Just as she herself had ascended to the throne as her father's most direct descendant and therefore rightful heir after their brother Edward's death, Elizabeth would follow her to the throne. The law of succession (and the support of the English people) guaranteed Mary's position by her birthright. Henry VIII had by legal decree restored both daughters to the succession: after Edward, the crown was to pass first to Mary, then to Elizabeth. He did not, however, explicitly and legally remove the taint of illegitimacy that had been imposed on each of them. Perhaps he just neglected to think of it.

Henry's will left them both very wealthy women. Each had the equivalent today of one and a half million dollars as an annual allowance, in addition to a dowry of over three million each. Mary also owned thirty-two houses (or grand estates and manors) and, perhaps most importantly, she had been given lordship over the lands of Norfolk, Suffolk, and part of Essex. These properties gave her something that she had not had before: an "affinity"; that is, she now had lands, money, and men—a group of supporters with local ties—whose loyalty was hers by right. She could—and would—call on the men of these counties when she made her bid for the throne. Finally, Mary now had, like her grandmother and her mother, an army to lead.

An incident during Mary's younger brother's earlier reign gives insight into her character throughout her reign: often forgiving of others yet periodically hesitant about many of her decisions, religiously she was always uncompromised and uncompromising. When, unlike his father, Edward VI outlawed the Catholic Mass and resolutely refused to allow Mary to continue to attend Catholic services in private, her deep Catholic faith, long her main solace, stiffened her resolve. Edward's absolutist strictures on her religious practices put into effect an impulsive scheme of hers to have herself rescued from England on two ships sent by her powerful uncle, the Holy Roman Emperor Charles V. The plan was for the imperial ship to slip into England at night, take Mary on board, and spirit her away to Brussels to the court of Mary of Hungary, another Hapsburg relative of hers. (Mary of Hungary, niece to Catherine of Aragon, was then ruling the Catholic Netherlands on behalf of her brother Charles V.)

On the brink of executing her scheme, Mary thought more prudently of the idea of flight, which would have irrevocably disabled any chance she might have had to succeed to the throne. Perhaps she decided that although she had now lost the private use of her Mass, by staying she might be able, on gaining the throne, to restore that Mass to the people throughout England. (Those who were then worshipping as Catholics had to hold services in secret; they built "priest holes" in their houses to hide the Catholic clergymen who risked their lives to say Mass.) When word got out that Mary Tudor had aborted the plan, Mary of Hungary judged her English cousin to be a weak and indecisive woman, suffering from self-pity, incapable of courageous action. At the time, most people assumed she had been overcome by timidity. But she may well have been motivated not by weakness but by the strength of her desire safely to secure the throne and return England to the true church.

In London, John Dudley, Duke of Northumberland, could reasonably have assumed that, given her divagations about fleeing, Mary would be a pushover when he made his bid for his daughter-in-law Jane Grey Dudley to be crowned queen after Edward's death. He was thus quite unprepared when Mary escaped from the castle of Hunsdon, where she had been sent to live under the close watch of her brother's council; she ultimately fled to one of her own holdings, Framlingham Castle, a moated stronghold, where slowly, bidden by Mary in letters and called on by her servants, a large army assembled itself to support her strongest claim to the throne of England. In fact, when the Privy Council in London came out in favor of Mary's accession, Northumberland gave up without a fight. Because of the English populace's immediate and massive support of Mary, she did not need to shed blood on her way to the throne. But she took the risk: she boldly sent out a declaration calling the people to her cause. An upwelling of loyal soldiery in her home county of Norfolk, her home "affinity," began a tide that quickly flooded in her favor.

This massive manifestation of loyalty to Catholic Mary only ten days after the death of the radically Protestant King Edward on July 6, 1553, was a stunning surprise to the radical Protestant Earl of Northumberland. He had been de facto ruler of England for four years during Edward's minority. But Princess Mary had been her father's heir for seventeen years; the nation had known her for almost two decades (and had known her mother Queen Catherine far longer than that). In contrast, few of them had ever even heard Jane Grey's name. The Protestant cabal in London led by the Duke seems to have been tone deaf about how much the common people would remember with fondness their traditional Catholic rulers. It was not merely a question of a shared religion (although many in the hinterlands

remained disappointed by all of the metropolitan elite's new Protestant practices that had been abruptly instituted during Edward's
reign—no ringing of bells, no incense, no brocaded vestments, no
Latin, no statues of saints to whom they could daily pray). What
they were persuaded by was that Mary was her father's daughter and
therefore was now their queen. Her declaration read:

> By the Queen. Know ye all good people that the most excellent
> princess Mary, elder daughter of King Henry VIII and sister to
> King Edward VI, your sovereign lord, is now by the grace of God
> Queen of England, France and Ireland, . . . and to her and to no
> other ye owe to be her true Liege men.[8]

When, five years later in 1558, Mary's sister Elizabeth I came to
the throne, she always said that it was the people of England who
had loyally supported her for queen and not any royal factions from
abroad. Doubtless this is true. But their loyalty had first been sponta-
neously (if not as famously) given to her older sister Mary. The politically astute Elizabeth might well have remembered Mary's lesson
and learned from it (as she learned from many of her sister's successes,
and, of course, her failures).

In 1553, Mary I proved herself the granddaughter of Isabella and
the daughter of Catherine at a crucial moment when her burgeoning
army began massing at Framlingham Castle, ready to battle Northumberland's rebels. There was no immediate fighting to be had, and the
men were growing restless. Mary rode out to the soldiers' camp on a
magnificent white horse to survey her troops arranged in formation.
Her horse, however, became skittish among the crowd of soldiers,
and while she was an excellent horsewoman, she chose to dismount
and walk among her troops, speaking to them individually with such
exceptional kindness and with an approach so wonderfully relaxed that
she completely won everyone's affections. Elizabeth I's appearance in
armor before her troops at Tilbury in 1588 may owe something to
Mary's courageous address at Framlingham thirty-five years earlier.

Because Mary showed herself a Tudor and a queen, she was acclaimed by the nation. However, she did more than simply prove herself her father's (and mother's) daughter. She generously secured recognition of Elizabeth as another of her father's daughters, worthy of the highest place in Mary I's court. In claiming her throne as the *elder* Tudor sister against her brother's wishes, Mary I made a safe path to the throne for Elizabeth as well. She assumed the crown as Henry VIII's eldest daughter, thereby nodding toward the younger daughter in the wings. Mary I's celebration at her coronation of Elizabeth as her sister and her heir recognized the legitimacy of their connections by blood to Henry VIII. Without Mary, there might never have been Gloriana.

In her elaborate coronation procession, Mary I's entourage wound its way through London from the Tower to Westminster Abbey, where the queen was to be crowned. Leading the procession, Mary I rode in a chariot draped in cloth of gold. Princess Elizabeth, prominently given pride of second place, followed immediately after her, wearing silver that matched her chariot. Former queen Anne of Cleves (briefly married to Henry VIII before he quickly had their marriage annulled but who had become a close family friend) rode in the carriage with Elizabeth.

Along the path to Westminster Abbey at every turning, from Fenchurch to Gracechurch to Cornhill, there were pageants produced by foreign cities to entertain the queen; many in the crowds thronging the way were impressed by Florence's very tall structure that supported an angel all in green, who blew a "trumpet" that sounded whenever a trumpeter hidden out of sight sounded his horn. Some pageants provided giants and dragons, and fountains at Cornhill ran with wine. Choirs of children sang, and poets chanted poems of praise.[9] It was a grand parade in which the people of London could join with their new sovereign to celebrate the Tudor monarchy that had restored order after a century of bloodshed in the War of the Roses. On that day both Tudor women were on display as the rightful granddaughters of Henry VII, the daughters of Henry VIII, and the sisters of Edward VI.

After the procession wended its way through London, Mary descended from her carriage and walked the rest of the way to the Abbey for her crowning. The ceremony used holy oil for her anointing specially brought into Protestant England from Catholic Brussels. Mary I was dressed in crimson velvet with crimson cloth of gold slippers decorated with ribbons of Venetian gold. The gold coronation ring, known as the "wedding ring of England," was put on her finger, and she was given the sword and spurs of kingship. She held the orb and *two* scepters, as she was—for the first time in English history—both king *and* queen. The second scepter was one that had, in fact, been held by her own mother, Catherine of Aragon, at her joint coronation with Henry VIII, he as king, she as queen consort.

During Mary I's banquet following the ceremony, Elizabeth sat in a place of honor at the queen's table. But however much Mary favored her sister, in succeeding months and then years, old conflicts remained that irrevocably divided them. At the core of these conflicts was the fact that in order to recover her own legitimacy, Mary had to insist on Elizabeth's bastardy. While they could both be proclaimed children of their father, they could not both be legitimate. In a letter to his English ambassador, Holy Roman Emperor Charles V, Mary's uncle, tells us that Mary I was making every effort to restore her past as well as her present legitimacy:

> It is apparent from your last letter that declaration by Parliament of the Queen's legitimacy, and Elizabeth's illegitimate birth, is well on the road to success.

Although Hapsburg Charles V, at the age of twenty-two, had been betrothed to his first cousin Mary Tudor when she was six years old and the legitimate daughter of Henry VIII, he had done nothing to aid her in her claim to the English throne. He did, however, stay in touch, and supported her when she had won it for herself. For her part, she considered him to be a powerful father figure.

> The Queen wishes . . . that the sentences pronounced in Rome
> by the Pope in Consistory in favour of the validity of the mar-
> riage of the late King Henry with the late Queen Catherine, our
> good aunt . . . , may be recovered and sent to her.[10]

The Emperor duly sent the packet of documents to Mary, but asked
that they be returned. So the sisters were still locked in the same double bind. Mary had long deeply loved her mother (she was an adult,
only a month shy of twenty, when Catherine died). Very differently,
Elizabeth was just two years, eight months old when Anne Boleyn
was executed. Moreover, Elizabeth had spent much of that infancy
not in court with her mother but far off at Hatfield, a beautiful Tudor
brick compound just south of Cambridge, surrounded by elaborate
knot gardens and rolling fields, with the delegitimized "Lady Mary"
essentially serving as her lady-in-waiting.

If Mary had always been legitimate, then Elizabeth could never
be. And if Elizabeth were legitimate, then Mary would not be. This
draconian choice was not a quandary of their own making, but the
result of their father's drive to beget a son as heir, as a result of which
he had both to divorce his first two wives and to bastardize his first
two legitimate living children. From this overriding impasse flowed
all the personal acrimony his two daughters suffered from, for the
rest of Mary's life.

Added to that personal conflict was the deadly internecine
Protestant-Catholic divide that Henry had introduced into his realm
by his break with the pope in order to marry Anne Boleyn. Mary was
Catholic and Elizabeth was Protestant, and although Elizabeth—
probably disingenuously—continually suggested to Mary that she
might be willing to convert to Catholicism, their differing views on
religion kept them at odds. As noted, if only Henry had resolved the
issue by straightforwardly declaring them both legitimate *and* the
heirs who would succeed their younger brother, then perhaps Edward
would not have overridden Henry's will with his "Device" and Mary

would not have had to insist on Elizabeth's bastardy in order to estab-
lish her own legitimacy.

But would a simple declaration have satisfied the emotional wound
that had been inflicted on Mary? As queen, married to the very Catholic Philip of Spain, she clearly was insisting on documentary cer-
tification of her legitimacy not merely to lift the stain of her own
bastardy but because she also wanted to legitimate the "annulled"
marriage of her father and Spanish Catholic mother. When, during
Wyatt's rebellion, Elizabeth became a magnet of resistance for English
Protestants who hoped to crush the rule of a Catholic queen, Mary I
grew ever warier of the popular appeal of her still illegitimate and still
Protestant sister. Despite Elizabeth's regular attendance at Catholic
Mass, Mary could hardly avoid noticing that she often came late, and
often nodded off during the service, clearly dishonoring the sacred
communion by which Mary had managed to survive the years of
exile from her father's favor. Such obvious and easy hypocrisy by Elizabeth must have rankled; Mary had risked much when she resisted
her father's call to abjure her Catholic mother.

After facing down the Protestant Wyatt's rebellion, Queen Mary
sent Elizabeth to the Tower of London, a gothic block of white stone
looming above the river Thames, both fortress and prison, with water
gates for easy entrance and exit of dignitaries and prisoners. Was
Elizabeth guilty of conspiring against her sister and thereby guilty
of the capital charge of treason? The rebels were indisputably using
her name. Mary easily could have then tried and executed her sister
just as she had finally executed Jane Grey. Not far from the scaffold
where Jane had been put to death on Tower Green, Elizabeth sat in
her own Tower cell and waited for her sister's decision about whether
or not to behead her.

Before Mary could bring herself to condemn Elizabeth, however,
she felt she must have proof that her sister had *actively* colluded in
Wyatt's rebellion. While Mary sought that proof, Elizabeth, fearful
for her life, kept asking if Jane's nearby scaffold was still standing.
On it was the execution block that the blindfolded Jane had had

so much trouble finding before she could lay her head down on it. Elizabeth knew all too well that relatives of royals died. Her father had her mother Anne Boleyn beheaded on Tower Green. Elizabeth probably knew about the fine-edged French sword that had been used in place of the axe, offering, so it was thought, a less painful death when wielded by a highly skilled French swordsman. (The axe often failed to do its job cleanly, as it would fail over thirty years later, when the axe-man botched the beheading of Mary, Queen of Scots, so that it took three blows to sever her head entirely, while the head's lips continued to move. Some said they moved in prayer throughout the ordeal.) Elizabeth knew that kings and queens could order the deaths of those they had once loved. Her father had done it a number of times.

Queen Mary, possibly answering Elizabeth's pleas for a chance to give her own evidence to counter the accusations of the queen's counselors, demanded that the men find real physical proof that Elizabeth had conspired with Wyatt, especially that they find it in her sister's own handwriting, before she could be brought to trial. Under intense interrogation in the Tower, Elizabeth refused to confess. She argued that while Wyatt might have written asking her to join his rebellion, she had never written to him in reply. Therefore, where was her fault? Ultimately, there was no incontrovertible proof produced—no eyewitness, nothing in writing, no confession. Then when Wyatt swore on the scaffold that the Princess Elizabeth had had no dealings with his rebellion, Elizabeth was finally saved.

Because Wyatt had faced a traitor's death—that is, to be hanged by the neck, then cut down before he was dead, his intestines ripped out of his body and his body axed into four different "quarters," which were then hung up in prominent public places (this is what "drawn and quartered" means)—it was assumed he would tell the truth. Many prisoners said whatever the authorities wanted because by this means, while they could not avoid the gruesome end, they could spare their family's entire loss of all their wealth, the further punishment for treason.

Through many hours of badgering by Mary's Archbishop of Canterbury, Stephen Gardiner, the twenty-year-old Elizabeth had resolutely refused to confess to anything. No incriminating letters could be found. When tempted by Gardiner to confess, be freed, and trust to her sister's clemency, she retorted, "I had rather be in prison with honesty and truth than have my liberty and be suspected by her majesty." Ultimately, when she could not be found guilty due to lack of evidence, she was freed from the Tower. She was not, however, declared innocent.

Released from her prison fortress, Elizabeth remained under house arrest for two more years in a remote village, Woodstock, near Oxford, where she was surrounded by forty soldiers, who guarded her every move. One day she scratched a poem with a diamond on a windowpane that years later would be quoted in John Foxe's *Book of Martyrs*, his famous compendium of Protestant "saints."

> Much suspected by me.
> Nothing proved can be.
> Quod [said] Elizabeth the Prisoner.

After Elizabeth became queen, she reinstated Wyatt's family to the lands and wealth they had lost by his treason. Her action created a lasting suspicion that she and Wyatt the Younger had in fact colluded in a rebellion against her sister. For one thing, people remembered that Wyatt's father, Sir Thomas Wyatt, the poet, courtier, and ambassador, had written exquisite and famous poems that appeared to be about his passionate desire for Anne Boleyn, Elizabeth's mother.[11] But she might just as well have rewarded him for his valor in not being forced by torture to name her as an accomplice, simply to end the pain.

Queen Mary had hated Anne Boleyn, but in the end spared her daughter despite years of conflicted feelings about Elizabeth (unwilling either to execute or to free her). Years later as queen, Elizabeth I would feel the same conflict about her cousin Mary Stuart, but in the end, after years of delay, she would make a different decision. In 1568 at one moment of extreme peril for the Queen of Scots when Elizabeth's counselors were clamoring for her blood, Elizabeth refused to find the Queen of Scots guilty of murder. Nevertheless, she continued to imprison her "sister queen" as a potential threat to her throne. Indeed, she kept her cousin and fellow monarch prisoner for eighteen years before she finally signed the order for the Scottish queen's execution.

Just as Mary I had been reluctant to execute her sister and heir without compelling proof in a trial, so Elizabeth I remained for decades committed to keeping alive Mary of Scotland, her next of kin, as long as she could, even when, after long years, there at least appeared to be accumulating (written) proof that the Queen of Scots was involved in plots to overthrow the queen of England and replace her on the throne. Mary I had tried to do the same for Jane Grey, sparing her life for over a year until her father's and brother's violent rebellion made clemency too great a risk.

Elizabeth often cited the years of her imprisonment by Queen Mary as the main reason for her not wanting to name an heir to her throne. In a speech to Parliament in 1566, she argued that she was sure "there was not a one of them that ever was a second person." That is, none of them had ever been direct heir to a throne. She vehemently confessed that she "had tasted of the practices (plots) against my sister."

> I stood in danger of my life, my sister was so incensed against me.
> I did differ from her in religion and I was sought for diverse ways.
> And so shall never be my successor.

It is true that Queen Mary had learned to mistrust Elizabeth so greatly that only when childless on her deathbed, in her last moments, could she be brought to name her sister as her successor. (In comparison, on her own deathbed Elizabeth could not bring herself to name *anyone* as her successor. King James was only "named" by Robert

Cecil, William Cecil's son who had inherited his father's place as chief counselor.) By imprisoning Elizabeth for her suspected complicity in Wyatt's uprising, Mary I gave her sister a harsher but much shorter version of the harassment that she had herself suffered at the hands of their father.

A strong-willed woman, Mary was the most legitimate of all the Tudors, descended as she was on her mother's side from both Plantagenet kings and Spanish kings and queens, Hapsburg monarchs, cousin of a Holy Roman Emperor. (In fact, all European kings and queens currently living share blood with Catherine of Aragon's parents, Isabella I and Ferdinand II.) So Mary had reason to be proud. Nor had she ever been treated as badly as Henry VIII had treated four of his wives (two of whom he beheaded, two of whose marriages he had annulled). Yet while he never committed Mary to the Tower, she was exiled from court, she was put under house arrest, and she was hounded mercilessly to obey Henry's implacable will and Anne's petty commands, both intended to demean her. During her father's reign and also during her younger brother Edward's brief kingship, multiple interrogators continuously hammered at Mary to relinquish her religion and to accept her bastardy. She refused resolutely to do either. Henry VIII had executed his very good friend, Catholic Thomas More, because he would not assent to Henry's divorce from Mary's mother. When Mary refused to acknowledge that her parents' marriage was illegal, she risked that same deadly rage from her father.

Finally, however, in June 1536 she caved in to her father's wishes. She came to the realization that by her refusal she was jeopardizing not only her own life but also the well-being of the vast number of people who were dependent on her, and that she was also possibly destroying any opportunity to restore the English church to what she deeply believed to be the true faith. At the time of this decision, she had not seen her father for five years. When she finally submitted and publicly displayed her abject obedience to him, she was restored to life at court and was given an immense income.

Henry's then wife, Jane Seymour, presented Mary with a diamond ring when she bowed to her father's will. A pleasant-faced, quiet-minded woman (the opposite of Anne Boleyn), and far more conservative in religion, Jane befriended the unhappy young woman. Recent biographer Linda Porter comments that, despite the restoration of harmony with her father, "This supreme act of denial [of her mother's legitimate marriage and of the Pope's authority in England] remained on her conscience for the rest of her days."[12]

Mary and Elizabeth never had the reconciliation enjoyed by Mary and Henry. Elizabeth was not released from her house arrest and brought back to court until Mary, sure she was pregnant, allowed her sister to be summoned to be present for the birth of England's heir. At that moment Elizabeth would cease to be a "second person" and become a "third person," that is, third in line to the throne and, presumably, less of a threat to Mary. But Mary was not, in fact, with child, although she had ceased to menstruate and had grown heavier. It was a false pregnancy; the loss of a child was a tragic blow to the queen and to her husband, King Philip II of Spain.

Philip II of Spain, wearing the Order of the Garter.

It had been, in fact, through the urging of Philip, the expect-
ant father of the desired heir to Mary's throne, that Elizabeth had
finally been allowed back to court. Following English argument and
Spanish precedent, Philip had been denied any right to inherit the
crown from Mary; he could not become king after his wife's death.
(His great-grandmother Isabella of Castile—who was also Mary I's
grandmother—had made just that arrangement of spousal exclusion
with her husband, Ferdinand of Aragon. At Isabella's death, Castile
had passed to her daughter Juana, Catherine of Aragon's older sister,
and not to her then living husband.) Moreover, as a Catholic and a
foreigner, Philip had been from his arrival deeply unpopular with the
common people (he never learned a word of English), although he
succeeded in making a very positive impression on members of the
court, who were swayed by his intelligence and good manners.

As a young husband, Philip was very solicitous of his even
younger sister-in-law Elizabeth, who—far from the Gloriana Regina
she would later become—was still living under house arrest in rus-
ticated Woodstock and in fear for her life. In March 1555, while she
was still imprisoned near Oxford, the Spanish ambassador Simon
Renard wrote to Philip advising him:

> It would be wise for you to send for Elizabeth before you leave
> England and admonish her to continue to serve and obey the
> Queen.

Although many of Queen Mary I's Catholic councillors wanted Elizabeth to be taken out of the country and married off to some foreign
Catholic prince in order to get her out of the way, Philip appears to
have been against that strategy. One might well ask why he should
be. Renard wrote next to Charles V, Philip's father, explaining that
Philip desired to continue Elizabeth's presence at court. Feria wrote:

> But it seems to me that the king considers that it would be better
> to keep her here until after the queen's confinement.

Clearly Elizabeth had become a key figure for a foreign husband who could not inherit his wife's crown should that wife's life be compromised by childbirth or should their child not thrive. Count Feria, a special envoy from Philip to Elizabeth, wrote to Philip in May 1558:

> I do not think the Queen will wish to prevent Elizabeth from succeeding, in case God grants no issue to your Majesties.

Feria might well have been extrapolating from his own sense of Mary's commitment to her sister. Even so, during the spring of 1558 Philip appears to have opened a secret conversation with Elizabeth through his envoy Feria. Feria wrote to Philip in June:

> I went to visit the Lady Elizabeth, as your Majesty instructed me to do. She was very much pleased; and I was also, for reasons I will tell your Majesty when I arrive over there.

Philip wrote back:

> I was glad to hear that you had gone to see the Lady Elizabeth. When you come, you will report what happened between her and you.

It seems likely that what King Philip wished (in the event Mary died childless) was to keep her sister Elizabeth squarely first in the line of succession so that another Hapsburg prince (or he himself) could marry her, thereby maintaining the Spanish-English alliance that he had made by marrying Queen Mary Tudor. After Mary did die childless in November 1558, Feria wrote to Philip that he should make clear to the pope that any Catholic meddling by Rome into the English succession would invite disaster in England.

> I am very much afraid that . . . if [the Pope] should take into his head to recall matters concerning the divorce of King Henry there

may be a defect in the succession of this Queen. . . . I think it well
for you to write to Rome and get the Pope sounded about it.

Philip later claimed to Elizabeth that he had done a great deal to protect her place in the English succession. It is clear from these commu-
nications that he was telling the truth. He had indeed worked hard
on her behalf. Of course, he did so in order to further his own geopolitical agenda. When Count Feria wrote again to Philip in December
1558 after Elizabeth had been crowned, he described his attempts to
seduce Queen Elizabeth for Philip:

> I see she is very vain . . . I fancy I can get at her through this
> feeling. We must begin by getting her into talk about your Maj-
> esty . . . [and not] to hold herself less than her sister, who would
> never marry a subject. We must . . . then place before her how
> badly it would look for her to marry [a common Englishman]
> while there are such great princes whom she might marry.

The vanity of which Feria speaks must have been the desire he sensed
in Elizabeth not to marry a mere subject, but to match with someone
who was himself royal. Decades later, her late-life interest in Catherine de' Medici's youngest son, François, Duc d'Alençon, demonstrates not vainglorious perimenopausal vulnerability but rather a
strategic desire to marry a royal, should she ever decide to wed anyone. In that regard Feria was probably right about her disinclination
to marry beneath her royal class.

However, the Spanish envoy's rather amusing assumption that
Elizabeth could be manipulated simply by his fostering feelings of
jealousy in her over the Spanish king's love for her now dead sister seems almost laughably naïve, as if he were dealing with an
unschooled girl and not the highly educated, independent twenty-
five-year-old who would go on to become arguably the most
successful ruler of England in its entire history.[13] Wildly underes-
timating her commitment to a savvy geopolitical agenda, he seems

to have been quite unaware that she might even have an agenda of her own. The Spaniards knew she was Protestant, but they seem also to have assumed that once married to a Catholic, she would become one herself. To Feria, Elizabeth was a mere woman who would always be incapable of rule by herself, unaided by a man. (Even the redoubtable Queen Isabella of Castile, Philip's grandmother, had always co-ruled with her husband, King Ferdinand of Aragon, although during her lifetime he had no authority whatsoever over her kingdom of Castile.)

Philip was among kings perhaps uniquely comfortable with the idea of reigning queens; he clearly thought them capable of rule, as exemplified by the Hapsburg female regents he himself appointed. Yet Philip's continued failure to anticipate Elizabeth's political genius would in the long run change the fates of both their empires.

# CHAPTER TWO

ᔧᕗ

# The Mary Tudor Pearl

Philip neglected to return to England for his wife Mary's funeral not because of a careless lack of feeling, or an unusual failure in etiquette, but because at that very time he was dealing with two other family deaths. He was also beginning to shoulder the burdens he had to take up when half of his father's empire fell to him to govern. His father, Holy Roman Emperor Charles V, died in September 1558; his aunt, Mary of Hungary, Regent of the Netherlands, died in October; Mary died in November. Not long before he died, Philip's father had abdicated his throne as emperor, splitting up the empire, granting to Philip the Spanish lands while granting the Germanic lands to his brother Ferdinand, Archduke of Austria. The governance of the Spanish Empire (including Naples and Sicily, the Netherlands, and the New World) had thereby fallen squarely on Philip, as had the prosecution of his father's current war with France, in which Philip had enlisted English forces and which he subsequently worked very hard to conclude with a peace. Philip was also supposed to take up his father's war against the Ottoman Empire, as well as manage the clearance of Protestants from Catholic lands, by forced emigration or conversion—what we might call "ethnic cleansing." They were all huge tasks.

Philip confessed that 1558 was the worst year of his life, not only because the death of his father had left him alone, facing the immense responsibilities that had become too much even for Emperor Charles

V, but also because the death of his wife Mary Tudor, who died childless, lost England for the Hapsburgs, for whom it had been a great
strategic prize. Thus added to his burdens was the need to woo Elizabeth for his wife.

Later, Elizabeth explained that she had been very "glad to be rid
of the motion of the King of Spain for himself," telling the French
ambassador that she rejected Philip's marriage proposal because he
was her brother-in-law; not because he had caused her sister to lose
Calais in the late war with France; not because the arrogance of the
Spaniards had turned the people against Mary; and certainly not
because she never wanted to marry.

Martin Hume, the editor of the English *Calendar of State Papers*,
suggested that this explanation about marital options was in fact a
fake and that Elizabeth really had said no because of the complica-
tions of current politics or "far more weighty reasons." Yet I am not
so sure that the editor is right to second-guess Elizabeth. I suspect
the queen was telling the ambassador the absolute truth. The matter of potential sibling incest would be to her, as Henry VIII's and
Anne Boleyn's daughter, a very weighty matter indeed.[1] Elizabeth's
whole legitimacy, and therefore her chance ever to become queen,
had depended upon the right that her father Henry had created for
himself to marry her mother on the grounds that his first marriage
was void because he had committed incest in marrying Catherine
of Aragon, his brother Arthur's wife. Were Elizabeth to marry King
Philip, she would be committing exactly the same sort of incest as
that for which, or so Henry VIII had claimed in numerous universities in Europe, God had punished him by denying him a living
legitimate male heir. In order to make right this sin, punished with
such danger (as he saw it) to his dynasty, Henry had put aside Catherine and married Elizabeth's mother. In a similar manner, having
been formerly married to Elizabeth's older sister Mary Tudor, Philip
would indeed need a dispensation from the pope to marry Elizabeth:
he had already received one for his marriage to Mary, because being
first cousins once removed, they were within the forbidden degrees

of affinity (not as close as Henry and Catherine, brother-in-law and sister-in-law, but close enough).[2]

While the falsely alleged crime of incest for which Anne was condemned to death was supposedly with her own brother George Boleyn, the fact remained that by the rules of the day, it was Henry's earlier affair with Mary Boleyn that made *his marriage with Anne* incestuous. Henry had forthrightly acknowledged this fact when he asked the pope for a second dispensation for incest because he was planning on marrying Anne. Elizabeth might well have known of her father's other liaison, for she remained close friends with her maternal aunt, Mary Boleyn, favoring her children—Elizabeth's first cousins—throughout their lives. (Mary Boleyn's daughter Catherine Carey might even have been Elizabeth's half-sister, the product of Henry VIII's earlier affair with Mary Boleyn.)

Elizabeth I's first principal counselor (then secretary of state and lord treasurer) William Cecil was reported to have told Count Feria, the Spanish ambassador (an envoy whom Philip greatly preferred over Renard), that Elizabeth "would have married" his Majesty King Philip, had it not been for this "impediment of affinity." The situation was especially problematic, Cecil confessed, because it involved questions about the pope's "dispensary powers," which, he said, it would be fruitless to discuss now that the offer had fallen through. Only a quarter century earlier, England had been transformed from Catholic to Protestant very specifically over Henry VIII's challenge to the pope's "dispensary powers"; Henry had argued then that the pope had never had the power or authority to grant a dispensation against marrying a brother's wife, an act directly against God's laws, for which the pope could never offer a dispensation. In Henry's view, the pope had thus condemned him to a reign without any legitimate living male heirs. Cecil's mild reference to the pope's "dispensary powers" glosses over the torturous events of the king's "Great Matter." It ignores the abruptness of the top-down "reformation" by which King Henry ripped the English people away from their former community within the Catholic Church. Only thus was he able to marry Anne without the pope's assent to a dissolution of his first marriage to the very Catholic Catherine of Aragon.

Given that Mary Tudor's reign had aimed to undo the transformation to Protestantism, when she strove to bring her people back into the Catholic Church (by the cruel force of burning them alive when necessary), Count Feria's bland summary of Cecil's explanation of Elizabeth's rejection of her brother-in-law the Catholic King of Spain seems laughably to understate the catastrophic problems caused by those "religious questions" such as the "dispensary powers" of the pope.

For the first three years of her short five-year reign, Mary burned heretics alive, many of them common people but some of them Anglican bishops and archbishops, such as the famous "Oxford martyrs" Jasper Ridley, Hugh Latimer, and her father's appointed Archbishop of Canterbury, Thomas Cranmer. A mere dozen years later across the Channel, in 1562, the neighboring kingdom of France would be engulfed by the first of the Wars of Religion between Catholics and French Protestant Huguenots, bloody conflicts that would drag on for three decades. So from Secretary Cecil's point of view, it really would have been "fruitless to discuss" the pope's power on the matter with Spanish ambassador Feria, not merely because Philip's marriage offer had not been accepted, but because under Elizabeth, England was inevitably going to return to being a Protestant nation. The realm was very unlikely to embrace Catholicism again, unless invaded and decisively conquered by a European Catholic power willing to force the nation to return to a faith that their king had rejected a generation earlier. Philip's Armada aimed at just such an invasion to restore England to the Catholic Church. He dreaded the possibility of England's returning to Protestantism, and this fear was one of the fundamental reasons he had offered marriage to Elizabeth.

Was the very Protestant William Cecil being ironic with the Spanish ambassador about this "impediment of affinity"? Feria was not at all ignorant about English history, and had worried a great deal about Elizabeth's status as an illegitimate heretic in the eyes of the pope. Because of the aftermath of King Henry's "Great Matter," it would have been absolutely impossible for Elizabeth to accept marriage with her brother-in-law without undercutting every argument for her own legitimacy. And that fact may have been the underlying point of Ambassador Feria's comments: his assumption that Elizabeth's legitimacy—about which both he and Philip were already worried—could be easily settled by "fruitful discussions" among the men involved in negotiations on the marriage matter, were that to have gone ahead. Was Cecil simply flattering Feria when he blamed the "impediment of affinity," as if this "impediment" were not the fundamental cause of England's transformation into a Protestant nation, a nation professing a non-Catholic religion to which Cecil was even more devoted than he was to his own queen?

King Philip had himself already relied twice on the pope's power to dispense with the rules against incest, once in his first marriage to his cousin, a princess of Portugal, and again for his second marriage to Mary Tudor. And, of course, he would have assumed that the pope had every power to grant him such a dispensation. Why did not Philip's deep Catholic faith make him decide that Henry's divorce or annulment from his great-aunt, Catherine of Aragon, had been totally bogus? Ultimately, he did decide that very point, but at the time Philip worked actively to marry Elizabeth, even though in his Catholic Church, she was deemed a bastard who could never be a true successor to the English throne. It appears that for Philip, Elizabeth's blood tie to her father (confirmed in his Act of Succession) was more compelling than her technical illegitimacy and her Protestantism. Indeed, her being the direct heir (however Protestant) meant that her cousin, the very Catholic Mary, Queen of Scots, at the time queen of France as well as of Scotland, was second to Elizabeth in line for the English throne, and therefore could not inherit unless Elizabeth failed to marry and produce an heir. If that happened, England would be swallowed up by France, something Philip could not allow.

Apparently in Philip's eyes, Elizabeth Tudor was a viable, in fact a far more preferable marriage candidate for him to choose, because she would act as a bulwark against a French takeover of England. Were a takeover to happen, France would be able to menace the Spanish Empire's financial center in the Netherlands from both sides of the Channel.

Philip may well have looked to a marriage with Elizabeth with far more appetite than when he had entered into his marriage to Mary; at twenty-five Elizabeth was six years younger than he (while Mary had been eleven years older). The younger sister was clearly very healthy, and far more likely than Mary to produce an heir to the throne.

We know Feria had been talking about *something* important with Princess Elizabeth even before Mary died (it may, of course, have been about the active courting of Elizabeth by the king of Sweden for his son). Philip clearly respected and was not afraid of rule by women, a Hapsburg family habit: although he disappointed Mary greatly, he was fundamentally a good husband. He later cosseted his very young third wife, Elisabeth de Valois, daughter of Catherine de' Medici; he developed a profound affection for his Hapsburg niece, Anne of Austria, his fourth and last wife; and he made unending efforts to find a throne for his much beloved daughter Isabella Clara Eugenia, even battling the French over the Salic Law. She would in the end be made, along with her husband as king, queen of the Spanish Netherlands. Equally clearly, Elizabeth did not care for him—she was either personally repelled by him as suitor or she guessed that, as rich and as powerful as he was, he would ultimately overcome all the restraints the English Privy Council had placed upon him when he had married Mary, and would come to dominate the court, and her.

Ambassador Feria had clearly guessed that Elizabeth would be governed by no one but herself. So he would not have been surprised when she vehemently claimed, "I will have but one mistress here and no master!" Throughout her reign, Gloriana used eloquent rhetoric to turn the traditional weakness of an unmarried, childless female into a singular power that acknowledged no obligation to the continuation of dynasty. Ambassador Feria obviously saw the danger that Henry

VIII's divorce posed for Elizabeth's legitimacy; he worried that the pope might officially declare her a bastard, and deny her a place in the succession to her sister's throne. (Eleven years later, the pope in fact did excommunicate Elizabeth I as a bastard and a heretic; he thereby officially pronounced an anathema against her, bestowing his holy permission on anyone who could—now sinlessly—assassinate her.) So Philip may well have done what Feria was advising him to do: write the pope to warn him against such a radicalizing move as excommunicating Elizabeth. But given Elizabeth's desire for autonomy and clear resistance to his proposals, it is hardly a surprise that the king of Spain, after spending nearly two years trying to persuade Elizabeth to marry him (doing so even, one suspects, during the last months of Mary's final illness), suddenly dropped his suit for her hand.

Instead, Philip married a French royal princess, Elisabeth de Valois, sealing the peace created by the Treaty of Cateau-Cambrésis (April 3, 1559). Philip could thus allay French aggression against his interests in the troubled Low Countries, just as he had been desperate to block the French by having Protestant Elizabeth retain the English throne instead of Catholic Mary, Queen of Scots and of France. He was then eagerly willing to overlook her Protestantism in order that the British island he had once ruled over through his wife Mary would not come under the power of the French crown, however Catholic that crown might be. Instead, his marriage to the young Catholic teenager would cement a truce with France. He might well have predicted that Elizabeth would never marry and thus none of the Valois sons who might be suitors would make it to the English throne. His wager was that England would not become French.

Twenty-five-year-old Elizabeth apparently had strung Philip's overtures along perhaps even before her sister's death, making Feria think she was pleased to hear whatever talk they were having about a possible marriage. One suspects that her receptivity was not (as Feria and Philip assumed) because she was interested in trumping her sister's marriage to a great king by marrying him herself. True, Philip *was* at this time the most powerful European monarch, ruling an empire that stretched around half the globe. But all Elizabeth appeared to have wanted was whatever aid she could garner from Philip in keeping her safe as the sole legitimate heir to the English throne during the perilous last months of Mary's life. Philip himself thought he had already offered her great service not only with the pope but with Mary's Council, when Mary clearly did not want Elizabeth to succeed.

While Mary lay ill with the influenza that would soon kill her in the early fall of 1558, Philip was busily engaged in complicated treaties to conclude the recent war England had entered, at his request, against France. The final treaty resulted in England's losing Calais, its last remaining outpost on the continent. Although Philip worked very hard to have the French return this uniquely valued city port to England, his efforts proved futile. The British were very bitter about the loss they had sustained on his behalf. He well understood their anger, having admitted honestly, in November, the month Mary died, that

> To conclude peace without the return of Calais would make the whole kingdom of England rise in indignation against me, although they lost the place by their own fault. . . . But as England went to war on my account, I am obliged to pay great attention to this matter.

After Mary died and while Philip's suit for marriage to her sister Elizabeth flared briefly, he was careful to return the jewels Mary had given him during his years as her husband. A list of these items is annotated in Philip's own hand. Even as a young man (he was only thirty-one at the time of Mary's death), he was meticulous about details. The list begins with Philip's comment to Feria:

> I have a *ring* which the Queen sent to me. . . . I think you saw it. Let me know whether it should be given back so that I may send it to you.

The list of jewelry goes on at length, including the regalia given him for his membership in the Order of the Garter.

> 1) A rich garter, with two large facetted diamonds, a large pearl, five flat diamonds set in a rose pattern, twelve flat rubies round the garter . . . The Earl of Arundel attached this to my leg on board ship at Southampton.
> 2) A chain of fifty-eight links, each link carrying diamonds or rubies . . . together with a St. George in armour made of diamonds, and the dragon formed by a pearl.
> 3) Another French robe of cloth of gold, with the roses of England and pomegranates embroidered on the sleeves . . . given to me by the Queen for me to wear on our wedding day . . . but I do not think I wore it because it seemed to me ornate.

If a royal marriage ends, a groom returns his wife's gifts to her royal house. This is not international law, but the proper decorum required by membership in a specific class of people who rule the world by accepting a shared responsibility for doing so collectively, and who are, moreover, themselves a family: related in however distant a fashion, but often related closely, by blood.[3]

Demonstrating her shared understanding of appropriate noble gift-giving (and returning), Mary I in her will gifted back to Philip an especially important jewel. Before their wedding, Philip had given his wife-to-be a table diamond. The diamond's top was square like a "table"; as such, it was very fashion-forward in the sixteenth century. Over the centuries it has been assumed that the portraits done by Hans Eworth and Antonius Mor around the time of her wedding show Mary wearing Philip's gift, the diamond she returned to him in her will.

The gem has a large embossed gold frame around a large "table" diamond, with an unusually large pear-shaped pearl attached beneath. This is the famous "Mary Tudor Pearl," which it has long been supposed (quite erroneously but also quite significantly) to have ended up, via

*Left:* Mary I; Hans Eworth, 1554. *Right:* Detail.
© *Society of Antiquaries, Burlington House, London*

generations of owners of the Spanish crown jewels, in the collection of
Elizabeth Taylor, a gift from her husband Richard Burton on their marriage. However compelling such a poetic legend, Mary Tudor's prominent jewel does not, in fact, appear in the many portraits of successive
Spanish queens, although they all wear a piece of jewelry that looks
almost exactly like Mary's brooch. That crown jewel, however, is clearly
*not* the diamond that Mary returned to Philip. Instead, careful scholarship has proved that the prominent piece of jewelry worn by Mary
in her wedding portraits came to her from her father's great collection
of jewels as listed in Henry VIII's 1547 inventory. She wears it in the
portrait painted of her by Hans Eworth in her wedding dress in 1554.[4]

The brooch clearly shows two clothed human figures set in the
filigree of the gold frame "holding" the table diamond. Henry VIII's
1547 inventory specifies a table diamond encircled by a gold armature
with figures, or "antiquities," who represent Roman soldiers dressed
in armor. The portrait of Mary painted by Antonis Mor also shows
the same detail in the pendant.

Mary I; Antonis Mor, 1554. The recently cleaned portrait reveals two figures in the filigree frame that surrounds the "table" diamond, matching
the Eworth portrait jewel. © *Museo Nacional del Prado, Madrid*

The jewels celebrated Mary's inheritance from her mother and
father, as the Tau cross pendant at her throat had belonged to Catherine of Aragon before she was forced to return it to the crown jewels
when Henry annulled their marriage. The table diamond with "anty-
ques" and a "large" pendant pearl is listed as part of Katherine Parr's
jewelry collection in the 1547 inventory.[5]

Because of its size, the pearl had been an important attraction
at Mary's court. A gold medal Philip had cast during her queenship
clearly stresses the pearl, the pendant forming a very significant part
of the high relief embossing of the coin.[6]

Even if the jewel had *not* been the gift from Philip—or the one
from his father, Emperor Charles V—the gem clearly formed an
important symbol of Mary's royal—and even imperial—lineage, one
deriving not only from her father but also from her mother, who was
the great-aunt of her groom. (The fact that she was marrying the

Mary I; after Jacopo da Trezzo, gilt electroplate, nineteenth century,
based on a work of 1555. *British Museum, London*

Holy Roman Emperor's son might have prompted her to select this
particular gem, with its Roman reference.)

Yet there could have been still another motive for Mary to choose
this jewel to wear for portraits of her. A newly discovered portrait
thought to be of Lady Jane Grey, which features two separate jewels
similar to the "Mary Tudor Pearl," suggests that the pendant may
have first been given to the teenaged "Nine Days' Queen" by widowed Queen Katherine Parr. Parr was known for her thoughtful gifts
to younger women. She had given her own personal prayer book to
Jane Grey when she was dying shortly after giving birth to a baby she
had with Thomas Seymour, her third husband (following her marriage to the king). Jane Grey had been very close to Parr and served
as chief mourner at her funeral. If indeed one of the two gems is a
bequest from Parr's collection, worn by Jane as part of her claims to
royalty, then Mary may well have taken it from Jane as a signal part
of the official crown jewels.[7]

Much confusion has resulted from the legend claiming that Mary

Lady Jane Grey; 1590–1600, unknown artist.
© *National Portrait Gallery, London*

Tudor's pearl was the one that had famously entered the Spanish crown jewels after it was found in the 1560s by a slave in Panama (who thereby, the legend has it, earned his freedom). However, this pearl was not discovered until at least six years after Philip and Mary's wedding in 1554, and Philip only purchased it well after Mary's death. Subsequently called "La Peregrina," it has had a famous and well-documented history, only leaving the possession of the Spanish Hapsburgs when Spain was conquered by Napoleon Buonaparte.[8] The Panamanian pearl indeed appears in the portrait of Margaret of Austria, the wife of his son Philip III; Philip II had included it in the Spanish crown jewels. In the painting, the queen unmistakably gestures to the pearl, indicating its importance.

In a quite real sense, when the Hapsburg dynasty lost "La Peregrina" to Napoleon, they not only lost this famous closely held "inalienable possession," they also lost all their power. That political fact is what made it necessary to surrender the pearl out of the

Margaret of Austria; Juan Pantoja de la Cruz, 1605. The queen's hand
calls attention to the famous pearl. *Royal Collection Trust /
© Her Majesty Queen Elizabeth II 2020*

family, to the Buonapartes. The pearl itself has retained its special
value because of its history of royal and imperial owners. (As such,
it became a worthy wedding gift from one renowned movie star to
another, however mistaken they were about its history, always believing that the pearl had been Mary Tudor's.)[9]

There is a portrait of the newly crowned Queen Elizabeth from
the first year of her reign that shows her wearing a table diamond and
drop pearl brooch almost identical to the one that Mary wore with
the pendant pearl in her wedding portraits. It would seem absolutely
proper that Elizabeth would inherit from Mary and then wear a gem
descended from their father. However, if one looks closely at Elizabeth's pin, it is possible to see that the gold frame is in fact embellished
not by two fully armed Roman soliders, but by two *naked* figures, a
man on the left and a woman on the right. Apparently, Elizabeth
decided not to wear something her sister had made so ostentatious

"Clopton" portrait of Elizabeth I; unknown artist,
English School, 1558–1560.

a part of her royal accessories and so specifically associated with the
time of her marriage to the Catholic king of Spain.

In his "sieve" portrait of Elizabeth, Quentin Metsys adds a detail
that seems somewhat discordant with this genre of imagery. The
"sieve" portraits of Elizabeth all refer to the story of the Vestal Virgin Tucca. Tucca was famous for being able to carry a full portion
of water in her sieve from the Tiber River to the temple of Diana
without losing a single drop of water, thus miraculously proving her
virginity. There were many "sieve" portraits painted of Elizabeth by
a number of artists.

In Quentin Metsys's version of the "sieve" picture, in which Elizabeth's pendant has become a brooch, the two figures holding the
diamond are even more clearly a nude male and a female (though
they have switched places); the female is quite naked and in a lan-
guid pose, her white skin notably contrasting with the pinker color
of her equally naked partner. Whose choice was this? The painter's?
Elizabeth's?

*Left:* "Sieve" portrait of Queen Elizabeth I; Frederico Zuccaro, 1583.
*Right:* Detail. *Pinacoteca Nazionale, Siena, Italy*
© *Granger for British Library, London*

Clearly this favorite close copy of a gem, worn so prominently by her sister Queen Mary in the portraits celebrating her marriage to a Hapsburg, remained a beloved and treasured item among Elizabeth's jewels. It is as if Elizabeth's "self-made" eroticized gem proclaims the choice of autonomy that she always made. In contrast, Queen Mary had chosen a jewel from her father's collection that spoke of *her* father's imperial imaginings, her marriage also a marital alliance with a relative of her mother's, from the most powerful family in Europe, the son of an emperor. Throughout her reign, in contrast, Elizabeth Gloriana used eloquent rhetoric to turn what was the traditional weakness of a childless, unmarried female into a singular power that owed nothing to dynasty: "My children are my people." "Men fight wars. Women win them." "If I were turned out of the realm in my petticoat I were able to live in any place in Christendom."

In the course of her life Elizabeth, kindly but firmly, turned down proposals from other royals; to the king of Sweden, for example, she said, "We do not conceive in our heart to take a husband but highly commend this single life, and hope that your Serene Highness will no longer spend time in waiting for us." Her sister Mary's personal motto had been *Veritas Temporis Filia*, "Truth, the Daughter of Time"; not surprisingly, the motto allegorizes a daughter's relationship to an older, parental (pre-Reformation) past. Elizabeth's motto was far more straightforward and solitary: *Semper eadem*, "Always the same." And so she was. If as a young woman Elizabeth had chosen to marry Philip, she might in time have received the Panamanian pearl. But her saying no to that alliance did not, it appears, mean she had to go without her own great drop-pearl jewel. Instead, she just had her own version made. That this version is so much more erotic than her married sister's pendant suggests much about Elizabeth's own sense of the sexual power of her virginity: first wearing the gem when she came to the throne at twenty-five, she was sexually mature. Yet forever unattainable, she could remain the seductive center of her court well beyond her prime reproductive years.

That these gems can symbolize so much is no fiction-like accident. Families are defined by their inheritance patterns, and their status is enhanced as they assemble more and more treasure to pass down to their heirs through multiple generations. The Hapsburgs amassed whole continents in the New World to pass along.

The reappearance of yet another table diamond and a pear-shaped pearl in one particular late portrait of Elizabeth, a most celebrated one, seems almost to nod ironically at this Hapsburg power. It is the Armada portrait, painted to celebrate England's triumph over Philip of Spain's attempted naval assault on England in 1588. A number of copies were made, differing slightly from one another in various details.

The portrait that hangs in the Maritime Museum in Greenwich, England (which is a copy of what is the supposed original in Woburn Abbey), shows a pearl decorating the bottom of Elizabeth's bodice that in part resembles Elizabeth's version of the "Mary Tudor Pearl." All copies of this famous portrait, decidedly not painted from

Armada portrait; unknown artist (formerly attributed to George Gower),
1588. The version of the portrait in the Maritime Museum is said to have
belonged to Sir Francis Drake, who was one of the triumphant naval
commanders in the victory. *Michael Bowles / Getty Images*

life, show a pear-shaped pendant pearl hanging from a bow tied to
a gold pin with a table diamond. The multiple bows and knots on
Elizabeth's garment, like so much of Elizabethan clothing, impart
important messages. They assert the meaning of the singular placement of the large ribbon bow holding a pear-shaped pearl. It appears
over Elizabeth's genital region, insisting on her pearl-like sexual
purity as Virgin Queen, the pink bow representing, along with all
the other bows, her "virgin knot" never touched by man. Just as the
Spanish Armada was unable to penetrate England's martial defenses,
Elizabeth remains an untouched island entity unto herself. The pearl
and bow are also painted in the same place as the large codpiece, fes-
tooned with a large bow, that appears in the famous Holbein portrait
of her father, Henry VIII.[10]

This giant pearl "of great price" represents Elizabeth's virginity,
as powerful as, if not indeed more powerful than, her father's virility

The "Ditchley Henry VIII," after Hans Holbein, 1600–1610.

as a conqueror of the globe. Resting under her right hand, the globe shows the western hemisphere, with North America nestling, protected, under her palm (Raleigh's colony in current-day North Carolina had been founded in 1584, only four years before the Armada). Central and South America lie open to the hand's potential grasp.

The Armada portrait of the Virgin Queen is a statement that she did not need to be her father to wear her father's imperial jewel, nor did she need to marry Philip in order to have a pearl of her own or to possess her own part of the New World.

Inalienable possessions—in essence heirlooms—are those that a family is never forced to sell, lend, or give away to a non–family member. They are the treasures that give that family its place in the social hierarchy, its class status. In the pre-capitalist society that anthropologist Annette Weiner studied in the Trobriand Islands in the South Pacific, the treasured items were cloth mats woven by women. As we shall see, the association of women with weaving across many

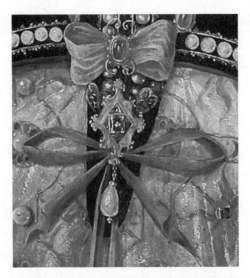

Detail of Armada portrait. *Michael Bowles / Getty Images*

cultures throughout history is relevant to the kinds of power that high-status women are able to accrue and maintain: the very word "heirloom" refers to the mechanism on which cloth is woven; what is made on a loom is passed down to "heirs." But as we have seen, inalienable possessions can be made of stuff other than cloth.

Here is a thought experiment: compare the crowded tours that have patiently threaded through the Tower of London in order to see crown jewels that are locked in a vault, and only brought out to be worn by the members of the royal family on special occasions. Now imagine a TV advertisement by the investment firm Goldman Sachs. In the latter, dollar bills flutter down into a vault filled with dust as a question appears on the screen: "Is your bank just storing your money?" We sense how different the treasure of royalty is from the working wealth that Goldman Sachs offers to build for its investors. The crown jewels stay locked up, only passing down as possessions from one royal family member to the next generation. Money—rightly called "currency"—must circulate (flow as in a river's current) in order to become more valuable. Goldman Sachs will make your money work in the world, rather than just let it sit idle in a vault like some inert lump of metal and stones, however precious. While one can say that the jewels do become more valuable over time, their increase in worth does not match what capital investments would garner. These are two very different systems of wealth, the one increasing capital, the other increasing the hierarchical social status, or "cultural" capital, of successive generations of a family, bringing it to the peak of social power.

"La Peregrina," the pearl from Panamanian fisheries, was in the twentieth century finally transformed into an *alienable* possession, although it somehow still circulates among royalty (of sorts). After it passed out of the Spanish crown jewels during the reign of a Buonaparte, it was sold into England and came into the possession of the Hamilton family, a notable family of peers, fairly closely allied to the Spencers. (Lady Diana Spencer was a Hamilton cousin, and hence the Hamiltons are distant cousins of the current younger members of the British royal family.) The Hamiltons sold the pearl in 1969. When it was bought by Richard Burton for his new wife Elizabeth Taylor, they erroneously assumed it to be Mary Tudor's pearl given to her at her wedding by Philip II. So certain were the Burtons that they possessed "Mary Tudor's pearl" that they purchased Eworth's famous seated portrait of Mary I wearing the pendant with drop pearl. They had been shocked to learn that the English government did not own a portrait of Mary I, so the celebrity couple arranged for the valuable oil painting to pass into the collection of the National Portrait Gallery. The Panamanian pearl from the Spanish crown jewels subsequently sold for $36,000,000 in 2011, when it was remounted by Cartier among a raft of diamonds and sold as part of Elizabeth Taylor's jewelry collection.

Unlike "La Peregrina," the Tudor and Stuart (and earlier) British crown jewels did not survive into modern times; the current-day crown jewels in the White Tower's "Jewel House" themselves only date back to 1660, when royalty was restored to power after the Commonwealth period, during which Oliver Cromwell had finished sell-ing off or melting down all the crown jewels. It was a practice Charles I of England had started when defending his throne (and his life). Only one spoon and three swords remain from the pre-Civil War era. With the abolition of the monarchy in 1649 (only forty-six years after Elizabeth's death in 1603), the entire royal collection was turned into cash, Elizabeth's gems included. Mary Tudor's pearl may have left the collection before then, as it appears on no inventory past Henry VIII's, but if not before, then surely it was gone by the Interregnum.

Although the monarchy was restored to the Stuarts in 1660 at the accession of James II, they had to begin over again, with their royal powers vastly reduced by Parliament. All the treasures that have safely come down from the pre–Civil War Stuarts into modern times had already traveled to the continent and therefore were safe from the destruction of treasures during the Interregnum.

I stress the importance of inheritance embodied in such jewels because their descent from one generation to the next makes visible the inheritance of blood (we would say DNA) through the ages. At this moment, Kate Middleton, the wife of Prince William, wears the same ring worn by Lady (formerly Princess) Diana, which Diana gave to her firstborn son William to give to a future bride. Meghan Markle wears a ring with diamonds left to Prince Harry by his mother, added to one diamond from Botswana, Africa.

In contrast, the Spencer tiara, which Diana wore at her wedding to Prince Charles, was on her death returned to her natal Spencer family, and is back in the custody of her brother Earl Spencer at Althorp, the family seat since 1508. (Similarly, her body was interred there on the castle grounds.)

As the daughter of an earl, Lady Diana was already a member of the British aristocracy before she married Prince Charles. In contrast, Kate Middleton became Duchess of Cambridge only by marriage to Prince William, Duke of Cambridge. Similarly, Meghan Markle, although (like Grace Kelly) an American media star who married a prince, could only share in her husband Harry's inherited title. As is only appropriate for a constitutional democracy, such

Princess Diana, in India, wearing the Spencer tiara. © *Princess Diana Archive, Hulton Royals Collection, via Getty Images*

titles are *specifically* outlawed by the Constitution of the United States of America.

If monarchy has anything to offer as a political structure, it is the certainty that everyone knows who will be the next ruler, and the next after that, and the next after that, so that power will be transferred (at least in theory) without the need for conflict or warfare (or expensive and possibly contested elections). Such generational inheritance promises the peaceful transfer of power. "The King is dead. Long live the King." Hence the frenzy of Elizabeth I's parliaments to force her to marry and produce an heir who would be visibly next in line for the throne. Queen Mary had died heartbroken that she had not been able to give birth to an heir, and so achieve this central objective of monarchy.

In France, when Catherine de' Medici finally came to power as regent in 1560, she had already produced seven living children: three girls, two of whom married kings, and four boys, three of whom became kings themselves, and the last of whom almost married Queen Elizabeth of England.

Mary, Queen of Scots had only one son, but he survived to become James VI, king of Scotland and then, ultimately, James I, king of England. (The current royal family is descended from him via his daughter Elizabeth.)[11]

Giving birth to kings is what queens are supposed to do. It is, of course, what Queen Elizabeth I resolutely refused to do, if only because doing so would have required a husband and she clearly stated that she did not want to have to share power with a man, whom everyone would consider to be superior to her in authority. (Even sixteen-year-old Jane Grey had refused to have her husband Guildford Dudley be equal with her as queen.)

However much the myth of Mary Tudor's pearl is not a story of historical fact but a legendary narrative, its power as a myth speaks to our sense of how deeply we seem to know that female agency is inherited from generations of forebears. However different Mary Tudor and Elizabeth Taylor are—and they are very, very different—it seems fitting that the English-born American movie star should become possessor of jewels belonging to the first independently ruling Tudor queen.

# Three Queens, One Poet, and the Republican Counselor

lizabeth's "rivalry" with yet another Queen Mary—the Queen of Scots—had also begun before Mary Stuart had been born. Although they often called each other "sister," Mary, Queen of Scots and Elizabeth, Queen of England were only first cousins once removed. As with Mary and Elizabeth Tudor, the conflict between the two women was not personal, although the popular story has been told through the centuries as if it were— that they were jealous of each other's beauty, stature, and popularity.[1] Fundamentally rooted instead in religious differences stemming from Henry VIII's abrupt initiation of the Protestant revolution in England, their "conflict" was first and foremost the conflict between Catholic Scotland and Protestant England. It began when Henry VIII began pressuring his nephew, James V of Scotland, to turn his realm Protestant, as he himself had recently done to England, touting the windfall of money that could come with all the appropriated church property.

Even though James V's own mother, Margaret Tudor, was Henry VIII's older sister, he rejected his uncle Henry's overtures. As a good son, he held off from attacking England until his English mother died. With Margaret Tudor now dead and no longer able to plead for peace between her son and her brother, the Scottish nephew and English uncle were free to go to war. The fateful end of that conflict was the battle of Solway Moss (1542). The English forces won a decisive victory. While King James V was not slain in battle, he did succumb to a raging fever when told of the Scots' defeat. When he died, his daughter Mary Stuart was only six days old. She was immediately crowned queen.

When the baby Mary had reached the ripe old age of six months, her great-uncle Henry VIII tried to force Mary's mother, Marie de Guise, to accept a betrothal between the infant queen and Henry's baby son, Edward, who was the king's only legitimate male child. Henry VIII had never given up trying to join the two realms of Scotland and England. With an English future king betrothed to a Scottish infant who was already a queen, the more powerful England could easily engulf Scotland and turn it into a Protestant satellite.

However, Mary's mother was not only French, she was also staunchly Catholic, loyal to her husband King James V in his fight to keep Scotland Catholic. Her Guise family was vehemently Catholic, and fought hard to suppress the growth of the heretic Protestant Huguenot faction in France. Earlier Henry VIII had asked to marry

Marie de Guise; Corneille de la Haye, 1550. *Courtesy of the Indianapolis Museum of Art at Newfields*

the highly competent, strong-willed Marie de Guise himself, after his third wife Jane Seymour died following childbirth. But the French-woman wittily replied that although she was a big woman, she had a "little neck," joking—perhaps a bit tastelessly—about Henry VIII's recent beheading of Anne Boleyn. Marie then married the Scottish king instead, who was, like herself, Catholic.

Vowing to keep Scotland an independent Catholic kingdom, as it then was (and had been intermittently for centuries), totally free of English domination, Marie de Guise enlisted the aid of France, which sent an army to help defend the country. In retaliation, Henry VIII sent soldiers not only to attack the Scots but also to kidnap the baby Queen Mary as a fiancée for his son, in a series of military aggressions that came to be called "the Rough Wooing" (1544–48). In fact the invasions were more like total war, as the English razed the capital city of Edinburgh almost entirely (save for the castle), burning, looting, leveling villages and towns, even setting fire to a manor house while the lady of the house, the servants, and the children were still inside. In consequence of this violence, in 1548 Marie de Guise, like any careful mother, shipped her young daughter, the Queen of Scots, off to the safety of her de Guise family in France.

Safely ensconced in the luxuries of the Valois court, the child Mary was under the care of her rigorously Catholic de Guise uncles, who helped arrange a marriage contract between her and the future king of France. The Dauphin François, Catherine de' Medici's first son with Henri II, King of France, was only three years old at the time of their betrothal, while Mary was five. The marriage arrangement was a great coup for the de Guise family.

As for the motives of the Valois rulers, the betrothal of the two children helped to bolster the French-Scottish "auld alliance," a traditional connection begun in the thirteenth century to provide mutual protection against England's continual threats to both nations. But the Valois also reasoned that they could thereby mount a French take-over of England by pressing Catholic Mary's claims to heretic Elizabeth's throne through her grandmother, Margaret Tudor. In Paris,

*Left:* François de Valois; François Clouet, 1549.
*Right:* Mary Stuart, Queen of Scots, as a child; François Clouet, 1549.
*Yale University Art Gallery*

the French king soon began quartering Mary's arms with the arms of England, as if she were already the Catholic queen of England, thus earning the undying ire of William Cecil, Elizabeth's radically Protestant secretary and treasurer.

An affectionate child, Mary came to love her toddler fiancé François. For the next twelve years they grew up together at the French courts of François I and of Henri II. When Mary (aged seventeen) and François (fifteen) finally married, Catherine de' Medici, queen consort of Henri II, gave the young bride a famous set of pearls (seen in both portraits by Clouet) that she had received as a wedding gift from her own uncle, Pope Clement VII.

In the summer of 1559, a jousting festival was arranged to celebrate the marriages that cemented the Treaty of Cateau-Cambrésis. Henri II suffered a gruesome accidental death when a splinter from his opponent's broken lance flew into his visor, piercing his eye and brain. The wound became abcessed and the king died some excruci-

*Left:* Catherine de' Medici; François Clouet, 1555.
*Right:* Marie, Queen of France, aged 17; François Clouet, 1558–1560.
The pearls may be those Catherine de' Medici had given to Mary for her
wedding, which Mary was allowed to take to Scotland with her.
*Royal Collection Trust / © Her Majesty Queen Elizabeth II 2020*

atingly painful ten days later. Fifteen-year-old François became king
and seventeen-year-old Mary became queen of France. This is not
to say that they had any real political power. True power was exercised by Mary's two maternal uncles, François, Duc de Guise, and
Charles, Cardinal of Lorraine. The ardently Catholic and militar-
ily powerful de Guise family had been using their niece Mary Stuart to further their religious and political ambitions ever since her
betrothal to the dauphin. As queen, she could help to further their
goal to disable the Protestant House of Bourbon, next in line after
the Valois for the French throne, and to take the crown for themselves if they could. The de Guises were against the Bourbons not
only because of their precedence as First Princes of the Blood (next
in line for the throne) but also because the royal Bourbon family was
by then loyal to the new radical Protestant religion, of which they
had become staunch and often violent defenders.

The equally extreme ideology of the de Guise family fueled their attacks on French Protestant Huguenots and thus ensured the destruction of any peace in France. François, the Duc de Guise, was a famous war hero in the long conflict with Spain. He had captured Calais from the English and had in time become the celebrated leader of the Catholic faction in France. However, he became infamous among Protestants when he incited a bloody attack on an assembly of peaceful Huguenot worshippers, opening a period of violent warfare between Protestants and Catholics. The event became known as the "Massacre at Vassy."

In 1562, while riding through the village of Vassy, de Guise heard the sounds of singing coming from a barn within the city limits. He heard the singing again when he attended a Roman Catholic Mass in a church in town. The duke realized that they were singing psalms in French, not in Latin, and that he was overhearing a Protestant religious service; the new religion refused to use the language of the corrupt Roman Church. The barn where the Protestants were congregating stood on land belonging to his young niece Mary, Queen of Scots, who had departed France, having begun her direct rule as queen in Scotland. Protestant services, while allowed and legal in the Protestant territories of France, had been outlawed on Catholic lands. Enraged, he assembled a troop of his men and bore down on the assembly as they were in the midst of their peaceful religious service. The Huguenots violently defended themselves against the attacking soldiers, and the fight that ensued left seventy-four Protestants dead and one hundred more wounded. The dead included many women and children, who had not been spared among the worshippers by the Catholic troops.

Not long thereafter, the Huguenots exacted their revenge when the Duc de Guise was assassinated by a youth in the pay of Gaspard II de Coligny de Chatillon, admiral of France, one of the foremost military leaders of the French Protestant faction. Confronted with such escalating violence, Catherine de' Medici, now ruling France as La Reine Mère, tried to keep a balance between the Huguenot and

Catholic forces that would stop them from tearing France apart. She ordered the de Guises *not* to retaliate against the murder of their family member, and they obeyed, at least temporarily.

Following this catastrophic and well-propagandized bloodshed at Vassy, widely disseminated by the new technology of printed pamphlets, Elizabeth I of England began sending financial support to the Huguenots, her Protestant coreligionists, out of sympathy for their innocence in the face of the Catholic violence against them. A "war of religion" had begun. After bloodshed that lasted two years, a treaty was finally signed in 1564 between Elizabeth I and Catherine de' Medici, finally ending this first "war of religion." There were to be more.

Many students of this period have unfortunately taken very seriously the offhand remark in a letter by a papal ambassador that Mary, Queen of Scots had once publicly spoken contemptuously of her mother-in-law: "Catherine de' Medici is nothing but the daughter of a merchant."[2] According to Adolphe Cheruel, writing in the middle of the nineteenth century, this seemingly offhand remark was the origin of Catherine's undying "hatred" of Mary; almost every historian and biographer repeats this anecdote to prove Catherine's lifelong detestation of her daughter-in-law. In this version of Catherine's story, the Italian queen was never able to forgive her Scottish teenaged daughter-in-law for making such a demeaning comment. Much is also made of the fact that Catherine demanded that Mary give back the crown jewels only one day after François II died, which does seem cruelly swift. So too, Catherine scotched the idea of wedding Mary to her second son, the young widow's former brother-in-law, who became Charles IX. Catherine also worked mightily to impede any negotiations between Philip II and Mary's de Guise uncles for a match between the teenaged widow and Philip's son, Don Carlos—who ultimately grew into a homicidal maniac, then died at a young age; perhaps it was just as well plans did not proceed. Catherine clearly did not want Mary and her uncles to make an exalted international marriage. But was it just pique against someone who might well have acted like a spoiled brat because she had been treated as a queen since she was six days old, always given precedence over all other children at court? Would Catherine, herself mother of three teenaged daughters, not have been able to understand her daughter-in-law's adolescent boorishness? Might there be other reasons beyond personal pique and female jealousy that motivated Catherine's reluctance to have Mary remain in France?

In his *Memoires*, James Melville, the Scottish ambassador to France and England, made clear that the "hatred" Catherine had supposedly shown to Mary after François II's death was, in his view, part of her attempt to dig the monarchy of France out from under the power of Mary's rabidly Catholic de Guise uncles.

> The King's death made a great change . . . he being wholly counseled by the Duke of Guise and the Cardinal his brother, the Queen our mistress being their sister's daughter. So that the Queen Mother was much satisfied to be freed of the government of the house of Guise; and for this cause, she entertained a great grudge against our Queen.[3]

If Catherine were to take up political control of France in order to protect the Valois dynasty, she needed to neutralize the de Guise brothers, as well as the Bourbon Huguenot faction. Yet her "grudge" did not extend to asking for Mary to return personal gifts. Although Mary had been asked to return the crown jewels of France, Catherine did not ask her to return the "Medici pearls" she had given to Mary for her wedding. Mary was able to take them with her to Scotland.[4]

꙳

WHEN, AS A NEW (and quite possibly still virgin) widow, the eighteen-year-old Mary returned to Scotland, life there proved as tumultuous as it had been in her earliest years, and very different from the practiced civilities of the French court. Her mother, Marie de Guise, had died of pleurisy shortly after being deposed from her post as ruling

Catherine de' Medici; workshop of François Clouet, 1565.

regent by the Scottish barons in 1560, so Mary was on her own. The Scottish Lords of the Congregation, who had transformed the Church in Scotland from Roman Catholic to a Protestant "Kirk," had lived without a sovereign for almost a year. With the financial aid of Elizabeth's secretary, the very Protestant Cecil, plus the moral support of the influential radical Protestant preacher John Knox, the "Lairds" of Scotland felt that they could justly rule themselves. And they seem to have assumed they could continue to do just that, without interference from another female ruler.

In the face of such challenges, Mary immediately instituted a program of toleration toward the brand-new Protestant Kirk of Scotland, reserving for herself only the right to attend her own Catholic Mass at court. She clearly had learned something from her mother-in-law about religious toleration and did not pursue the rigidly intolerant religious programs of her Catholic de Guise uncles. She also reached out to Elizabeth in England to try to make peace between that country and Scotland. Even so, John Knox railed at her wildly, exhorting her to give up the beastly, idolatrous, corrupting ceremony of the Catholic Mass, which to him was an abomination that totally negated her right to rule Scotland.

Not dissimiliar to Catherine's problems with Mary, Elizabeth's difficulty did not result from her dislike of Mary's "seductive," "reckless," and "passionate" personality. Their famous conflicts were not personal but fundamentally geopolitical. The pope could have very easily at any time excommunicated Elizabeth and sent an army against her as a heretic and installed Catholic Mary Stuart on the throne in her place, thus restoring England to Catholicism. As we have seen, Philip II of Spain worked hard to stop any threatened challenge to Elizabeth's legitimacy by the pope after Mary Tudor died.

The historical evidence for Elizabeth's womanly jealousy of Mary begins with Scottish ambassador Melville's testimony in his *Memoires*. Describing Elizabeth's extensive questions about Mary's height, hair color, and other aspects of her appearance, her studies, her horsemanship, her dancing, and her ability to play the virginals (a predecessor of the piano), Melville clearly was struck by Elizabeth's competitiveness with Mary. The ambassador was "hard-pressed" to figure out a way to answer such questions that would please Elizabeth without traducing his own queen. To be sure, Elizabeth had at this time strangely proposed her beloved Robert Dudley—soon to be made Earl of Leicester—as her preferred bridegroom for Mary; this proposal was, in fact, the purpose of Melville's visit to Elizabeth, so he may perhaps be forgiven for seeing Elizabeth's questions as jealousy regarding Mary's sexual allure in the event of a possible marriage to Leicester. Melville's scene has had a lasting impact.

For example, eighteenth-century historian David Hume, after describing the supposed rivalry, offered his opinion that "where there entered so many little passions and narrow jealousies . . . [Elizabeth] durst not avow to the world the reasons for her conduct scarcely to her ministers and scarcely even to herself."[5] Hume does, however, go on to suggest that part of the motivation for Elizabeth's hesitancies to approve of a groom for Mary was her reluctance to carry out her own part of the royal bargain that, were Mary to marry to Elizabeth's liking, she would in recompense officially name Mary to be her successor. The geopolitics of the problem were always more troublesome than any personal dislikes. (One wonders if Elizabeth were not in part teasing Ambassador Melville, testing his diplomatic dexterity just for fun.)

Yet there existed in 1565 alternate ways to look at the relationship, ways that are different from the narrative offered by the conventional perspective on their personal "jealousy" of each other. For example, the view of Catherine de' Medici, mother-in-law to Mary through the years of her childhood and adolescence, offers us a very different perspective. Catherine was a woman ruler who understood that there could be a parity between royal motherhood and virgin governance.

Catherine obviously assumed Elizabeth would ultimately marry. Royal women conventionally did, their reproductive powers ensuring the continuation of dynasty; indeed they were one of their country's most valuable assets (just as the "traffic in women" makes clear), most treaties being sealed with a marriage contract between the two parties. Although she expected Elizabeth to marry, the queen mother also allowed for the possibility that single womanhood could be a powerfully virtuous and empowered state. She could envision Elizabeth and Mary on separate thrones, together a pair of ruling queens, in concord, sharing the single isle of Great Britain, and with Mary patiently continuing to tolerate her people's choice of a different religion from her own.

In 1565 Catherine had many reasons to court Elizabeth, with whom she began negotiating a marriage to her second son, Charles de Valois, or Charles IX, who had become king on the death of his older brother François II in 1560. Now that François's young widow Mary was safely in Scotland, she was no longer helping to empower the de Guise family at home in France, so Catherine could entertain a useful liaison with Mary as well. Despite the differences in faith among the three queens (two Catholic, one Protestant), in nationality

Pierre de Ronsard, *Elegies, Mascarades, et Bergerie.*

(one Scottish, one English, one Italian and French), and in age (one twenty-two, one thirty-two, and one forty-six), Catherine believed that Mary, Queen of Scots, Elizabeth I, and she herself could effectively join forces to govern and achieve peace amid the tumult of masculine wars.

At Catherine's suggestion (or her command), Pierre de Ronsard, one of France's most distinguished poets and arguably its most popular as well, produced a book in 1565 that he dedicated to Elizabeth I of England. Its text makes an eloquent defense of monarchal rule by women. Ronsard forcibly insists not only that queens are well able to rule but also that they often prove to be far better sovereigns than kings. Ronsard explains in a direct address to Elizabeth that Catherine, the queen mother, had commissioned him to write this volume of poems, which he has now dedicated and sent to the English queen. It is thus safe to assume that the gift volume also represents Catherine's royal opinions about governing, richly loaded as the text is with elaborate praise of Catherine at every turn: Catherine the wise ruler, the tolerant, the creator of great festivals, Catherine who had erased the conflict between Protestant and Catholic, bringing peace to France.

It is therefore a bit of a shock to see that the central poem in this book is a work of dramatic verse dedicated neither to Elizabeth nor to Catherine but to Mary, Queen of Scots, *La Reine Éscossoise*. Such an inclusion in a book created for the queen of England suggests that Catherine utterly discounted any personal jealousy between the two. She certainly wanted to embrace the two younger queens by giving Elizabeth a book forthrightly arguing in favor of rule by women, as a cooperative group.

Having Ronsard include a dedication to Mary, fronting a poetic piece that is centered on Catherine's children, in a book dedicated to Elizabeth, at a time when Catherine was trying to negotiate a possible marriage between Elizabeth and one of her sons, was a subtle way of telling Elizabeth that Mary was still connected to Catherine's family. Mary, Queen of Scots was still her daughter-in-law (as Elizabeth too might become), and she was still a treasured sister-in-law, who had been playmate to all the Valois children who appear in the masque Ronsard dedicated to her. Catherine was thereby quietly urging the two queens to cooperate with each other in peace, as she herself and Elizabeth were now doing by together signing the Treaty of Troyes.

Years before, Catherine's personal astrologer-fortune-teller, the famous and often eerily accurate poetizing prophet Nostradamus, whose work has never been out of print since the sixteenth century, had predicted that the son of Mary, Queen of Scots would inherit the throne of England. At that time, Mary was the child fiancée of the dauphin and future king François II. Catherine de' Medici and her husband, King Henri II, naturally assumed the astrologer's prediction meant that their own grandson would rule Scotland and England. Although Nostradamus was in fact proven right—Mary's son *did* inherit the throne of England—it was James VI of Scotland, a son Mary had borne not to her former childhood playmate, François II, but to her entirely different and very problematic second husband, the Englishman Lord Henry Darnley.

By 1565, the two unmarried women, Mary, Queen of Scots and Elizabeth Queen of England, had already been ruling on the same island for some years: Mary for four and Elizabeth for seven. If the queens were such implacable rivals, why would Ronsard (and through him, his patron Catherine) address Elizabeth and Mary together as "twin suns" who illuminated the island of Britain with their royal twin authorities and beauty? It was true that because Elizabeth did not allow Mary a passport to travel through England to Scotland (although she had many times allowed Mary's mother, Marie de Guise, to do the same), Mary had to sail to her kingdom through the rough waters of the Channel and the North Sea. It was true, as influential historian James Anthony Froude, in the eighth of his twelve-volume history of Tudor England (1858), comments on Elizabeth's predicament, that "One rival only possessed claims [to the English throne] which would bear inspection," and that was Mary, Queen of Scots.[6] Mary had refused to sign the Treaty of Edinburgh (1560) in which she was required to renounce her place in the line of succession to the English throne. Hence Elizabeth's refusal to issue her a passport through England. Yet Froude goes on to condemn Mary as a "wild cat," possessing a "cynical proficiency" capable of "sustained and elaborate artifices," always insisting on having the "power of gratifying herself," ignoring what was Mary's simple and resolute insistence on the rights she had inherited through her grandmother, Margaret Tudor.

Ronsard's equal praise of the physical beauty of both queens seems strangely maladroit in the face of history's sense of Elizabeth's pronounced jealousy of the Scottish queen. But if the two were forced by circumstance to stand as claimants to the same British throne, they were also already both ruling queens, and Catherine implicitly asks them (through Ronsard's emphasis on their shared royal authorities) to sympathize with each other's similar predicaments in a threatening patriarchal world that held that no woman should rule.

The French poet's 1565 collection of poems is a small volume, an "octavo" (the printer's paper folded eight times), small enough to be carried about easily in a lady's pocket, like the book of lyric poetry it was. Titled *Elegies, Mascarades, Bergerie,* the little book contains within it poems addressed to each of the three queens: Queen of Scotland, Queen of England, and La Reine Mère of France. However small physically, the octavo edition is a pivotal work of Renaissance artistry that speaks volumes about at least Catherine's sense of what she shared with her younger royal ruling sisters. The stature of Ronsard in France at this period was preeminent. Lyric poets were, if you will, the rock stars of the sixteenth century, teaching the language of love to generations throughout Europe. (This language could also speak eloquently, if very subtly, about politics as well.) So far, no historian has thought to consider what Ronsard's poetry can tell us about the relations among the three most famous women rulers of Renaissance Europe.

The poem Ronsard dedicated to Mary is a masque, a small court dramatic piece, one he had written a year earlier for four of Catherine de' Medici's young children, then ages nine to thirteen. It is not certain that the children actually did perform the "Bergerie" during a forty-day-long festival the French royal court celebrated at Fontainebleau. If indeed the event took place, their performance would have been staged as a presentation to their elder brother, thirteen-year-old King Charles IX, for whom his mother Catherine served as regent. For Catherine, however, the English and Scottish readers of the whole book on the British island may have been far more important than any French audience for the volume's one piece of drama.[7]

The occasion for the gift of the dedicatory book was a treaty Elizabeth and Catherine had just concluded in 1564, the Treaty of Troyes, which ended the first "war of religion" between French Catholics and Protestants, to the latter of whom Elizabeth had given significant financial support. In honor of this treaty, Ronsard's dedication to Elizabeth insists on the peaceful power wielded by *both* queens in what he names a "prudente Gynecocratie" ("prudent woman-rule"). He seems quite specifically to challenge those who think men are better rulers simply because they are male: although men in the "best and biggest part of Christendom" then claimed women were incapable of ruling, this misogynist opinion was entirely benighted. Europe, Ronsard argues, "is governed today by princesses, whose [accomplishments] have shamed kings." He says forthrightly that it would be better that "a princess of gentle and sharp spirit would reign" than that there be rule by "a lazy, do-nothing King who has in himself nothing of the magnanimity of a Prince than the mere name." Ronsard goes on to castigate roundly the assumptions of many centuries of misogynist tradition.

Elizabeth would certainly have appreciated Ronsard's lavish compliments to her and to Catherine for achieving what no historical king had ever been able to do: lasting peace between France and England. The 1520 Field of the Cloth of Gold summit between Henry VIII and François I, intended to end war forever, had certainly not done so. The Treaty of Troyes did.

> For truly, that which the kings of France and England . . . did not know how to do, two queens . . . not only undertook but perfected: showing by such a magnanimous act, how the female sex, previously denied rule, is by its generous nature completely worthy of command.

Ronsard celebrates female rule and claims it to be *the* hallmark of the sixteenth century.

> Our century [is] so well ordered, where women, some by bearing children, others by virtue, have come to the summit of supreme power.

Ronsard here makes Elizabeth's virginity (virtue) equal to Catherine's motherhood (bearing royal children); so too, for Ronsard, the power of Catherine's rule as queen mother is equal to Elizabeth's autonomous rule. To equate them is to make Catherine's power appear as legitimate as Elizabeth's direct dynastic authority (a sovereignty that Catherine, as a woman, not to mention as a foreigner and a commoner, could never have exercised on her own in France). Ronsard is careful to compliment the French queen regent as both mother of kings and ruler of the realm. He underscores Catherine's fundamental achievement as a victory against the forces of intolerance: "The words Papist and Huguenot are dead!"

Conversely, the value of Elizabeth's virginity as a means to underwrite her personal power in her realm in the latter half of her reign should not blind us to Ronsard's different assumptions about the legitimizing force of kinship, motherhood, and fleshly succession for female rule. Even if Elizabeth wanted no successor, she had succeeded to the throne on the foundation of consanguinity—her family blood. Blood was the very thing the Protestant "democracy" of Knox rejected as the basis for rule.

Both the content of the *Bergerie* (a play about children) and its dedication to Mary, Queen of Scots (a presumed challenger to the English throne) may seem strange gifts to send to the Virgin Queen. But when the book was written, everyone assumed Elizabeth would someday marry and have a child for her successor. It is indeed a central assumption in the *Bergerie* volume itself: Ronsard's expectation is the celebration of both Mary's and Elizabeth's coming marriages, to whomever their consorts might be:

> But when [a queen] meets one like her in beauty,
> Fertile, she procreates a race through duty,
> A rebirth of herself. *[lines 854–57]*

Ronsard ignores kings altogether, not mentioning them, only implying they are involved in a queen's rebith of herself, procreating a dynasty. When Elizabeth received the poet's volume in August 1565, Mary Stuart had married Lord Henry Darnley only one month before. And Elizabeth had only just declined Catherine's offer of marriage to her son Charles IX, the fifteen-year-old king of France:

Elizabeth had said Charles was both *"trop petit et trop grand"*: both too little (he was half her age) and too great (as a foreign king of a much larger realm).

So, clearly, when Ronsard placed the *Bergerie* masque in his 1565 volume, he did so in support of Catherine's planned program of dual marriages for both Mary and Elizabeth. Many things had changed since Ronsard had written the central verses in the *Bergerie* in 1564, but the *gift* of the book the following year remained an offering of Catherine's assumptions not only about successful marriages for both Mary and Elizabeth, but also her belief that as women they were fully capable of governing their countries as well as, if not better than, mere men.

Perhaps even more fundamentally, the masque staging Catherine's royal Valois children was an exemplum to the two British queens of the reasons they *should* marry, that is, they should produce a group of children similar to the ones to whom Catherine had given birth.

The collected royal progeny in Ronsard's masque display in their variety and charm the fundamental fact upon which any family dynasty rests: birthright is the means by which kings rule. That centerpiece of the volume Catherine sent to Elizabeth is filled with children and so insists upon the same crucial centrality of a political fact as the one that Elizabeth's parliaments were trying mightily to drive home to her: that she should not only rule, but also reproduce.

Ronsard's play has a simple plot: the shepherds of the kingdom bring gifts to a young king "Carlin." Charles IX's two brothers—the future Henri III and the younger Duc d'Alençon (whom Elizabeth later nicknamed her "Frog" and seriously considered marrying)—are both shepherds; they give the king a stag and a goat, respectively; two other young courtiers, the Duc de Guise, "Guisin," and the young heir to the king of Navarre, "Navarin" (the future Henri IV), give the king a shepherd's hook and a richly decorated vessel carved out of a single tree root. Navarin's vase has the image of a rough satyr carved upon it, who is in the process of ravishing a maiden. Navarre himself was descended from a man notable for his roughness, and his

Catherine de' Medici and her children; Workshop of François Clouet, 1561. Left to right, Hercule-François, Catherine herself, Charles, Margot, and Henri. *Lebrecht Music & Arts / Alamy Stock Photo*

kingdom, lying in the Pyrenees, was thought by the French to be on the rough edges of civilized France. And in fact he was to become a notorious womanizer. He apparently also had a lifelong love of garlic and so therefore stank a bit more than the usual courtier.

Guisin, of the Guise family that had fought against the Huguenots in the just-ended first war of religion, offers a shepherd's crook, much like the pope's own crozier. While this crook is decorated with pagan figures, the papal reference would not have been lost on the audience. The play's moral is the same lesson of divine right that Ronsard offers directly to young Charles in the poem "*Qui resist au roi, resist à Dieu*": "He who defies the king defies God."

There are two other important poems in the book. One is written to Sir Robert Dudley, who holds a very prominent place with a dedication that immediately follows the dedication to Elizabeth. This pronounced emphasis suggests that while Catherine may have given up on marrying Elizabeth to her son Charles IX, she may well have suspected (as did many) that Elizabeth planned to marry her longtime favorite Dudley, a former childhood companion. (The younger son of the Earl of Northumberland and brother of Guild-ford Dudley, Lady Jane Grey's executed husband, Robert had also been imprisoned in the Tower at the time of Mary's accession but had been later released.)

In one of the truly bizarre episodes in the relations between Mary Stuart and Elizabeth, Elizabeth herself suggested shortly after Mary returned to Scotland that Mary should marry her beloved Dudley; indeed, Elizabeth made Dudley the Earl of Leicester so he could woo Mary, and sent the man suspected to be the love of her own life up to Scotland to be an official suitor to her. Instead, Mary chose Lord Henry Darnley, a man who (unlike Dudley) had royal blood of his own (and who was a potential heir to *both* the English and Scot-tish thrones). Mary's choice of Darnley angered Elizabeth, because the union with another close heir doubled up Mary's claim on the English throne. But it also left Dudley free for Elizabeth—which may have been one of the reasons Elizabeth risked allowing Darnley to accompany Dudley to Scotland in the first place.

While the *Bergerie* clearly suggests kings as the proper spouses for Mary and Elizabeth, Ronsard lavishly compliments the lower-ranked "Robert Dudlé." Ronsard offers quite fulsome praise to the noble-man: Dudley's famous support of poetry makes his name mount to the skies, victorious specifically over kings. Perhaps only a poet would think the support of poetry could make a mere earl supe-rior to a king. It was true that Dudley had over a lifetime patron-ized many artists and had received more dedications of books than any other member of Elizabeth's court save for Elizabeth herself; the earl's nephew and sometime heir Sir Philip Sidney was one of the leading poets of the age.[8]

More prosaically, at the time Dudley had been seeking support among Spanish Catholics for his projected marriage to Elizabeth, promising to send English representatives to a Church council if Spain

Robert Dudley, First Earl of Leicester; Steven van der Meulen, 1560–1565.
*Universal History Archive, Universal Images Group, via Getty Images*

were to support his match with the queen. Catherine (and therefore Ronsard) probably knew about Dudley's secret dealings with Spain. Whether they married or not, it looked as if Dudley was destined to retain power as Elizabeth's marked favorite.

Thus, a dedication to Dudley, in the midst of the French poet's display of the dynastic strength represented by Catherine's Valois progeny, was not entirely out of order. If not a king himself, Dudley could be father to kings.

Ronsard's praise of Dudley suggests that the French court did not care about the huge (and in England, disabling) scandal that Elizabeth and Dudley had suffered only five years earlier. In 1560, Dudley's wife, twenty-eight-year-old Amy Robsart, had died in suspicious circumstances from a fall down a (very short) flight of stairs at her house in Cumnor, on a day when all of the servants had been sent off to a fair in the village. Her husband became the chief suspect in rumors of a possible homicide.

After a thorough inquest that ruled the death to be an accidental fall, Dudley was cleared of murder. But suspicion lived on. The rumors made it impossible for Dudley and Elizabeth ever to marry, for their wedding would seem to prove that Dudley had every reason in the world to do away with his wife, suggesting that he had gotten rid of her specifically so that he could marry the queen. Rumors quickly abounded and formed part of the "fundamentally Catholic" attacks on Dudley (who had become a protector of English Puritans). They formed the basis for a bad reputation that lasted through three centuries of history writing, according to which Dudley not only murdered his first wife, Amy Robsart, he also supposedly murdered his mistress Lady Shelton; then he married Lettice Knollys, whose husband he murdered; then he ruined his neighbors by false litigation; and in the words of epic slanderer Edmund Bohun (1693), "he gave himself up entirely to the exercise of most wicked and universal Luxury . . . and brought into England from Foreign Countrys, many new and unheard of pleasures. . . . He would drink dissolved pearls and Amber to excite his Lust."[9]

In 1870, using historical documents other than the scandalous *Leicester's Commonwealth*, George Adlard argued that Amy may have committed suicide. When a famous Scottish surgeon took up the case in 1946, he argued that Amy Robsart may have actually been suffering from breast cancer that may have progressed to her bones, so that when she slipped and fell down even a short flight of steps, the fall was sufficient to break the compromised bones in her neck. (Among others, Froude emphasized the report of Amy's illness in her breast in 1863.) Since there is no record of any physician's attendance on Amy for breast cancer, it seems unlikely that she was suffering from the disease, as it was known and treatment attempted at the time. (DNA evidence might help, but it would be difficult to find it, as the cemetery where she was buried has been substantially disturbed over the centuries.)

Recently, in 2008, Alison Weir has pointed to William Cecil as a murder suspect; he was the one person who would profit from a scandal that compromised Dudley, his political rival. The evidence against Cecil relies primarily on a report by Alvaro de la Quadra, the Spanish ambassador, who wrote to the Duchess of Parma, Hapsburg ruler in the Netherlands, on September 11, 1560, outlining some very provocative things Cecil had said to him.[10]

Apparently Quadra, a great and not always reliable gossip, said that Cecil had asked him to speak to Queen Elizabeth, then in her midtwenties, regarding her quite public (and scandalous) intimacy with Robert Dudley. Cecil said that the queen "surrendered all affairs" to Robert and "meant to marry him." Cecil then asked the ambassador "to point out to the Queen the effect of her misconduct, and persuade her not to abandon business entirely but to look to her realm." Cecil apparently ended this conversation by saying that "Lord Robert would be better in Paradise than here."

The Spanish ambassador ended his report by saying bluntly that according to Cecil, Robert Dudley was thinking of killing his wife, who was publicly announced to be ill, although she was quite well, and would take very good care they did not poison her. He said "surely God would never allow such a wicked thing to be done."

Quadra also reported that Elizabeth herself said to him directly that Dudley's wife was dying and would most certainly be dead soon; this might have been after the news of Amy's death was already secretly known at court, or even—far more problematically—before the event itself. (Froude argued that Quadra's letter makes Elizabeth's statements about Amy take place before the news had arrived at court, but that has been shown to be his mistranslation from the Spanish.) Quadra does not make clear the day when Elizabeth spoke to him, saying only that she asked him to keep the news to himself. He summarized: "Certainly this business is most shameful and scandalous, and withal I am not sure whether she will marry the man at once or even if she will marry at all, as I do not think she has her mind sufficiently fixed."

Quadra's suggestions about timing, especially his insinuation that the queen knew beforehand of the death (thereby implicating her in whatever murderous machinations had gone on), are the most problematic part of the Spanish ambassador's report. He narrates the conversations with Cecil and then with the queen in the same paragraph, only adding, in a separate paragraph afterward, that Elizabeth had officially announced the death of Amy Robsart. The sequence of statements seems to imply a similar sequence in time: (1) Cecil's warning of Dudley's intent to kill Amy; (2) Elizabeth's knowledge of the impending death; and (3) the fact of Amy's death. But is it Cecil who is concocting a tale of Leicester's murderous plans? Or is it Quadra who seems to suggest Cecil's foreknowledge and therefore his potential guilt? At the very least (if we are to trust Quadra's account) Cecil seems to be planting seeds of suspicion about Dudley's guilt in the Spanish ambassador's mind.[11]

On the one hand, we will never know if Cecil took the immense risk of having Amy Robsart done away with, particularly since it would have left Dudley free to marry Elizabeth—an outcome he deeply feared. On the other hand, the scandalous nature of Amy Robsart's death would give—and did give—the politically cautious Elizabeth immense pause. Court gossip about the suspicious circumstances of the death of Dudley's wife had quickly spread throughout Europe on the whistling wings of ill fame. If Elizabeth had married Dudley, she herself certainly would have become compromised. How well did Cecil know his queen?

Quite well, it seems, for Cecil was immediately returned to full favor, and Robert Dudley was exiled from court until the gossip finally died down.

By 1565, when the *Bergerie* volume was published, the gossip about Dudley's having murdered his wife seems to have died down almost completely. Ronsard's praise of Dudley suggests that his sponsor Catherine de' Medici assumed either that Dudley was innocent of his wife's death, or that she simply didn't care whether he had murdered his wife. Elizabeth clearly thought Dudley was innocent, or she could never have suggested him as a suitable match for Mary, Queen of Scots.

Elizabeth's sacrifice of any possibility of wedding this most beloved man may well have contributed to her horror some years later at Mary's apparent decision to marry the Earl of Bothwell, who—all assumed—had just murdered her previous husband Darnley. Just as Elizabeth had feared that a marriage to Dudley would ruin her reputation, so Mary's marriage (however forced it might have been) to Bothwell, her abductor and one of the murderers of Darnley, absolutely did in fact destroy hers, quite utterly. It led to her losing her reputation, her crown, her freedom, and ultimately her life.

OF FAR GREATER IMPORTANCE than the poem to Dudley, Ronsard's poem to William Cecil is absolutely crucial to a new understanding of Catherine de' Medici's concerns for the peril to monarchy at this time. It is also central to my argument that Catherine took pains to communicate with Elizabeth (and also with Mary Stuart) about the challenge to their collective monarchal rule as women by the patriarchs of the radical Protestant Reformation. While the poem is not at all subtle, it does depend on taking seriously a pun Ronsard plays on Cecil's name that sounds like "Sicily." All queens were, of course, well versed in the humanist language of classical myth that Ronsard deploys so elegantly, and they would easily have understood its political warning about the republican threats surrounding them. It has been entirely overlooked in the study of the relationships among the queens, and deserves careful scrutiny.

Catherine's intimate knowledge of Elizabeth's court may surprise us even more than the existence of a poem praising Mary Stuart in a book for Elizabeth. The strange piece of poetry Ronsard dedicated to Cecil underscores the threats queens faced from societies preferring the rule of men, who had, moreover, been "elected" by other men. The poem asserts that Catherine (and Ronsard) understood the threat that Cecil, Elizabeth's secretary of state, posed to the foundation of Mary's rule, based on the divine right of kings. Elizabeth herself staunchly believed in the divine right of kings: they were beyond any earthly reproach and held complete authority over their subjects as God-appointed rulers; the people over whom they ruled had no rights whatsoever against their authority. Ronsard's poem suggests how much Cecil doubted that absolute divine right sovereignty was sufficient in itself as a foundation for good government.

Catherine and Ronsard clearly knew of Cecil's secret financing of the Lords of the Congregation in Scotland and his alignment with John Knox against Marie de Guise. Even more fundamentally, they seem to have suspected the two Protestant leaders' shared coolness toward the divine ideals of monarchy itself. The Treaty of Edinburgh (which Mary refused to sign) did away with her sovereignty in favor of an oligarchic arrangement between men.

Ronsard's poem cleverly insinuates that Cecil, like Knox, was fundamentally no friend to kings (or queens). Cecil had long been a supporter of Knox, and was a sworn enemy of Catholic Mary, Queen of Scots ever since her coronation as queen of France—when her

William Cecil; unknown artist, English School, 1572. © *National Portrait Gallery, London*

father-in-law Henri II claimed for her the right to Elizabeth's throne. Mary's most recent biographer, John Guy, calls Cecil a "spider weaving his web in London," with regicide against Mary Stuart "already in his sights" in 1560.[12]

Early in 1559 (only a year after the *First Blast of the Trumpet against the Monstrous Regiment of Women*), while Mary was still queen in France, Cecil had written out a plan for Scotland: the realm was not to be administered by a governor or regent in the case of an absentee ruler (such as Mary then was), but by a council of nobles appointed "to govern the whole realm." And if she "shall be unwilling to this," then quite simply, wrote Cecil, she should be deposed. "Then is it apparent," that Almighty God "is pleased to transfer from her the rule of that kingdom for the weal [good] of it."

In essence Cecil was advocating a government of aristocratic men, such as would have also been preferred by John Calvin, who had argued in the *Institutes of the Christian Religion* (first published in 1536) that monarchy was not the most hospitable of political arrangements to the practice of the true Reformed religion, but rather a mixed aristocracy-democracy would be. Such an oligarchy would not be one of birth but a meritocracy, a government of superior (male) spirits. (The founding fathers of the United States of America posited just such a group of men; they were, however, selected by fellow superior colleagues, whose qualifications depended upon the amount of property they owned—including in some instances other human beings—and not on their selection by God.) Calvin taught resistance to evil rulers, but unlike Knox—who championed outright armed violence in support of a purified religion against the blasphemous idolatry of Catholics—Calvin called for resistance to be passive, nonviolent, and nonmilitary.[13]

Opening with some elaborate and bizarre punning on Cecil's name, the Ronsard fancifully posits that his name derives from the island of Sicily. ("Cecil" was pronounced "sissel" in Renaissance England.) To anyone with a humanist education and therefore versed in Greco-Roman mythology, Sicily was the island where the Titan

Typhon, having rebelled against the sovereign gods, was defeated, pinned forever by Jupiter beneath Mount Aetna. The volcano's continual eruptions warned of the giant's attempts to free himself in an effort to overthrow divine sovereign power once again.

Ronsard's humanist joke on Cecil's name has a profoundly serious point: rebellion against sovereign authority never really dies.[14] As if the myth suggested by the name "Sicily" might not have been enough to indicate the poet's warning about Cecil's Knox-like rebellious tendencies against kingly sovereignty, Ronsard underscores the point by creating an original legend of his own in which Jupiter, worried about a possible resurgence of the Titans, creates a new political feature: monarchy. Jupiter rains down on the world with his seed, so that earth is made pregnant: "She conceives a race of kings, / Who God's justice mirroring, / Are formed to crush the Titan's crimes." The rest of the poem to Cecil is given over to a vision of how kings will obliterate the giants, should they ever rise up again against Jupiter or against the kings themselves. In the poem, "Sicily" is the preeminent battlespace between the earthborn forces of rebellion seeking self-rule and the celestial power of hierarchically ordered divine sovereignty.

Centuries would pass before the revisionary moves of twenty-first-century Tudor historiography finally discovered proof of this fundamental fact about which Catherine and Ronsard had tried to warn Elizabeth, that her secretary Cecil's real politics were, even at this early time in Elizabeth's reign, not fully in support of the divine right of kings. He needed to be reminded how it came to be, ordained by God. Exquisitely educated as she was, Elizabeth doubtless got the point, but trusted that Cecil's pronounced personal loyalty to her— for she was a brilliantly successful and properly Protestant queen— might override his personal conviction that politics needed to take second place to religion. At least as far as Scotland was concerned, for him it was better to have no queen than a Catholic one; better, indeed, to have a group of Protestant men. They clearly agreed to disagree about their different ideas concerning Mary, Queen of Scots' divine right to rule, however problematic her claim on Elizabeth's throne might be. As it turned out, Elizabeth trusted Cecil too much.

Ronsard's poem dedicated to Cecil, about the power of kings to prohibit rebellion against divinely authorized rulers, also forecasts Catherine de' Medici's urgency about reminding Elizabeth to hold firm to shared royal loyalties in the cause of Mary, Queen of Scots. Three years after Ronsard's volume was sent to Elizabeth, in 1568, after losing a final battle with the Confederate Lords, Mary made a dash to safety in Elizabeth's realm. Ten days after that desperate escape, Catherine wrote to Elizabeth about her concern for the safety of the Scottish queen, whom she continued to call her "daughter-in-law" (*belle-fille*). She appended to a formal letter a note she wrote in her own hand:

> You can understand—not that I doubt your good will, never hav-ing another opinion [of you]—and also that you remember how often we have sent [to each other] about the queen my daughter-in-law, as it is a cause which touches princes and principally prin-cesses. I am reassured that it is in your power to do in deeds what you have shown to her in words, so that you make me say that she would be happy to be in your realm.[15]

Aside from signaling to Elizabeth that Mary's safety concerns the fundamental issue of female rule—its being principally a problem for princesses ("principalement au prinsese")—the main body of the for-mal letter insists more clearly that it is not so much a question of Eliz-abeth's harboring Mary, but of the English queen's aiding Mary in her struggle against her disloyal subjects: "it is necessary for princes to help each other in chastising and punishing subjects which rise up against them." Ronsard's poem to Cecil had said the same thing.

Nevertheless, even though Elizabeth had apparently promised Catherine and her son the king that she would send troops to help Mary regain her throne, in fact she never did. Instead, she impris-oned Queen Mary Stuart in England for eighteen years. All that time, Cecil tormented her about the urgent need to execute her prisoner, another anointed queen.

Elizabeth did not need to read Ronsard's book to know that the legitimacies of the two queens on the British island were inextricably intertwined. But she did send the poet a diamond as a gift in response to his presentation to her of the volume of verse. Doubtless she read Ronsard's clever humanist warning about Cecil, and understood that the poet, along with Catherine de' Medici, genuinely supported the legitimacy of female rule.

# PART TWO

✥

## THE STUARTS

# CHAPTER FOUR

‍ᔕᕰᕫ

# "Sister" Queens, Mary Stuart and Elizabeth Tudor

*The Solid Gold Baptismal Font*

hen told in 1566 of the birth of the male baby who would eventually grow up to become her successor after she died in 1603, Elizabeth, the Virgin Queen, reputedly dropped to her knees and cried out, "The queen of Scots is this day lighter of a fair son, and I am but a barren stock!" This is at least the traditional story told of Elizabeth's response on the night the news of Prince James of Scotland's birth was whispered into her ear by her secretary William Cecil.[1]

The famous quotation again comes from the Scottish ambassador James Melville's *Memoires*; he was an eyewitness—but he only saw Elizabeth's reaction and presumably did not hear what Cecil had whispered to her. What then if we ask: What did Cecil say to the queen? If Cecil had chastised her about her long refusal to wed by pointing out, "Mary, Queen of Scots has fulfilled her queen's duty and you have not!," one can well imagine the reasons for Elizabeth's responding the way Melville reports she did.

We know Cecil now feared Mary even more than before, for her power had only been increased by her giving birth to an heir, especially a male one with royal bloodlines descending from both his parents. When Mary Stuart had married an English subject of Elizabeth's who was Catholic and also cousin to both queens and thus had his own claim to the English throne, she had done so without Elizabeth's official permission, although she had promised the English queen—as her closest kin—that she would obtain it.

Elizabeth had quickly made clear that she in no way approved of Mary's choice of a groom because he, like Mary, stood in rank too close to Elizabeth's throne. Henry Darnley's pedigree was deeply dangerous. Henry VIII's older sister Margaret had married King James IV of Scotland, to whom she had borne the father of Mary Stuart, King James V. Then in 1514, after the death of James IV, she had made a second marriage, to Archibald Douglas; the child of this (very unhappy) union was Lady Margaret Douglas, none other than the mother of Henry Darnley. So in the closely tangled gene-alogy of sixteenth-century royals, Henry VIII's sister Margaret was the grandmother of *both* Mary Stuart *and* Henry Darnley (just as Isabella of Castile was *both* the grandmother of Mary Tudor and the great-grandmother of Mary's husband Philip II).

At first the Protestant propaganda against Mary's marriage did not mention its threat to Elizabeth but focused on Mary's unseemly behavior during the courtship. Anti-Catholic Scottish courtiers attested to Mary's besotted physical lust for Darnley. The very Prot-estant Earl of Moray, Mary's illegitimate half-brother, broke with Mary over her choice of Darnley, ostensibly because of his Cathol-icism, but probably in part because he feared losing his place as adviser to his sister. Mary's Catholicism and thereby her "idolatrous" defects of character fed into her reputation for unrestrained pas-sion. Following the contemporary slander, Froude summarized her character:

> From the day on which she set foot in Scotland she had kept her eye on Elizabeth's throne, and she had determined to restore Catholicism; but her public schemes were but mirrors in which she could see the reflection of her own greatness . . . the passions which were blended with her policy made her incapable of . . . restraint.[2]

Before her portentous marriage to Darnley, Mary had been praised for her virginal purity and decorous elegance as queen; at the time her virtuous behavior provided a celebrated contrast to Elizabeth's reprehensible public flirtation with Robert Dudley. Later, however, Mary became the preeminent image of the lust-driven, passionate, and unreasonable woman ruler.[3] Unfortunately, the marriage to Darnley proved to be a catastrophic failure, not because of Mary's own flaws but as a result of her husband's narcissism, folly, and vengeful desire to take over the Scottish throne for himself. She had chosen him quite blindly, not understanding his weak character and his alcoholism. His personal intellectual and moral frailty, however, would have little effect on the pedigrees of their children. Catholic Europe could still be expected to find the Catholic Queen of Scots and her Catholic husband attractive as successors (or alternatives) to Elizabeth: Mary would still have a (Catholic) dynasty in the making, while Elizabeth might end up the last of the Tudors (as in fact she did).

At the time of the baptism of the baby who would become James VI of Scotland (and subsequently James I of England), the two sister queens Elizabeth and Mary were more closely tied together than they had ever been before or would ever be thereafter. Having recovered from her jealousy (or indeed not truly having been as despairingly jealous of the Scottish queen as Ambassador Melville had supposed), Elizabeth I sent to Mary a significant gift, a solid gold baptismal font for use in the ceremony of the baby's baptism. This font was subsequently melted down, only six months after the festivities, when Mary, Queen of Scots needed its gold to pay troops to quell yet another rebellion of her nobles.

Easily convertible into cash, the font was clearly no inalienable possession. Yet while some have taken its destruction as an act of boorish ingratitude on Mary's part, Elizabeth herself may well have intended the gift to provide her sister queen quite specifically with emergency cash, understanding as she did how much poorer Scotland's crown was than England's. All we know now is that the font was made of solid gold and was said to weigh a full 333 troy ounces.[4] We don't know how tall it was or how elaborate the design of this "font of gold for a gift," as it was called by William Camden, the first to write a history of Elizabeth's reign.[5] We do know, however, the exact route taken to deliver it from London to Stirling Castle, some fifty-one modern miles northwest of Edinburgh, in time for Prince James's baptism on December 15, 1566.

And we also know that the goldsmiths who made the baptismal font used about twenty-two pounds of pure gold. Elizabethan poet John Donne reminds us that gold could be to "airy thinness beat," that is, to the width of a single molecule. (Such a thread of gold could reach across the English Channel from Dover to Calais two times over with length to spare.) Given that much potential gold filigree, the baptismal font could have been elaborate indeed. The Venetian ambassador, who attended the ceremony, wrote:

> It was a font of massive gold, of sufficient proportions to immerse the infant Prince, and of exquisite workmanship, with many precious stones, so designed that the whole effect combined elegance with value.[6]

Although it is not jewel-encrusted, a seventeenth-century Danish font may help to give some sense of what Elizabeth's gift might have looked like, especially the ewer (the water pitcher), which is made of solid gold. (The base of the font presents the Baptism of Christ in silver relief.)

Everyone who mentions the font Elizabeth sent notes its extravagant value, but might her gift have been saying something more particular about the relations between the two queens? It was a present totally appropriate for a baptism, of course, but given the penchant of all sixteenth-century educated people to delight in mottoes, impresas, conundrums, emblems, and secret coded language for all those who could decipher them, it is not an insignificant question to ask.[7]

Baptismal font, Rosenborg, Denmark, 1671; Christian Mundt II.
*The Royal Danish Collection, Rosenborg Castle*

While the apparently elaborate workmanship and bejeweled ornaments might have told a useful story—a story now lost to us—the fact of the font itself is still able to speak. What would Mary—and her court—have taken the specific message conveyed by Elizabeth's font to be?

The gold font traveled from London to Scotland overland on the Old North Road—which followed a Roman road most but not all of the way (the Romans had never conquered Scotland, so no Roman road reached as far as Edinburgh). The gift probably traveled by cart—no doubt, given its value, with a retinue of armed guards. A brief comment in a report to William Cecil from the Earl of Bedford, the nobleman in charge of the convoy, reported that "Some [thieves] that heard of the 'founte' and my 'caryage,' laid wait in a place or two, and missing it, did not trouble themselves with 'baser' things of less value."

The font had gotten no further than Doncaster on November 25, 1566, still about 221 miles south of Edinburgh, a little more than three weeks before the huge celebration of the scheduled baptism at Stirling set for December 15, 1566. (The road was, of course, the same one that King James VI of Scotland would travel to become James I of England in April 1603, thirty-seven years later. He would turn that journey into a royal progress south, a leisurely trip of thirty-two days—a fast rider could do it in four—whereby he could meet with the English gentlemen who galloped north to welcome him to England and to Elizabeth's now empty throne.)

Elizabeth herself long remembered the baptism gift as an important moment in her commitment to the child—and therefore also to his mother. When she wrote to James many years later, she made a very motherly sounding point of recalling her earlier care of him:

> As we have always, even from your birth, a special care over you, yes also great as if you had been our own child, for your safety in all your troublesome times, not having spared our treasure nor the blood of our subjects . . . and for a token thereof, considering that God has endowed us with a crown that yields more yearly profit to us than we understand yours does to you . . . we have lately sent to you a portion fit for your own private use.[8]

The solid gold baptismal font was Elizabeth's first down payment on this long-lived support of someone she considered in a symbolic way to be her own child. A recent biography suggests that Elizabeth was not overreaching in assuming such shared parenthood, because Mary had in fact asked her to become a *commère* in mothering the baby, as if she were a member of the baby's own family.[9] Rather than have Elizabeth stand merely as absentee godmother in this baptism, the Queen of Scots wished her to be a second parent. Elizabeth later told James she had from the first understood herself to be like a mother, so much so that James often said he had two mothers.

Mary originally asked Elizabeth to assume this awesome responsibility when the baby James was only three months old; she had just suffered a serious illness and an almost complete collapse and feared she might be dying. Knowing by now that Henry Darnley, the

boy's father—drunken and power-crazed (and probably syphilitic)—
would prove a disastrous guardian for their infant should he be left
sole parent, Mary decided that the duty of the "special care and protection of her son" should be given to Elizabeth. By this means, Mary
might protect her son's life—defending as well his dynastic right not
only in Scotland but also in England. It was a remarkable effort to
appeal to Elizabeth's potentially maternal feelings of family and
dynastic connection. By means of this "masterstroke" of woman-to-
woman request for co-mothering, Elizabeth and Mary finally started
negotiating, "queen to queen," to resolve the problems over Mary's
(and therefore her son's) place in the English succession. Years later,
Elizabeth repeated the exact wording of his mother's request for her
"special care" of him in the letter she sent to James.

It was during this closest point in relations between the sister
queens—as they called themselves—that the baptism took place.
Elizabeth apparently asked the Duke of Bedford, her ambassador to
the ceremony, to play down the size of the font as being too small
for a six-month-old baby—but to say that it would serve well for
Mary's future children. Such a wish suggests that Elizabeth either
was being disingenuous or had moved on from what we have been
taught to take as her first unhappy reaction to news of Mary's giving
birth to a son, when she apparently fell to her knees and complained
of her own barrenness. Her subsequent actions suggest that she had
at the very least shed her initial jealousy of Mary's motherhood and
that any first hysterical response (if true) did not represent her own
developing maternal feelings toward someone she came to think of
as her own child.

When the font arrived at Stirling Castle, it would have entered a
court readying for elaborate celebrations: Mary Stuart had planned
three days of festivities—including masques, dances, banquets, and
an outdoor mock siege of a make-believe castle. All these conviviali-
ties would end in a nighttime display of elaborate fireworks. Scotland
had never seen a fireworks display before, although they had been
frequent in the France of Mary's adolescence. The festivities had been

long in the planning. In September, a courtier had written to William Cecil that the Scottish queen "was in Holyrood House . . . and there sorted her jewels, and commanded the Lords to prepare for the baptism, and appointed every one of them to have a certain number in colours, and has given Murray a suit of green, Argyll red, and to Bothwell blue." The listing of their colors does not quite do justice to the Lords' suits, which would have been loaded with gold trim and jewels, for noblemen dressed as elaborately as women in this era, and for the same social and political reasons—to display status and power. A nobleman's suit would often cost far more than what Shakespeare ended up paying for the "second best" house in Stratford.[10]

On his way to Stirling Castle, the courtier reported to Cecil:

> The preparation for the baptism is making at Sterling. She [Mary] has borrowed of the town of Edinburgh 12,000 pounds Scot and intends to borrow of the rest of the borough towns certain money to set forward the baptism.

Why would Mary need to borrow so much money for this event? The size of the expenditure needed to match the importance of the birth of a male heir to the Scottish throne. In fact, it needed to be huge because, at this moment, the prince's birth would mean that he might also be heir to England's throne. Ever since the "Rough Wooing" two decades earlier, when Henry VIII had sent English warriors into Scotland to steal away the infant Mary in order to make her a wife for his son Edward VI; ever since the Scots under Marie de Guise had hustled Mary off to France at five years old to await marriage to the heir to the French throne; for decades, many thought the union of the two realms of Scotland and England (brought about by a royal marriage) to be a much more desirable outcome than any marriage with France. While the union between the two realms would not happen until 1701, another century and a half later, the marriage that had taken place in 1503 between Henry VIII's sister Margaret Tudor and James IV of Scotland had aimed at the same idea.

It was, of course, this very bloodline that would finally prevail to conjoin, at least in James's physical body, the countries upon Elizabeth's death; then James VI of Scotland became James I of England in 1603 and retraced southward the steps his baptismal font had taken north. So the borrowed money proved to be a wise long-term investment in a Stuart dynasty, although Mary herself would not be alive to see the day. And in the shorter term, it was also a worthwhile action on her part to put on a lavish display of royal estate, spectacle, and bounty, if the baptism extravaganza (like similar spectacles of her former mother-in-law Catherine de' Medici) brought Mary's intractable nobles into accord with her rule.

In the boy's birth, Mary had fulfilled one of the key obligations of monarchy; and her son's baptism proclaimed her achievement loudly to all and sundry. In contrast, providing for such a clear succession was the very thing Elizabeth had *not* yet done. So, although it is wildly speculative to theorize, perhaps this boy heir—surrogate child of Elizabeth—might have appeared to the Virgin Queen to offer an obvious potential solution to *her* succession problem.

Although the Protestant nobles asked that the baptism be conducted with the rites of the newly reformed Presbyterian "Kirk" ("church"), Mary decreed that the baptism would be a Catholic one following the religion in which she had been brought up, both in Scotland and in France. She had promised the pope she would do so. This may have been one reason why she chose Stirling Castle for the ceremony: it was the only Royal Chapel still consecrated as Roman Catholic, all others having been stripped of their elaborate (and to reformers, idolatrous and corrupt) decorations and accoutrements.

At the baptism, the Protestant Duke of Bedford, along with Protestant Scottish lairds, ostentatiously remained *outside* the chapel, possibly standing in the central courtyard, or already within the great banqueting hall that formed the northern side of the courtyard of Stirling Castle. They were thus exempting themselves from the ceremony, not so much as a form of protest, but as a sign of tolerance, acceding to Mary's royal right to have the Catholic ceremony for her son. Thus, Mary had a Catholic baptism for her son, just as she was allowed to have Catholic Masses at court. Although she was trying to persuade a number of her nobility to return to her faith, she never used force, and "separate but at this time equal" religious toleration was the note of the baptismal day. Catherine de' Medici's ambassador to Scotland, Philibert du Croc, explained that the baptism was to be a moment when the nobles would do their *deboir* or "duty" as far as religion went, and that they were "reconciled" to Mary; he did not see a "single division" in the court.

Mary had not only asked Elizabeth to act as parent, she had requested that Elizabeth give James one of his baptismal names. Bedford clearly felt the weighty burden of making this choice when on December 3 he wrote, "I trust the Queen's majesty's pleasure for the naming of the child be on the way to me, as I am looking to be called to come to 'that Queene.'" By asking Elizabeth to name the child, Mary was conferring a special honor on her sister queen, an honor that may well have been intended to cement the bond between Elizabeth and the child (and thus also with the mother).

The centerpiece of the banquet after the baptism was a procession in which the food-laden dishes, rather than being brought out singly by servers, were placed on a round mechanical table that rolled across the hall, operated by a number of elaborately disguised masquers, while musicians paraded after it. The round table was meant to recall King Arthur's acceptance of all his knights on an equal footing, when he made the table at which they all assembled circular so that no one was at the head and no one at the foot. Sir Lancelot, Sir Gawain, Sir Percival, Sir Kay, and the other eight knights were of equal importance in the sight of their king (a fourteenth-century replica of the legendary table, embellished by Henry VIII, hangs in Winchester Cathedral, visible today). In the same way, at Stirling Castle precedence was shared equally among the different national and religious groups: French, Scottish, and English. The round table insinuated Mary's (and her son's) far more continuous royal Scottish heritage (begun in 1371) into the Tudor myth, which claimed that the family counted King Arthur of Camelot, a Welshman, as one of the founders of the Welsh Tudor family. In fact, the first Tudor king, Henry VII, with some quite tangential royal blood of his own, took the throne by conquest in 1485. In order to shore up his royal credentials, Henry VII named his eldest son "Arthur," adding the power of the legend of Camelot to the Tudor myth of a generations-old royal ancestry. Sheer generational extension made for dynastic legitimacy. If your family had been ruling for a century or so, you must deserve the right to continue.

At Stirling the international actors and some of Mary's Scottish and French courtiers costumed as pagan semi-gods, each group of whom recited a few lines of Latin addressed to Mary, who was seated on a dais holding her infant son. The costumed ranks of satyrs, naiads, and oreads each addressed the infant prince, while the nereids and the fauns directed their speeches to his mother, the queen.

In traditional historical accounts, the importance of the masque has been overshadowed by an impromptu drama created when one of Mary's French courtiers wagged his satyr's tail obscenely in the direction of the English guests. A fistfight fracas quickly ensued that interrupted the feasting until Queen Mary and the Duke of Bedford managed to silence the two warring groups. Historians tend to stop telling the story of the baptismal celebration here because the combat underscores the simmering baronial violence always alive at the Scottish court.

The baptism was only a brief lull between crescendos of catastrophic conflict. Only nine months before the birth of the prince and the baptism, Mary's personal secretary, David Rizzio, had been dragged out of her presence still clinging to her skirts, into a hall and knifed to death by fifty dagger thrusts. And only two months after the baptismal festivities, the baby's father, Darnley, would be killed in a spectacular cataclysm when the house in which he was sleeping was blown up by multiple barrels of gunpowder hidden in the basement. It is no wonder that historians stop narrating any details about the baptismal masque when they must confront the historical impact of the appalling murders of Rizzio in 1566 and Darnley in 1567.

While it will be necessary to look again in some detail in the next chapter at the two interconnected murders—as Darnley himself had been the cause of Rizzio's slaughter—the impact of Mary's and Elizabeth's shared intentions with the baptismal ceremony had no less a far-reaching political impact than the violence itself. Pacific poetry is less exciting than gore, but is just as important in understanding what all the actors were trying to accomplish. What did Mary hope to achieve by including a performance of her (perhaps) still loyal court poet George Bouchanan's Latin masque, *Pompae deorum rusticorum*, "Parade of the Rustic Gods?"[11] Buchanan's masque spoke of the gifts the gods were giving to the Queen and her infant son:

> Valorous, wise Queen, happier to give form to the most fortunate: the fruit of marriage; but most happy are those foreign legates . . . rustic gods who reverence it with gifts inherited from the woodland satyrs and the fountains of the naiades.

Casting all the foreign ambassadors who attended the ceremony as an assembly of rustic gods, Buchanan's Latin poetry envisions Scotland as a humanist haven in and of itself. Historians have demonstrated that the baptismal celebration owed much to the festivals that had been mounted just a year earlier at Bayonne, France, by Mary's former mother-in-law Catherine de' Medici. That occasion had feted Catherine's daughter Elisabeth Valois, queen of Spain, and the duke of Alva, who stood in for her husband Philip II. It was held over a period of days in the middle of Catherine's royal tour in 1564–66. A book published soon after the tour allowed a wider audience to appreciate its many "magnificences," although it is likely that Mary heard even more directly about its various entertainments from participant eyewitnesses.

Catherine's elaborately staged events provide a measure by which to judge Mary's specific intentions, if not her success, both in their similarities to her former mother-in-law's extravaganzas and also, most pertinently, in their differences. First of all, Catherine's festivals took place in the French language, while Buchanan's Latin poetry importantly claimed a more international humanist audience for the Scottish festivities. Performing in Latin also sidestepped the issue of which vernacular language to use: French or English or Scots? George Buchanan was, like John Milton a century later, a poet famed for his achievements in Latin poetry (the two poets are comparable only in Latin; Milton is a major author in the English canon of literature). Aimed at a broader humanist culture of classicizing performances that could then be shared among the learned in the realms of France, England, and Scotland, the Buchanan masque subtly insists not only upon the giving of gifts, but also on the fact that those gifts were inherited.

The "Parade of the Rustic Gods" insists by its use of Latin that all European realms must and do play by the same rules of civilization—especially the rules of inheritance. The boy James will be king by virtue of the fact that his mother is queen. By the same rules, the "foreign" legates will bequeath gifts that they have themselves inherited. Mary's subtle point must be not only what her son inherits from her, but what she inherits from her bloodline, that is, her place (and his) in the succession to the English throne. Her inheritance underlies her authority spectacularly presented to the nobles and legates who attended the ceremony.

The giving of gifts is, of course, an entirely appropriate ritual for a baptism; the actual contents of the offerings are not specified in the masque, though the naiads explain that their gifts to the king will not seem so small if, instead of using gifts to value the heart, the heart gives value to the gifts. Such elegant rhetorical devices as this one—balancing gifts and hearts—are the stuff of humanist compliment. (The specific rhetorical figure is called a *chiasmus*, from the Greek word for cross, and was much favored by Virgil, Rome's most revered poet.) The relationship of gift-giving and kingship was, of course, a very old English tradition; the word "lord" derives from the Anglo-Saxon word *hlafford*, bread-giver. The lord was he who consolidated the material goods of the culture and apportioned them back to his people. The reciprocity of the exchanges is fundamental to most social connections, and so gift-giving is a signal ritual in demonstrating the loyalty of Scottish subjects to their queen and infant prince, as well as, of course, the acknowledgment by foreign powers of the importance of Scotland among the kingdoms of Europe.

When Henry VIII went on his royal tours throughout his realm, sometimes showing off his entire retinue, sometimes in smaller hunting parties, gifts to him usually took the form of food, implements for the hunt, or hawks, as suited his masculine pastimes. In the earlier part of her reign, Elizabeth instead received silver and gold plate and coin. The convertibilty of the font into similar cash gifts, like her later gifts of money to James, may have been due to Elizabeth's knowledge that Scotland was a poor country. The gold font could easily be melted down, as it subsequently was, without entirely losing the meaning of the significance of the gift when originally given.

Accompanying the masque, the central event of the baptismal festivities for Mary's infant James was a surprise to the guests: a mock battle that took place outdoors. In it, diversely disguised groups of noblemen assaulted an enchanted castle: bands of Moors, Highlanders, centaurs, German knights, and fiends were all successfully repelled.

Specifically modeled on the "magnificence" enacted in Bayonne, the place where Catherine had hoped to meet the king and queen of Spain on the French-Spanish border the year before, this "triumph," as even John Knox called it, was designed to do what Catherine de' Medici's celebrations also always aimed to accomplish: produce a reconciliation among competing factions at court and in Europe. The Valois tapestry of the Bayonne "Tournament" shows the Bretons and Irish in mock fighting. The Valois tapestry scene will give us some idea of what Mary was copying in this dramatic siege of a castle. Following Catherine's lead, Mary was using open-air festivals to transform military combat into art, to make battle into theater, resplendent with exotic costumes and weaponry.

Catherine had suppressed all jousting performances in France after her husband Henri II's death from the wound he'd taken during

Detail, Valois tapestry, "Elephant"; unknown atelier, ca. 1575. Celtic warriors wear a continental conception of plaid; note also some confusion kilts. Other fighters wear turbans. *Gallerie degli Uffizi, Florence*

a joust, and in place of these dangerous combats, she had presented brilliant musical concerts, classical ballets (the elaborate geometric patterns of which she often personally choreographed), and various feats of equestrian skill, such as running at the quintain, a small metal ring hanging from a swiveling armature. She thereby created a direct translation of the test of jousting skills into a feat far less likely to cause the death of any participant. The fireballs thrown into the mix in the mock "melee" game in both Catherine's and Mary's performed castle attacks would have added to the excitement and potential danger of the festival events without actually threatening human life (or, indeed, even serious injuries to the horses).

So, like Catherine's French spectacles at Bayonne, Mary's baptismal festivity to celebrate James's christening at Stirling in Scotland was an event by which she could consolidate her monarchal authority in the face of an increasingly violent honor culture, practiced to the

Detail, Valois tapestry, "Tournament." *Gallerie degli Uffizi, Florence*

point of death by her Scottish barons. Just as Catherine attempted to allay hostilities between her Roman Catholic and Huguenot nobles by making them participate together in civil pastimes such as feasts, masques, balls, plays, concerts, and other festivities, so her daughter-in-law Mary Stuart, now ruler of the Scots, did for Roman Catholic and Protestant nobles.[12]

The finale at the Stirling ceremony was a coruscating display of fireworks—the first ever performed in Scotland. The preparations for the show had been elaborate and time consuming. A record of payments mentions the work of four men involved in bringing the barrels of gunpowder and one small barrel of brimstone by cart from Dunbar; they note that the Laird of Quhitlaw was to be reimbursed for the use of his horses. A special gunner at the castle at Dunbar was brought in to create the fireworks. He was asked to write to Mary explaining how the pyrotechnic project had been executed specifically to her own design: "Inform hir highness of the foresaid fyrework conforms to hir grace's precept there upoun." The cliff upon which Stirling Castle sits rises far more abruptly from the plain than Edinburgh Castle, so the fireworks show would have been visible for miles in every direction. It was a perfect site for a nighttime display.

It was also highly significant in that Stirling had been the site of two of the most important battles in the history of Scottish independence: the victories of William Wallace at Stirling Bridge (1297) and of Robert Bruce at Bannockburn (1314), when each hero decisively defeated far larger English forces. So the gunpowder would not merely have provided a beautiful nighttime spectacle but also a display of the martial power of Scotland that had in history twice prevailed over its far stronger neighbor to the south and had done so near the very spot now occupied by the present royal stronghold.

The gift of the baptismal font tells us much about an aspect of the relationship between Elizabeth and Mary, monarchs of those two ancient enemy kingdoms, a relationship that we have misunderstood through lack of attention to particulars and through our misplaced preconceptions about their rivalry. Why did Elizabeth choose to give as a gift the baptismal font itself, the centerpiece of the ceremony? The answer, I think, is that Elizabeth's font insists, with a quite pronounced emphasis, on the same unity and toleration everywhere highlighted in Mary's ceremony and its surrounding banquets. Because the visiting Venetian ambassador testified that the font was highly elaborate with jewels, we can guess that it might very well have had a story displayed upon it, probably a story concerning a biblical baptism. We will never know. But that does not mean that the font could not speak for itself.

Elizabeth's choice of the font, the implement in the church that centers the congregation's attention on sharing the vows of Christian commitment, also subtly insists that baptism was the one sacrament still shared without controversy between the two divided Christian churches. Even if the Protestants chose to remain outside, the font would have pointed straight to the heart of fundamental Christian

unity. Over the early decades of the sixteenth century, Protestantism had shed as unnecessary, and not biblically authorized, five other
Catholic sacraments (private confession, penance, marriage, last
rites, and priestly investiture), but had kept baptism, one of only two
holdovers.

The only other sacrament the two Churches still shared was
Communion, but that ceremony had become the fraught flashpoint
of the catastrophic conflicts over the nature of the host, that is, the
communion wafer served to the faithful during the worship service.
Wars were fought and martyrs were burned alive over what it meant
to take the host to eat. Was it to ingest a transubstantiation of
the *actual* sacrificed body of Christ, or rather to perform a Protestant *memorial* of the sacrifice of Christ? According to the Catholic
Church, only the celibate priesthood was endowed with the power
to transubstantiate the flesh of Christ "beneath" the appearance of
the communion wafer. Protestants may have mocked this power
by calling it "hocus-pocus" or a childish game of magic and decep-
tion. (The expression "hocus-pocus," still with us today as a sign of
magic, may have derived from a corruption of the Latin words *Hoc
est enim corpus meum* ["This is even my body"], said by the priest
during the Mass when the communion bread and wine are turned
into the body and blood of Christ.)

But unlike the controversies that engulfed Communion, the rite
of baptism remained the same through the transition from Catholicism to Protestantism. And so Elizabeth's font was the ideal uncon-
troversial gift from a Protestant Queen to a Catholic one. Elizabeth's
gift emphatically stresses what the two queens shared—an essentially
similar, tolerant Christianity (and a womanly care for dynastically
begotten children). The font in and of itself insists upon the centrality of the shared rite, making familial bonds across the Catholic-
Protestant divide by welcoming and giving a name to a new member
of the fellowship of Christianity. We do the history of Elizabeth and
Mary an injustice not to notice their sincere attempts to consolidate
a strong sisterly, familial bond that would include a new generation,

through the baptism of Mary's son James, the prince who would become the heir to them both.

Mary gave the baby the first name "Charles," which she'd chosen to honor not a Scottish forebear, but her brother-in-law, Charles IX, the Catholic king of France for whom Catherine de' Medici had first taken up the rule of France as regent. In Mary's asking Elizabeth to name her son, and in Elizabeth's naming him "James" for the five Scottish kings before him, the two women were underscoring both his mother's French royal connections and the boy's British inheritance. They were therefore signaling that the baby prince might become heir to Elizabeth's throne, but also that the "sister" queens could align with each other when seeking comity rather than conflict, therefore creating a single family to rule the island. Paying attention to Elizabeth's gift of the font helps us to understand an entirely different history of this pivotal moment in the creation of a greater "Britain." We can hypothesize that Mary and Elizabeth were preparing to herald a new nation on the island, but such a goal was unrealistic given the global conflicts of the time and the prejudiced fears and aspirations of those who served the two monarchs.

In time, popular preference renamed the king "James Charles," and so in history he is usually titled "James VI of Scotland, I of England." His claim to the English throne ran through the bloodlines of both his parents, Mary Stuart and Henry Darnley, both descendants of Henry VIII's elder sister Margaret Tudor from her marriages to two husbands, one royal and one not. His parents were therefore both related by blood to Mary's "sister" Queen Elizabeth.

James's birth fulfilled all the demands of monarchal succession in Scotland and ultimately in England, as well. Why then, did it not protect Queen Mary's throne as she clearly expected it would?

# CHAPTER FIVE

૱ஜ

# Regicide, Republicanism, and the Death of Darnley

There was one key person missing from the Stirling Castle baptismal festivities: the baby's father, Henry Darnley. He had refused to attend. He was angered because Mary would not grant him the crown matrimonial, which would have allowed him to remain king of Scotland were Mary to die, and would have given him more power than even Philip II of Spain had been granted by Mary I of England. More intimately, Darnley was frustrated because once Mary had become pregnant by him, she no longer accepted him as a lover. With his drunkenness, unreasonable behavior, and outrageous ambition, Mary was forced to conclude that her handsome groom had proved a catastrophic choice for a husband.

Yet at first Darnley had seemed a very apt consort for the young widowed Mary, especially as he had been reported by Michel de Castelnau, the French ambassador who had been sent to Mary's court by Charles IX and the queen mother Catherine. Castelnau had described the young man in glowing terms:

> It is not possible to see a more handsome prince, who gives himself over to honest exercises, and (who) would like very much to begin his enterprise to travel to France to see the king.[1]

Somewhat naïve, like Mary herself, Castelnau assured the French majesties that Darnley was worthy of receiving the Order of St.

Michael from the French king. His pedigree was impeccable. The grandson of Henry VIII's sister Margaret, he was royal, and he was good-looking and taller than Mary (who, like her mother, was a "big" woman, though perhaps not, as some have reported, over six feet). He had grown up in England, the son of the Fourth Earl of Lennox, who owned land in both England and Scotland. As Margaret Tudor's grandson from her marriage to Archibald Douglas, he was Mary's first cousin once removed, and like her also stood in direct line for the throne of England, as well as less directly in the line of succession for the throne of Scotland.

True to his royal blood, Mary's young consort did genuinely and enthusiastically join her in pleas to have the French king Charles IX and queen mother Catherine send troops to aid them in a war that Mary sensed was going to be waged by the republican Scottish lords against their royal majesties. French ambassador Castelnau airily waved away the young couple's fears. Biographer John Guy, usually very sympathetic to Mary, strangely follows Castelnau's (one guesses) masculinist dismissal of her worries about the challenge to monarchy

Henry Stuart, Lord Darnely, 1545–1567. Consort of Mary, Queen of Scots; unknown artist, 1564. © *National Galleries of Scotland*

in Scotland, calling them a "narcissistic view" of her predicament and not the astute political analysis that, I would argue, underlay not only her very legitimate but also quite prescient worries. Mary placed her anxieties about the rebellion she faced in a broad historical context that Castelnau clearly thought was naïve. She maintained that her subjects refused her rule, not for the sake of their religion but out of their desire for more power of their own: they "left all obedience to her more for an evil and hideous desire of which they were ever and plainly full, than for in this case any hindrances concerning religion, [where she, Mary,] had no desire whatsoever to seek after and to prevent them in any way." Mary insisted that although Scotland had long been a monarchy, her subjects had never stopped wanting to make it a republic: and she used that specific word—"republic."[2]

Such a desire on the part of the Queen of Scots' people was "a thing which touches all princes of the world to see a subject rebel against his sovereign prince." She would rather die than witness such an event in Scotland. I would like to argue that, in making this argument to the French ambassador, Mary displayed a very informed political understanding of the forces marshaled against her. The not merely religious, but also republican, menace that faced her would, in two short generations, sweep her grandson Charles I from the English throne. Mary clearly felt that it was not only she who was at risk, but monarchy itself—in England and in France as well as in Scotland. And she was right.

For his part, Castelnau reported to Charles IX and his mother that he had spent four hours attempting to calm the two youthful royals, who seemed together to worry excessively about the rebels' intent to kill them both. He counseled the pursuit of peace rather than war; and he suggested that the rulers of France (including, apparently, Catherine La Reine Mère) did not think things were in such an extremity as the young monarchs supposed. Castelnau noted that Darnley was only nineteen years old at the time of this lengthy interview and might well be excused on the basis of his inexperience. Castelnau did not mention specifically either Mary's gender or her youth in dismissing her concerns about the anti-monarchist tendencies abroad in Scotland, but he did mention that during this conversation Mary had shed a few tears. Could they have been tears of anger at Castelnau's patronizing attitude? Long after September 1565, when Castelnau thought he had easily dismissed the young royals' concerns, Mary remained intransigent in her belief that a republican menace threatened her throne.[3]

Her trepidations proved Cassandra-like. Only a year and a half later, in February 1567, Darnley was assassinated; and only four short months after that, Mary was forced to abdicate her throne. The two young royal majesties were not entirely wrong, then, in their sense of imminent peril. Mary was well-enough educated to have understood Ronsard's warning to Elizabeth in the 1565 volume of poetry she'd been sent, and she might well have remembered it. Much has been written about the disastrous choices made by Mary and Darnley and in fact, they each did a great deal individually to bring on the catastrophes that overwhelmed them. While it is fair to say that they deserve considerable blame for their tragic lives, they were also right to fear a rebellion by nobles who thought little of murdering or deposing royalty.

Mary's historical sense of her kingdom's anti-monarchist tendencies proved extremely well founded. She understood that her conflicts with her nobles were not about religion but about power. Although his own masculinist assumptions about his wife's inferiority to him as husband made him vulnerable to the powerful factions that were set against them both, Darnley may never have understood how easily the Scottish lords could compass killing him, a king consort even if he did not wear the crown matrimonial. Mary's expectations of obedience from the lords would doubtless have been even greater, having been queen of Scotland since infancy and also having grown up as the only crowned child at court during the stable reigns of François I and Henri II, where she took precedence over the other royal children.

The rules and the rights of monarchy in Europe had for a very long time simply been assumed: one-person rule was best. The diplomat Castelnau appears to mock Mary's reference to imperial Rome, using it to counter her argument that she could only protect her throne by meeting violence with violence. He assured her that peace, as the Roman Empire understood, was always more effective than war. Leaving aside the violent civil wars of Rome's transformation from a republic to a dictator-dominated empire, Mary might effectively have pointed out the remains of two Roman imperial walls still extant in the north of England that marked the limits of Roman civilization, ruins left there first by the Emperor Hadrian and next by the Emperor Antoninus Pius, both of whom had failed to conquer Scotland. Quite differently, France had been colonized by the Romans; Gaul had been a major component of their empire for millennia. But two separate Roman rulers had been unable to bring the Pax Romana to Scotland. Because Rome had never prevailed, the walls had been built instead. Hadrian's wall marked the limit of Roman rule, which had included their long governance of modern-day England and Wales, from 403 BCE to 43 CE.

Roman forts on the south side of these walls had indoor plumbing. North of the walls there was none. The Romans had developed the water technology they inherited from the Etruscans in 200 BCE, along with their aqueducts and massive stone-covered drains and sewers. Such civilized amenities had accompanied the expansion of Roman power everywhere. After the collapse of their empire, there ceased to be any indoor plumbing anywhere in Europe until the nineteenth century. Such are the evanescent limits of some aspects of true civilization. Hadrian's Wall still boasts the remains of a Roman bath, hypocaust-heated water and all. But Scotland, never conquered, had never had such amenities.

It is perhaps not surprising that Scottish war leaders easily defied the rule of a teenaged female from France, a country that had been civilized by Rome centuries earlier. Before Mary had arrived from Fontainebleau to assume rule over a kingdom she'd left at the age of five, a treaty had been drawn up in 1560 between Scotland, France, and England in which it was arranged that a group of Scottish barons would rule for Mary in her absence, a situation that was doubtless expected to last through fifteen-year-old King François's entire lifetime, another forty years perhaps. (He died within a year of his crowning.) As recorded in the English State Papers, the barons had insisted that they

> do declare that they nor any of them mean by this compact to withdraw due obedience from their sovereign lady the Queen, nor the French king her husband and head, during the marriage, but in maintenance of their ancient laws and liberties.[4]

While they may have honestly felt they could offer this sort of obedience to Mary, when she returned widowed at eighteen, she found that the Scottish lords were far more interested in preserving "their ancient laws and liberties" than in showing reliable obedience to her as their sovereign. The case was made more fraught by the fact that they had recently changed their religion from the one she still devoutly professed. They were also influenced by the most notable leader of their new religion of Presbyterianism, John Knox, who had just recently blasted out his belief that women should never rule.

The toxic mix of politics and religion in all the upheavals of these times is rather aptly captured by the title "Lords of the Congregation," chosen by the Scottish barons. The "congregation," as it turned out, was a group of men who had first banded together to move the Scottish Church away from its Roman Catholic form and dogma. These Lords then went on to agree to formulate Scottish foreign policy, negotiating the Treaty of Edinburgh in 1560, a political agreement among the governments of three separate countries. While "Lords of the Congregation" first meant a religious body, it quickly came to specify a political faction. Later the Lords renamed themselves the "Confederate Lords," indicating an even looser collection of like-minded political men.

The Catholic Stuart, Valois, and de Guise families had early on understood how both the Protestant French Huguenots and the Scottish barons were using religion as a cloak to hide their politically subversive desires to challenge royal authority. Hence religion, as is so often the case, was at this moment far more about tribalism and power than about paying devout attention to the divine.

In 1559, Mary and François, as king and queen of France, had written officially to Mary's mother Marie de Guise, Regent of Scotland, their understanding that "religious" rebellion in both Scotland and France was politically rather than spiritually motivated—and that it was ultimately aimed at the suppression of monarchal authority.

> Under the name and the cloak of religion, they force to draw to their party many of our subjects of the said realm, and intending, as it is discovered by their actions, to oppress little by little our authority in order to attribute it to themselves and to appropriate it.[5]

We might suspect their letter to be more Catholic propaganda (initiated by the de Guises) than astute political analysis. But the young French Catholic royals were not wrong to assume the Congregation's quest was not merely for religious freedom but for a change in the political structure of Scotland's government. In light of John Knox's contemporaneous sermons in Scotland on royal rule, it seems the youthful Mary and Darnley also had a surprisingly realistic sense of the lay of the land. At this time, Knox was arguing bluntly that the mere inheritance of a title from a biological forebear did not authorize a person to rule a nation. His argument undermined the fundamental tenet of royal dynastic succession by blood. According to Knox, by then a renowned and rancorous castigator of women rulers, who thundered every week his theories of radical reformation from his pulpit in Edinburgh, a proper candidate for a ruler needed to be chosen by a Protestant people inspired by God, and not by having been born the child of a king. (Knox's view was a fundamental anti-monarchist position that would, in two centuries' time, evolve into the American Revolution against the tyranny of King George III.)

When Mary returned to Scotland from France, John Knox was already holding sway in Edinburgh at St. Giles' Cathedral, a looming brownstone gothic structure halfway down the "royal mile" between Edinburgh Castle and Holyrood House, an elegant royal palace situated in a large park, where Mary often resided. The young Queen would have passed by it often. After being famously hectored by Knox at court, she did not attend his Protestant sermons at the cathedral but kept to her private Catholic services. But her husband Darnley (who had flirted with Protestantism) did go to St. Giles after their marriage, and he was deeply offended by what he heard there. From the pulpit Knox was spouting doctrine that was diametrically opposed to the divine right of kings.

> Kings then have not an absolute power, to do in their government what pleases them, but their power is limited by God's word; so that if they strike where God has not commanded, they are but murderers; and if they spare where God has commanded to strike, they and their throne are criminal and guilty of the wickedness which abounds upon the face of the earth, for lack of punishment.[6]

The outcome of Knox's delivering this sermon was that he was prevented by decree from preaching whenever the royal party was in town—although Darnley and Mary left Edinburgh so shortly afterward that he was not much hindered in his arguments about the divine limits on royal rule. Knox had, moreover, written down this particular sermon, the only one for which he took the trouble to do so. He usually gave his sermons extempore and left no copy. But he published the sermon on Isaiah 26 so that as many men as possible would be able to read it in order to see for themselves that he had said nothing problematic, so he could argue that it was "for so very little" that their highnesses had taken offense.

But for those whose position in society was based on biological inheritance and not a God-inspired election, Knox's sermon would be troubling indeed. In it he repeated a point he had made earlier in a letter to Queen Elizabeth I, for whom one would suppose he might feel real respect, if only for her Protestant "martyrdom" under her Catholic sister "Bloody" Mary Tudor. But when Elizabeth strenuously objected to his *First Blast of the Trumpet against the Monstrous Regiment of Women*, Knox wrote a note of "apology" to her that instead bluntly restated his challenge to monarchy: "It is not birth only nor propinquity of blood, that maketh a king lawfully to reign above a people."

In Knox's view, any ruler should be nominated, appointed, or elected by the people of God, and should they decide that the ruler had become a tyrant, he could be deposed and executed. The people of God had that right. Elizabeth thoroughly disagreed, and made certain that none of her people were taught such radical doctrines. One of the original homilies in Elizabeth's reformed Anglican Church was a preset sermon "On Obedience." Her government required all preachers to deliver this homily from the pulpit at least once a year. In contrast to Knox's radical proposition of populist government and the right of the people to mount violent resistance, the Homily on Obedience insisted that even tyrannical and evil rulers must be obeyed. The second part of the homily emphasizes that Saint Peter taught that all people must be obedient to their masters not simply if the rulers are "good and gentle," but even if they are "evil and aggressive." The calling of the people is to be "patient" and long-suffering. Citing the foremost authority of all, the homily concludes: "Christ taught us plainly that even wicked rulers have their power and authority from God." [7]

The Elizabethan Church thus put monarchs beyond any legitimate reproach. Knox and the Scottish Reformed Church, in contrast, asserted that monarchs served the people, not vice versa, and the people could "unelect" them at will. This is in fact the foundation of modern democratic theory and was quite rightly understood to be a fatal enemy to absolute royal authority. As we have seen, even more than John Knox, George Buchanan, the poet who wrote the Latin masque for Prince James's baptism at Stirling Castle, was a republican outright, centering his political theory directly on the natural right of a people to "unelect" and even in favor of the people's right to execute a ruler who had not obeyed the law that put the people's authority over the ruler's.[8] When Buchanan and Mary read the Latin historian Livy together, they doubtless discussed the Roman author's worries about Caesar Augustus's transformation of the Roman Republic into an autocratic empire as an incidence of the fundamental tension in Rome's founding. Livy's lurid scene of the rape of Lucretia by King Tarquin's son would have been an unforgettable lesson in the conquest of decadent monarchy by republican morals: thus a formerly quiescent man snatched the knife, still dripping with her blood, out of the wound Lucretia had made when she committed suicide in shame at her violation, and holding it up, announced, "By this blood—most pure before the outrage wrought by the king's son—I swear . . . that I will drive hence Lucius Tarquinius Superbus [then king] . . . and I will not suffer them or anyone else to reign in Rome."[9] Thus, the republic had been mythically born out of the destruction of kingship.

Buchanan's *De Jure Regni apud Scotos*, written immediately after Mary's escape to England (although not published until 1579), clearly indicates the ideas he had held perhaps even while writing tributes for the royal infant James's baptism. Going further than Knox, Buchanan did not rest his argument in support of the people's rights on divine authority, but on natural law itself, of the sort that he and his pupil would have found in Roman literature and law.[10] Mary's complaints to Castelnau were thus far more intellectually and historically informed than the dismissive French ambassador realized. She claimed bluntly that Buchanan was, simply, "an atheist." (Buchanan subsequently did his best to imbue his royal pupil, Prince and then King James VI, with his political theories, and even though he often physically beat his student, he failed miserably in the end to radicalize him, as King James VI staunchly held to Divine Right as the basis for his rule in Scotland and England.)

While Darnley wholeheartedly shared Mary's political views on monarchal authority in Scotland, he turned out to be a murderously jealous partner of his queen's sole supremacy, scheming for an equal (if not greater) share of her authority. His most infamous act of defiance took place in early March 1566, when Mary was almost six months pregnant with their child. Darnley instigated and then took part in the assassination of Mary's Italian secretary, David Rizzio.

Angry that Mary would not grant him the crown matrimonial giving him equal right to rule, Darnley decided that it was Rizzio, Mary's favored secretary, who had advised her against him; for good measure he'd also decided that Rizzio was sleeping with Mary (even though Darnley apparently had himself been one of Rizzio's sexual partners, and even though Mary—then beginning her final trimester and probably quite visibly pregnant—was unlikely to have been involved sexually with anyone). Darnley had been assisted in his plot against Rizzio by a number of the disloyal lords, who bargained that if they helped Darnley to the crown, he would as king pardon all of their fellow lords then in exile for an earlier rebellion. Meanwhile in England, William Cecil, Elizabeth's chief counselor, had full knowledge of the plot to kill the Italian secretary but did nothing to alert Elizabeth (or Mary) to the danger that was then stalking Elizabeth's sister queen.[11]

In Holyrood House, on the early evening of March 9, 1566, using his private back stairwell lit only by candles, Darnley silently led a few rebel lords into Mary's most private chambers, where she and her ladies, along with Rizzio, were eating dinner.[12] Some moments later a large group of armed men barged into Mary's outer rooms, whose doors had been unlocked earlier by someone in Darnley's party. The men laid violent hands on Rizzio and began to haul him out into the hallway, where a mob of eighty more men was waiting. Mary tried to shelter Rizzio against the assault as he clung to her skirts with such tenacity that the assassins had to begin stabbing into his body before they could loosen his grasp. After the frenzy of knifing out in the hall, where Darnley's own dagger was pointedly left in the body, there were more than fifty dagger wounds in the Italian's flesh. To this day, the spot where Rizzio's body was supposedly dragged is marked on the chamber's floor in Holyrood House.

Mary managed to escape the palace, even taking the weak-willed Darnley with her despite his perfidy, after she had persuaded him that he was the dupe of the lords and would be menaced by them. They were helped in their escape by the Earl of Bothwell, who brought them horses. The queen immediately wrote on March 15, 1566, to Elizabeth about the assault, saying that one of the many murderers had aimed a pistol at her belly, threatening her unborn child, to stop her from struggling to protect Rizzio: "The rebels took our house, slayed our most special servant." She explains that she and Darnley had to escape from Holyrood House at midnight, riding through the night to a place also of great danger through "fear of our lives, and evil estate that ever princes stood in." She apologizes that she would have written the letter with her own hand, but she could not manage it, having become exhausted from riding for forty miles in the dark, with frequent stops due to the sickness brought on by her being in the final months of her pregnancy.[13]

The most pertinent point of Mary's dramatic letter to Elizabeth was, of course, its assumption that such heinous acts against a sovereign ruler should compel other sovereigns to come to their fellow sovereign's aid. Mary bluntly asked whether Elizabeth would support a fellow queen rather than (as Elizabeth had in fact been doing) underwriting the rebels of the realm.

> Which handling no Christian prince will allow, nor yourself we believe—desiring you earnestly to let us understand if ye mind to help them against us. . . . Praying you therefore to remember your honor and all princes should favour and defend the just actions of other princes as well as their own.

But the problem with regard to Elizabeth's sense of her honor was that she could not be sure that Mary's own acts were "just." The

Scottish queen had ignored Elizabeth's attempts to stop her precipitous marriage to Darnley, an English subject, and she had also begun attacking and harrying the nobles who would not accept her Catholic husband as their king. From Elizabeth's perspective, Mary rampaged across Scotland—or, to put it another way, selectively attacked the lords who had refused obedience—destroying nobles' property as punishment. It is at this point that the notion of a reckless and heedless queen began its vigorous circulation among Protestants both in England and in Scotland. Subsequently, once Mary realized that Darnley had been a ruinous choice as a partner for help in governing Scotland, she had turned to Rizzio, a foreigner and her secretary (and some thought a papal spy), to be her highest-ranking counselor. Her choices profoundly offended the Scottish nobles who had formerly ruled the country, and who had assumed it was their right to be her (reasonably loyal, or so they thought) native Scots counselors.

No one had warned Mary of the plot to murder Rizzio. She was astonished that Darnley turned out to have been a ringleader; although she had him declared innocent of the crime, she convicted and exiled all the others. Yet after the birth of her son, she was tragically persuaded to forgive all the rebel lords who had murdered Rizzio, and to allow them to return from exile to Scotland. No one warned her that this too merciful decision would work to undermine her royal rule entirely. In bringing back the rebel leaders, Darnley's coconspirators in Rizzio's stabbing, she unknowingly set up the conditions for the spectacular murder of Darnley himself.

The plot to murder Scotland's king consort was so elaborate and so clearly aimed at creating as memorable an event as possible that it might well have had as its ultimate intent the erosion of all trust in Mary's government as much as the murder of Mary's husband the king. Darnley was slain for having betrayed his coconspirators in Rizzio's murder when he testified against them at trial, falsely claiming his own utter ignorance about the matter "upon his honor, fidelity, and the word of a prince."

James Hepburn, Earl of Bothwell, was not one of the rebels who had refused to recognize the Catholic Darnley as king (indeed, he helped rescue Mary's party, including Darnley, in their escape from Holyrood the day after Rizzio's murder). He had also not been a part of the murder of Rizzio. He had always been a staunch and consistent supporter of the Stuart monarchy, first of Mary's mother reigning as regent, when he stole the gold that Cecil had sent to support the Lords of the Congregation in 1560; afterward, he was always loyal to Mary herself, as queen. He did, however, join with conspirators to carry out an elaborate plan to blow up the king, seeing Darnley's removal as a chance for him to take Darnley's place as king.

In preparation for Darnley's murder, at least twelve barrels of gunpowder had been placed beneath the rooms of the old provost's lodge where Darnley was going to spend the night while recuperating from smallpox (or possibly syphilis). Even more preposterously, the massive explosions, which rocked all of Edinburgh at 2 a.m. and leveled the old stone building, proved not finally to be the cause of

James Hepburn, 4th Earl of Bothwell, c. 1535–1578. Third husband of
Mary, Queen of Scots; unknown artist, 1566. This miniature is one of a
pair Bothwell had painted to celebrate his marriage to Lady Jean Gordon,
whom he subsequently divorced in order to marry Mary.
© *National Galleries of Scotland*

Darnley's death. Instead, he and his servant were found smothered to death, lying in their nightshirts out on the lawn, well outside the perimeter of the house. Why such a spectacular and clumsy way to assassinate a king? Why an overkill so excessive as to appear almost parodic?

Even though Darnley had never received the crown matrimonial, he was still King of Scotland as Mary's spouse. So his murder was in fact a regicide. When the murder happened, some of the ambassadors who had traveled to Scotland for the baptism of the infant James were still visiting in Edinburgh. Coming so soon after that large gathering of European dignitaries, the murder quickly became an international scandal.

Elizabeth's first response to the catastrophe was not concern over Darnley's demise but worry over her sister queen's authority—and her reputation:

> My ears have been so deafened and my understanding so grieved and my heart so affrighted to hear the dreadful news of the abominable murder of your mad husband and my killed cousin, that I scarcely have the wits to write about it. . . . I cannot dissemble that I am more sorrowful for you than for him.[14]

As if she had heard the citywide explosion of the gunpowder herself, Elizabeth reacts intensely to the staggering news of Darnley's regicidal death. But in the last analysis she retains her sympathy for Mary. However, when the news arrived at the English court that Mary had gone on to elope with, or had been abducted by, and in any case had married Bothwell, the man most people suspected of having been the principal player behind the murder of her husband, Elizabeth's sympathy swiftly changed from empathetic sorrow to emphatic coolness. And thereafter she distanced herself from Mary, writing on June 30, "We cannot fynd the old waye which we were accustomed to walk in, by wrytyng to you with our own hand." Elizabeth attributed the change to the "general report of you . . . and the evidence of your own acts since your husband's death." Nonetheless, she tried to hang on to her former warmth toward Mary and still stated that she personally felt "no lack of friendship."

Elizabeth's self-confessed "grief" over Mary Stuart hints not only at the breadth of the assault on Mary's reputation but on the English Queen's suspicions that Mary herself was complicit in the "abominable" plot to murder the "mad" Darnley, a relative of both women.

> Madame, to be plain with you, our grief hath not been small that in this your marriage . . . [you used] haste to marry such a subject who . . . public fame hath charged with the murder of your late husband.

Her hasty marriage, Elizabeth wrote to Mary on June 23, had made all suspect "yourself also in some part, although we trust that in that behalf, falsely."

The total collapse of Mary's reputation was caused by the speed of her marriage to the Earl of Bothwell less than four months after Darnley's death. Although Mary had already been castigated for succumbing to lust when she married Lord Darnley in the first place (a cover for political objections to his Catholicism and the feared loss of Protestant power), her precipitous wedding to Bothwell made her, in the eyes of propagandists and Protestant balladeers, something tantamount to a prostitute as well as a coconspirator in murder.

Much ink has been spilled over Mary's disastrous decision to marry Bothwell. The two had a long, complicated history. Even before she'd first arrived back in Edinburgh, Bothwell was no stranger to her. He had been the most loyal Scottish supporter of her mother, Queen Regent Marie de Guise. Earlier, in Paris, as the teenaged queen of France, she had facilitated Bothwell's being made a Gentleman of the King's Bedchamber, with a handsome stipend for his loyalty. She had indeed given Bothwell's bride sumptuous wedding clothes for her marriage to the Earl on February 24, 1566.

Now, word came from Scotland that Mary had been abducted by

Bothwell when she was on her way from Linlithgow Palace to Edinburgh. Accompanied by eight hundred soldiers, he had supposedly taken her by force to his castle at Dunbar where, it was said by some, he had raped her. Later she admitted, "We cannot dissemble that he has used us otherwise than we would have wished or yet have deserved at his hand."[15] The undecided question still remains undecided: Was Mary a murdering adulteress who plotted with Bothwell to blow up her inexcusable husband? Or was she an innocent wife and queen, traumatized by the spectacularly violent murder of her husband and king consort in an attack in which she clearly thought that she herself was also a target? Mary had left the lodge where Darnley was to sleep only hours before the explosion occurred. Two months later did Bothwell, a man she had learned to trust, physically assault her and force her to marry him? Or did she decide to exchange her disloyal drunk of a second husband for a third spouse, who might have the physical and psychological strength to suppress her rebellious nobles? Did she succumb (again) to lust? Or to despair?

For four hundred fifty years, the question of Bothwell's "rape" of Mary has been a vexed one. The most immediate evidence of an actual sexual attack on the queen comes once more from James Melville's *Memoires*. Melville was in the castle at Dunbar on the first night of Mary's abduction there by Bothwell. He does not say in his memoirs that he knew or even heard of any attack at that time. He does say, however, that he heard Bothwell boast that he was going to marry the queen, "Wha wald or wha wald not!" (whoever would or whoever would not [approve]), and add "yea, whether she wald her selfe or not" (whether she wanted to herself or not). Melville then mentions having heard about Bothwell's actual rape of Mary some days later, when all the lords were called together to sign a document testifying to their approval of Bothwell's marriage with the queen. One of the reasons given to the lords that they *should* sign the document was that the marriage was, in essence, a fait accompli: they were told that Mary had no choice but to marry Bothwell because he had already raped the unwilling queen. Melville reports the logic of the argument: "And then the Quen culd not bot marry him, seeing he had ravishet hir and lyen with hir against hir will."[16]

Melville also reports later in the *Memoires* that Mary was very changed in her appearance after her marriage to Bothwell, that she looked very ill, and said she wished to die, even if it meant killing herself. If one accepts the idea that Mary colluded with Bothwell in his kidnapping of her, and that she had with him planned his public announcement that he was going to rape her, and concurred in his claim that she definitely was going to marry him because he had already raped her and so she had no choice, then one can also believe that she also colluded with him in the murder of Darnley. If she was only pretending to be in despair after her marriage to Bothwell, fooling Melville into thinking she had been brutalized, then it is fairly clear that Mary was a perfidious and devious liar and an actress of the first water.

However, Melville's reported sequence offers evidence that Mary had indeed suffered from, and bore the psychological effects of, trauma of the sort her rape would have been. Women were then (as still even now) thought to be themselves guilty of inciting their own rapes, indeed desiring it; traditionally, the shame of the attack fell on them as its victims. Hence once the sexual assault had happened, Mary had—as whoever announced the rape clearly assumed, knowing the mores of masculinist Scotland—no other choice but to cover over her shame by marrying her attacker. Or, like Lucretia, by killing herself. The alternative options were in play because—and this is a consideration many men might not have thought of—she also could have worried that she might have become pregnant (as soon thereafter she did, in fact—with twins).

The abduction and shocking marriage fed into the lurid narrative John Knox had been telling about Mary ever since she had first attended Mass in Edinburgh and especially after she had married the Catholic Darnley. For their belief in the Catholic Mass, Mary and Darnley could be—and were—condemned for everything from lying, fornication, and adultery, to idolatry and whoredom, to being devoted disciples of the craft of the devil. Knox's objection to Mary's love of dancing and her lavish feasts, not to mention her faith, called forth his most vehement execrations. In his view she was guilty of the worst possible sin, a beastly abomination, simply by holding to the religion in which she had been raised.

In her letter of explanation to Elizabeth about the events following Darnley's death, Mary pointed out that she had done "nothing in that matter but by advice of the nobility," that is, she had not married Bothwell until he had been cleared of murdering Darnley by the Scottish nobles (many of whom were guilty of the murder themselves). Bothwell was exonerated not only by a trial but also by an act of the Scottish Parliament. Mary said she had been shown a bond to which a plurality of the nobility had signed their names, testifying that they all were in favor of her marriage to Bothwell. The means by which the lords were persuaded to sign this document, at least according to Melville's eyewitness account, demonstrates how quickly and potently they all seemed to assume that a rape would be so degrading to Mary that she would, out of pure shame, consent to marry her attacker.

Bothwell had hoodwinked Mary by saying all the lords were in favor of her marriage to him. She only later learned of Bothwell's deceit. He had served her faithfully for years. She clearly misjudged him from his past successful exploits in protecting her mother and also herself. Not only had he performed well during the Chaseabout Raid in 1565 when she pursued the rebel lords, he had also helped rescue her and Darnley from Holyrood. And finally, as she wrote to both the French and English courts, she realized that "this realm being divided in factions as it is, cannot be contained in order unless our authority be assisted and set forth by the fortification of a man, who must take pain upon his person in the execution of justice and the suppressing of their insolence that would rebel." She could not impose this order alone, being "already wearied and almost broken with the frequent uproars and rebellions raised against us."

Just imagine a comparable sequence of slaughter and sexual assault confronting Elizabeth. Imagine if a large gang of Robert Dudley's men had torn William Cecil's clutching hand from its clasp on Elizabeth's gown as he begged for her help, if eighty of Dudley's followers had stormed into her private chambers and had stabbed Cecil to death by inflicting on him more than fifty dagger thrusts. Imagine that Dudley had with his own knife thrust the last dagger into Cecil's body. Imagine that Dudley had abducted and then raped Elizabeth, and then forced marriage on her. Such outrageous possibilities seem so utterly and absolutely implausible that even to raise them somewhat risibly demonstrates the vast differences between the state of civilized order in the two realms with which Mary and Elizabeth had to deal.

In 1560, the Scottish Parliament had turned Scotland Protestant, exercising autonomous power after deposing Marie de Guise. The English Parliament sat for a *total* of one thousand days (close to three years) during Elizabeth's reign, which lasted forty-five years. England was an orderly monarchy; Scotland was not, nor did it, apparently, want to be. As the English queen haughtily informed her own Parliament when they were desperately trying to get her to name a successor, "The foot should not direct the head." Meanwhile, Scottish rebel "feet" were running roughshod over their "head," Mary, and thus also stomping into the mud the foundational principles of sacred monarchy. It was a threatening menace for any sovereign to see.

When Elizabeth heard that Mary's (and Bothwell's) forces had been defeated by the Confederate Lords in the Battle of Carberry Hill, which Mary ended to forestall further useless bloodshed, and that she had been captured and was imprisoned in Lochleven Castle by the collected Scottish lords, her sympathies shifted once again. The report in the *Calendar of State Papers* for instructions to Nicholas Throckmorton, written by a secretary for Elizabeth, explains that the queen's former stance had changed again:

But now finding from intestine troubles, [the Queen of Scotland] is restrained by her nobility and subjects from liberty, the Queen has changed her intention of silence and forbearing to deal in her sister's causes, to commiseration for her and determination to aid and relieve her by all possible means: "and not suffer hir, being by Goddes ordonnance the prince and soverayne, to be in subjection to them that by nature and lawe are subjected to hir."

At this point, Elizabeth then herself wrote directly to Mary, offering,

For your comfort in such your present adversity, as we hear you are in, we are determined to do all in our power for your honour and safety, and to send with all speed one of our trusty servants not only to understand your state, but thereon so to deal with your nobility and people, as they shall find you not to lack our friendship and power.

Mary entered her castle prison on June 17, 1567, less than a week before she heard from Elizabeth—who was clearly keeping a close eye on Scottish affairs. Lochleven Castle was set on an island in a lake, a half mile from the lake's shore at its narrowest point. It seems to have been chosen to parade before Mary's daily view the lords' collective masculinist power as it was ranged against her. Could it have been an accident that resident in the castle at that time was Lady Margaret Erskine, the mother of the Earl of Moray, Mary's bastard half-brother? Lady Margaret had been a mistress of Mary's father James V. She had always claimed she had married the king in secret and thus her child, and not Mary, was the legitimate heir of James V—and so the true King of Scotland.

Until this juncture, Elizabeth had trusted Moray, Mary's illegitimate brother, as a reliable Protestant bulwark in Scotland against the Catholic French. Now she finally became suspicious of Moray's machinations against his half sister, the queen. When Mary had married a Catholic and made him her king consort, Moray had started

James Stewart, First Earl of Moray; Hans Eworth, 1561.
Darnaway Castle, Scotland.

a rebellion against the queen's rule whose purpose was supposedly freedom of religion. Mary had put down the rebellion and had exiled Moray. In the guise of a purely Potestant militant, he had been receiving secret English financial support for his presumably anti-French agenda. In the second rebellion (the one after which the Confederate Lords imprisoned Mary), the barons, calling themselves "the States of Scotland," insisted that they were only rescuing and protecting Mary from Bothwell's malign capture.

For her part, Elizabeth complained to Moray that he seemed to be inexplicably slow in obeying her explicit commands to free his sister; in fact he now "looked to be dealing only for himself." The English queen was becoming increasingly incensed at the assault against the divine law protecting monarchy that she saw in the Scottish rebels' malicious imprisonment of their queen. In morally indignant rhetoric, she insisted that her ambassador lecture the Protestant ingrates whom she had supported for so long. She instructed Ambassador

Throckmorton in no uncertain terms that if these lords continued to deprive the queen "their sovereign lady of her royal estate," he should threaten them that Elizabeth would gather a cadre of like-minded Christian princes to take revenge upon them for their breach of obedience, "as an example to all posterity."

> Doubting not but God will assist us and confound them and their devices, for they have no warrant by God's or man's law to be as superiors, judges, or vindicators over their prince, whatever disorders they gather against her.

Threatening that she would convene a multinational army against them, Elizabeth was aghast at the lords' blatant refusal to honor the sanctity of kingship. "What warrant have they in Scripture, as subjects, to depose their prince?" Exasperated, she asked further: "What law find they written in any Christian monarchy, that subjects may arrest the person of their princes, detain them captive and proceed to judge them?" There existed, she exhorted them, no such authority anywhere in civil law. She thus accused the men, whom she had been favoring with financial support ever since Mary had arrived in Scotland, of committing "unlawful . . . acts of rebellion." Had she not realized that Knox's sermons would have had an effect on a Protestant assemblage of native nobles? Elizabeth was only just now learning what Mary had known long before, that both queens were battling an out-and-out rebellion against sovereign, monarchal authority.

However much the lords had accepted money from Elizabeth, who thought she was aiding them in their roles as anti-French Protestants fighting for freedom of worship, the native aristocracy of the Scottish clans, such as James Douglas, Lord Morton, and James Stewart, Earl of Moray, were no more intimidated or swayed by a foreign queen than they had been controlled by their own queen. They did not listen to the lesson the emissary Throckmorton had duly passed on from Queen Elizabeth. In fact, they continued utterly to ignore the presence of an appointed English statesman in Scotland.

Ironically, this defiant group included the men whom Elizabeth had advised Mary to pardon for their murder of Rizzio. And in the same letter to Throckmorton instructing him to lecture the lords, Elizabeth remembered that it was she who had insisted on pardoning them, specifically naming James Douglas, fourth Earl of Morton, not only one of the major players in Rizzio's stabbing but now irrefutably implicated in Darnley's murder—arguably far more central than Bothwell had ever been. Elizabeth now understood the Earl of Morton to be a—if not *the*—leader of the rebel lords: "Ye may tell Morton he had refuge when we might have delivered him to death . . . and he was pardoned at our ins[is]tance."

William Cecil, longtime supporter of the men whom Elizabeth had accused of "acts of rebellion," had in fact urged his queen to request the pardon for the men complicit in the Rizzio conspiracy. Cecil understood—as perhaps neither Elizabeth nor Mary did—that the rules of a Scottish blood feud would require that the murderers of Rizzio avenge themselves for Darnley's craven betrayal of them after he turned witness against his co-murderers in their trial. While in exile, they posed no threat to Darnley; when they returned to Scotland, it became only a matter of time before they exacted their revenge.

Recent scholarship helpfully explains that Mary's "policy towards the murderers was magnanimous" but that raised in a different culture entirely, "she had never really grasped the limitations of the honor culture in Scotland, where a stance of loyalty to the crown was an attractive option to lords wishing to advance their own ambitions"; any respect for the monarch was ultimately founded on stark "self-interest."[17] The Confederate Lords could now ignore the queen of England, possibly because they no longer needed her money, but also perhaps because she—like Mary—was only a woman ruler. They deposed their queen and made her infant son king.

Elizabeth seems to have understood the tribal male culture of the country to the North no better than the French-raised Mary. After escaping in a rowboat from Lochleven Castle in May 1567 and her army being defeated at Carberry Hill in June, Mary fled from Scotland to England. The Protestant lords quickly seized rule of most of Scotland, although there remained constant fighting with Mary's Catholic supporters. First the Earl of Moray ruled as regent for Mary's young son James. Moray was, however, assassinated in 1570 after only three years in office. Lord Morton then ruled as regent for six years; subsequently he too was removed from office. But he would not be executed for Darnley's murder until 1581, fourteen years after the crime, when Darnley's son, King James VI, then fifteen, had finally grown old enough to bring to justice his father's murderers. Everyone, however, had clearly known Morton was a major player in the crime all along.

Throughout this period of Mary's troubles, the main worry for Elizabeth—beyond the Scottish lords' open contempt for monarchy in general (just as Mary had warned her)—was the threat to Mary's child and heir, Prince James. Elizabeth had very recently accepted the responsibility of acting as second parent for him—just as Mary had asked her to do in the negotiations around the baptism—and she worried that the infant would be vulnerable to the lords' ambitions for rule. Mary had placed her baby under the protection of the Earl of Mar, whom she had put in charge of Stirling Castle. Moreover, she had specifically stipulated that he protect the prince from the intrusions of large bands of men.

> Suffer nor permit no noblemen of our realm or any others, of what condition soever that they are to enter or come within our said Castle or to the presence of our said dearest son accompanied with any more persons but two or three at the most.[18]

This caution was not merely to protect the prince from abduction by baronial armies, but also to force the overproud lords to shed their vast armed retinues and to approach the young royal scion as humble private petitioners. Her assumption, or hope, was that the practice would teach them at least a simulacrum of obedience to sovereign authority.[19]

But when Mary personally asked to have her son with her as his mother, the Earl of Mar refused, sensing that if Mary and Bothwell became keepers of the heir to the throne, the lords would revolt, perhaps already knowing that the prince was the key to their return to power. Because Mary very soon thereafter came under Bothwell's control, Mar's prudence was well warranted. (The prince remained at Stirling with Mar's family, which included a number of children to be his playmates. There, along with them, he was raised as a Protestant and given an excellent early education.)

Meanwhile Elizabeth was also trying to obtain possession of the child, and also failed. She instructed her ambassadors to offer a safe haven for the infant in England, as Scotland appeared to be subject to "sundry troubles from time to time," and therefore as it was clearly "manifest" that Mary's son could not "be free from peril," Elizabeth offered that "her son may enjoy surety and quietness within this our realm." She solemnly vowed to provide

> as good safety therein for her son as can be devised for any that might be our child, born of our own body.

Once again, Elizabeth's default mode for thinking of James as a baby was to imagine herself as his second mother, the mother Mary had asked her to be. Elizabeth seems thereby to dangle the real possibility of James ultimately taking his place in the English succession should Mary consent to letting him be brought up in England. Would Mary agree to have her son shipped out of the realm, as she herself had been at five? Should she consent, Elizabeth told her ambassadors to promise Mary that "she shall be glad to shew to her therein the true effect of natural friendship. And herein she may be

Mary's child, King James VI of Scotland;
Arnold Bronckhorst, 1574.

by you remembered how much good may ensue to her son to be so nourished and acquainted with our realm."[20]

FOR ALMOST A YEAR after being forced to abdicate in favor of her son, Mary languished in prison in Lochleven Castle, waiting for rescue. For almost an entire long year no rescue came. She then took events into her own energetic and capable hands: she escaped. Aided by the young son of the castle's owner, who had cleverly unmoored all the boats but one, Mary was able to sneak out of her island castle-prison on May 2, 1567, during the groggy aftermath of rowdy May Day celebrations. She was rowed to land, where a group of Catholic supporters waited with horses. Back in the saddle, she again gathered an army, as the lawful queen to whom the entire country owed fealty, just as she had before the battle of Carberry Hill. Before that battle it had been reported that "She minds to levy 500 footmen, and

200 horsemen. She has 5,000 crowns coined from the font Bedford brought to the baptism." The coins that had been minted from Elizabeth's baptismal gift had been worth three pounds apiece.

With a far smaller army, she lost the battle of Langside, and the Queen of Scots was finally out of both men and money. At that point she threw herself fully on the mercy of her sister queen in England, whom she trusted would cherish her as that sister had seemed to want to cherish her son; that sister whose gift of the gold font had sustained her wars.

When she fled to Elizabeth, Mary was just twenty-six years old. She never saw her son again.

꩜

# CHAPTER SIX

# Mary, Queen of Scots

*Eighteen More Years in Prison*

rench-allied Scotland had been tied to the larger wars between Europe's two major powers: France and Spain. Those wars had begun when the French king, Charles VIII, had invaded Italy in 1494 hoping to take over the rich Spanish lands there. The two realms continued to battle for control of Italy for at least half a century. Each time the French invaded, they were driven out by Spain and its allied forces. Then in 1525, the Spanish emperor Charles V not only conquered, he captured and imprisoned the French king, François I, at the Battle of Pavia. After Charles vanquished an army of 28,000 French troops, his imperial army sacked Rome and imprisoned the Medici pope. The pope's imprisonment by Charles's army was a core reason for his refusal to annul Henry VIII's marriage to Catherine of Aragon (Charles's aunt), which in turn led to Henry's overthrowing the entire Catholic Church in England in order to legally marry Anne Boleyn. Ironically, then, Charles's victory in Italy meant that the whole realm of England was forced to become Protestant, which expanded the very religion that Charles V had been fighting so hard to suppress in the Holy Roman Empire, that is, his extensive German and central European lands, including parts of Italy.

The emperor's victory also led to the destabilization of Italy generally, and most particularly Florence, where the members of the Florentine Republic took the opportunity to rise in rebellion against the ruling Medici family. As a child in rebel-torn Florence, Catherine de'

Medici suffered traumatic treatment at the hands of outraged Florentine republicans when, during the chaotic years of Charles V's invasion of her city-state, the populace had run the whole Medici family
out of town. They left eight-year-old Catherine behind to endure
house arrest. While for a time the young girl was housed without
harm in an elegant convent, she was subsequently paraded through
the streets of Florence, mocked, and threatened with being put into a
brothel for soldiers or being hanged naked from the city walls.

Such early violent trauma may have made Catherine far more
sympathetic regarding Mary, Queen of Scots' plight of imprisonment.
On May 26, 1568, only ten days after Mary's bolt to England, as we
have seen, Catherine de' Medici sent a strong, emotional letter to Elizabeth, urging her to foster Mary's case. She wrote with her own hand
a paragraph appended at the bottom of the last page—a sign of her
deep seriousness in composing the personal note. Continuing to refer
to Mary, widow of her son François II, as her daughter-in-law (*belle-
fille*), Catherine apologized to Elizabeth that her handwriting was still
feeble from a recent illness.[1] She explains that she writes in her own
hand because she wants to touch Elizabeth as immediately as she can,
person to person—thus the importance of her pressing the pen to the
paper with her own painful fingers. It's obvious that Catherine feels
some real urgency about enlisting Elizabeth's continued aid for Mary
Stuart, sensing that help from Elizabeth might be in jeopardy.

The body of the formal letter itself asks Elizabeth to help Mary
regain her throne: "I pray you to return her to her liberty and also to
the authority which God has given to her, that which by right and
equity belongs to her and to no other." Catherine and her son remind
Elizabeth to hold to her own opinion that "princes must aid one
another in chastising and punishing . . . subjects who rebel against
their sovereigns."[2] Although the *Calendar of State Papers* suggests that
Catherine had sent a harsh letter to Mary after Darnley's murder, it
does not appear in her collected letters. However, a letter still in the
archives shows that Catherine's first still extant response to news of
Darnley's death was quite sympathetic to Mary. Catherine had writ-

ten to the Constable of France on February 27, 1567 ( a little more than two weeks after the murder) to confide that she was happy for Mary to be rid of her husband, whom she called a "jeune fu" (young fool). She added that had Darnley been wiser, he would still be alive. Catherine had probably met Darnley when he came to France for installation into the Order of St. Michel, and La Reine Mère had clearly formed an ill first opinion of him. So, in some ways, it was a "grent heur" (grand or happy hour) for her daughter-in-law to be free of the "conditions" from which, as Catherine had heard from Ambassador Philibert du Croc himself, he had personally seen [Mary] suffer because of Darnley's drunken behavior.[3]

On March 8, Catherine wrote to du Croc that, on receipt of her letter, he should return to Mary and comfort the Queen of Scots as well as be of help with her affairs while she was in such pain and trouble. It was royal Mary who'd been overthrown, not merely royal-blooded Darnley. Catherine therefore understood Mary's deepest peril to be her own monarchal authority, specifically, as she later said, because in this case the challenged authority was being exercised by a female ruler: the danger was *"principalment aus princeses,"* "foremost for princesses."

While many assume that Catherine "hated" Mary Stuart because of some flippant derogatory comments, it is, I think, much more likely that—if only because Mary had married Catherine's firstborn son, and as her husband, while heir and then on the French throne, he had been happy with her—Catherine felt less personal animus toward her than has been supposed. As François II's widow, Mary had remained dowager queen of France even after she returned to Scotland, and Catherine seems to have felt it necessary to take on some responsibility for her former daughter-in-law. So did she really "hate" Mary as history has popularly concluded?

Like Mary, Catherine had lost her father as an infant (she was less than two months old when he died); Mary's father James had died only six days after her birth. Like Mary, in her own youth, Catherine had suffered at the hands of republican-minded men. Since Mary's return to Scotland she'd fought incursions of British soldiers, armed rebellions by various native lords, violent conspiracies, murders, and assassinations. Nearly six months pregnant, she had witnessed Secretary Rizzio (essentially her chief of staff) stabbed to death as he clutched in terror at the hem of her gown. She felt she had narrowly escaped dying in the explosion of gunpowder meant for her husband.

When she heard, like Elizabeth, that Mary was imprisoned by her rebellious republican subjects, Catherine felt real sympathy. She had been similarly imprisoned by Florentine republicans opposed to the autocratic rule of her family. Her lifelong commitment to preserving and strengthening the Valois dynasty may have been deeply rooted in her own sufferings as a child of an outsted ruling family. When Florence was finally reconquered by allies of the Medici forces, Catherine's fortunes vastly improved, especially after her uncle, Pope Clement VII, arranged for her to marry Henri de Valois, the second son of François I. However, in its beginning, and for many years afterward, her marriage to Prince Henri was no happier than the last days of Mary's marriage to Lord Darnley would be.

Catherine's husband Henri had himself also suffered greatly as a youth. He had been swapped, along with his older brother François, the dauphin, in a ransom exchange for his father, who was imprisoned in Spain by Emperor Charles V. As hostages, the two boys spent four and a half years in prison, until the signing of the Ladies' Peace of 1529, when Louise of Savoy, François I's mother, negotiating with Margaret of Austria, Charles V's aunt, managed a final version of the treaty that would release the boys. At ages twelve and eleven, the brothers returned to France, traumatized. So both Henri and Catherine de' Medici were collateral damage of the Valois-Hapsburg warfare and shared an unhappy history as pawns in a high-stakes game of imperial wars.

This stretch of pan-European battling did not, in fact, finally stop until decades later, when the peace of Cateau-Cambrésis in 1559 ended Henri II's pursuit of France's war against Philip II of Spain. The two young kings had both inherited their wars from their fathers, Henri II of France from François I and Philip II from Charles V. The second son, Henri, had come to hate the Spanish roundly from his time in prison there as a child.

When François I saw his two sons after their release from imprisonment by Charles in Spain, he noticed that Henri was severely depressed. Realizing the fragility of his second son, the French king asked a sympathetic court lady, the twenty-five-year-old beauty Diane de Poitiers, to take him under her care. She did so, and after a long platonic relationship during which the growing boy fell in love with her, when he reached puberty she began a sexual liaison with him. When Henri married at age fourteen, his Italian bride Catherine (also fourteen years old) had no chance to displace her husband's mature mistress, and gain a share of his love. She was unwanted by her husband, a stranger in a foreign court, and very unhappy.

The royal couple remained childless for the first ten years of their marriage. While her husband ignored her, Catherine found a welcoming place for herself in the retinue of King François I and his erudite sister, Marguerite d'Angoulême (later Marguerite de Navarre).[4] Just as Anne Boleyn may have developed her spiritual sympathies for the reformed religion while in the company of the king's sister Marguerite at Fontainebleau, so too Catherine may have learned her tolerance of the reformers' differing religion from conversations with Marguerite's poets, scholars, and courtiers. In the court salon, Catherine's natural wit and intelligence, as well as her excellent education and exquisite manners, allowed her finally to shine.[5]

Then around 1543, when it seemed likely that Catherine would be put away for her barrenness, Henri's mistress Diane (worried perhaps that a new wife would not be as amenable to her role as Henri's mistress as Catherine had seemingly been) commanded her lover to visit his wife in bed more often. He obeyed. It is said that after examining the couple's reproductive parts, a doctor prescribed that they try new techniques in their lovemaking. They obeyed his instructions. No hint remains of what the doctor's specific advice actually was, but Catherine quickly became pregnant.[6] In the end she conceived many times, and would give birth to ten infants, seven of whom lived to maturity. (In contrast, the Tudor queens had no children at all, and Mary Stuart had only one.)

When the de Guise uncles of Mary, Queen of Scots, then teen-aged wife of Catherine's teenaged son François II, took over the government after Henri II was killed in the famous jousting accident, Catherine (so long supplanted by Diane de Poitiers) was suddenly able to put the now aging mistress utterly out of power. And she did exactly that. But she remained immobilized politically by the de Guises until after the early death of her son François II at sixteen. At that point, in 1560, she took over the reins of government directly as regent for her second son, Charles IX. And then, like Diane before her, the young Mary, Queen of Scots was moved aside by La Reine Mère; Mary chose to return to Scotland.

Eight years later, in 1568, Catherine frankly seemed to care more about the imprisoned Mary Stuart, the de Guise niece, than the de Guises did themselves. The family apparently withdrew their support when Mary appeared to have been implicated in the murder of her husband Darnley. (While history has for the most part decided that she was innocent of this charge, English and Scottish propaganda machines had quickly spread news of her guilt.)

꧂

IN ENGLAND, ELIZABETH MAY well have had more reasons to help Mary than the philosophical affront to the monarchal principles about which she had asked her counselor Throckmorton to lecture the rebels. But the English sister queen in the end did very little to help. Mary wrote to Elizabeth shortly after her escape to England that Elizabeth herself was in part responsible for the catastrophe that had befallen her. On May 28, 1568, Mary reminded Elizabeth:

> You will remember that at your request I recalled these "ingrates" banished for their "crymes" against me, to my detriment as now appears. If then for your sake, I did what has all but ruined me,

can I not justly seek recourse with her, who with no ill intention has caused the damage, to repair her error?

Mary clearly understood how fatal that terrible decision to pardon James Douglas, the 4th Earl of Morton, and the other rebellious lords had been in precipitating the murder of Darnley (for which Mary also blamed her half-brother Moray—although at least of this one evil deed, he was in fact innocent). Historian John Guy argues that planting the idea of this pardon in Mary was, in fact, part of Cecil's plot against her, and one certainly made with the greatest ill intent.[7] Although the signal is very subtle, the idea to pardon and recall Rizzio's murderers was something that might well have been hatched by Cecil, for Bedford seems to imply the same in his report to Cecil on December 30, 1566:

> The Queen has granted to Morton, Ruthven and Lindsay their "relaxacion and dresse," wherein Murray has done very friendly for them to the Queen, as I have, *by your advice*.[8]

On January 9, 1567, Bedford again commented to Cecil that Morton was grateful to him: "Morton having obtained his "dresse," is *much beholden to you [Cecil]*."

Guy argues that Cecil well understood that were these conspirators allowed by Mary to return to Scotland (especially Morton), they would take the opportunity to wreak vengeance on Darnley, who had betrayed them when he testified against them for murdering Rizzio. Although he had been one of the chief conspirators in that murder himself (and the lords had papers to prove it), Darnley testified that he was in no way himself involved but knew of the guilt of all the others. Guy convincingly argues that Morton himself was the conspirator who enlisted Bothwell's aid in organizing Darnley's murder; and that he was also the person who later made available the "Casket Letters" to demonstrate that Mary had written poems and expressions of love to Bothwell that supposedly proved her collusion with him in the murder of Darnley.

There has apparently never been a shred of genuine, uncompromised evidence that Mary knew a single thing beforehand of the plans for Darnley's murder. Lacking such proof of her complicity, the Confederate Lords were forced to convict Mary of some sort of harlotry with Bothwell in order to persuade people of her guilt by sexual association as a co-murderer of her husband. While Elizabeth insisted that these compromising letters be kept from the public, Cecil leaked them in his continued efforts to blacken Mary's standing with the common people of both kingdoms. The Casket Letters—which weighed very heavily against Mary both in Scotland and then again in the "conference" held in England to debate the extent of her possible collusion in Darnley's murder—have now been definitively proven to be intricate forgeries.

Having quickly offered to act as arbiter between the lords and their anointed queen, Elizabeth held a conference (not a trial) to inquire into Mary's actions. She clearly hoped that there would be no convincing proof offered of Mary's collusion with Bothwell to murder Darnley. When doctored evidence, Casket Letters and all, began to mount against Mary, Elizabeth abruptly closed these proceedings. As a result, the Scottish queen was neither convicted nor proven innocent, rather like Queen Mary Tudor's treatment of her sister Elizabeth so long ago, during the Wyatt Rebellion: Elizabeth did not condemn Mary, but neither did she exonerate her.

Instead, Elizabeth officially recognized Mary's bastard half-brother Moray as regent of Scotland, while in the meantime still refusing to recognize Mary's child James as the crowned king while his mother the queen still lived. But she also took no step to restore Mary to her throne. Instead she complied with Cecil's insistence that Mary remain in England, and in even closer confinement.

All this while as an anointed queen unjustly deposed by her rebel subjects, Mary had been expecting and waiting for Elizabeth's help to put her back on the Scottish throne. Elizabeth had indicated to Mary that perforce she would do so; Elizabeth apparently had also promised Catherine de' Medici she would do so. In France, Catherine and her son Charles IX continued to send letters to Elizabeth, asking her to field an army to aid Mary in regaining her crown. As late as June 1570, Catherine was urging Elizabeth to "begin the pacification of the realm of Scotland, and the freedom of the queen our daughter-in-law."[9] Charles IX had also written to his English ambassador that

> he was to insist that Elizabeth take up arms, march into Scotland with a great force, and help her chastise her rebels.

Sometime after Mary first fled to England, the French king and queen mother enthusiastically supported a plan to have her wed the Duke of Norfolk, a Protestant lord but from a Catholic family, who held vast lands in the north of England, one of the most distinguished dukes in Elizabeth's realm. (Robert Dudley, Earl of Leicester also favored this plan, possibly misled into thinking that Elizabeth would also support it, based no doubt on her earlier idea of containing Mary by giving her an English husband—himself.) When instead Norfolk was arrested and sent to the Tower for the treasonous secrecy of his dealings with Mary (a betrayal of the sovereign's right to ratify marriages among the nobility), his near Catholic neighbors and supporters, the Earls of Westmoreland and Northumberland, broke out into open revolt against Elizabeth. In a short six weeks, the "Northern Rebellion," as it was called, was summarily put down by southern forces loyal to the English crown. Elizabeth exacted a terrible revenge by calling for (specifying the number) seven hundred executions of the common people, even though there had been no uprising of the general populace in support of the rebel earls of the North. (Her sister "Bloody" Mary had burned a total of 284 Protestants at the stake, including two babies; another 400 had died of starvation. So the sisters are somewhat even as to numbers of deaths directly attributable to their decisions, although Mary burned Protestants for reasons of

religion, while Elizabeth hanged Catholics for reasons of state secu-
rity. Mary's executions still historically defined her half a century
later as "Bloody Mary." Elizabeth remained "Gloriana.")

Although Elizabeth ultimately executed her second cousin the
Duke of Norfolk for his complicity in the 1571 scheme hatched by
the Spanish ambassador—the so-called "Ridolfi plot"—she apparently never blamed Mary Stuart for such plots, understanding that
as a prisoner Mary might rightly undertake to regain her liberty by
extreme means, but was not guilty of treason so long as she never
consented, in writing, to the death of Elizabeth.

The year 1570 proved a turning point for the conflicts between
Protestants and Catholics in Europe because it was then that the
pope excommunicated Elizabeth as a heretic—just as Philip and
Feria had wrongly worried the pope would do twelve years earlier,
when Philip had hoped to marry her. Now the Holy Father forgave
the sins of whichever Christian might manage to assassinate the
queen of England. In a sense, this decree moved the conflict between
Mary and Elizabeth from a set of tensions between two cousins ruling kingdoms on a single island into a global affair. Still, the "Enterprise of England" formulated by Philip II of Spain to invade England
was only in its beginning stages, and was not to become an overpow-
ering threat until the Armada nearly twenty years later.

FOR THE FIRST FIFTEEN years of Mary's imprisonment from 1569 to
1584 in various estates owned by the Earl of Shrewsbury (her reluctant jailer), Elizabeth made certain that her Scottish cousin was
imprisoned in the style befitting an anointed queen, with a retinue of
thirty to sixty attendants, and surroundings that included the most
elaborate and luxurious furnishings. The most painful part of Mary's
sequestration was the strict limits placed on her ability to take exercise
outdoors—where she would be most accessible to rescue by mounted
Catholic forces. As a woman able to ride horseback twenty miles in
the dark while pregnant, Mary's robust constitution would suffer

Bess of Hardwick; unknown artist, 1580.
*National Trust Images / National Portrait Gallery, London*

from nearly two decades of forced sedentariness; she not only gained weight, but her legs became particularly swollen with pain, and by the time of her execution at age forty-five, she could barely walk.

The wife of her jailer during these early years, the Countess of Shrewsbury, or "Bess of Hardwick," was at first a congenial companion who shared with Mary a passion for textile work. A close friend of Queen Elizabeth's from her former position as lady-in-waiting, Bess was a formidable woman in her own right, having amassed a great deal of wealth from her first three marriages, wealth that, by her own clever entrepreneurship, had grown into an even larger fortune. Involved in real estate, mining, banking, and general agricultural management, she ultimately became one of the richest women in England, second only to Queen Elizabeth.[10]

Bess had royal pretensions of her own, which she acted upon when she arranged to have her daughter from her second marriage, Elizabeth Cavendish, married to Henry Darnley's younger brother, the Earl of Lennox. The daughter born to this union, Arabella Stuart, was King James VI of Scotland's *only* first cousin. The Lennox-Stuart marriage caused some strain between Mary and Bess of Hardwick when Bess, descended from gentry, muscled her way into a royal bloodline that she shared with the Scottish queen.

For years the queen of Scotland and her warden Bess of Hardwick would sew and embroider together for hours on end, planning elaborate wall hangings and ordering fine cloths and golden threads from France, courtesy of Mary's contacts there.[11] This traditional female pastime sounds like an escape from all the melancholy of Mary's losses, but as the reader should now be ready to suspect, their shared creation of elaborate large and small cloth objects was a significant activity of an altogether different sort than simple recreation. Not only were they creating valuable cloth items slated to become inalienable possessions to be inherited along dynastic lines, Mary, Queen of Scots was also creating inalienable objects of political resistance.

Their pastime in textile work was not trivial; it is hard for people in the twenty-first century to realize how centrally valuable a commodity sixteenth-century finished cloth was, as almost all of our cloth and clothing is made in other countries by machine, predominantly out of petroleum by-products. How could a suit of clothes be a more valuable commodity than an entire house, say the house Shakespeare bought in Stratford when he retired from London?[12] But in the Renaissance, even mass-produced cloth (and there were many factories where workers produced fabric) was made by hand out of natural materials. Wool was the foundation of England's economic prosperity; in the sixteenth century, finished wool cloth comprised two-thirds of the country's entire exports. English wool cloth was the premier global brand, amid a market that was becoming more and more capitalist throughout Europe.[13]

On the one hand, the materials and highly skilled labor that went into making a gentleman's cloak would include not only the local wool, but designs worked in imported silks as well as intricate embellishments created with jewels and precious metals. A whole house, on the other hand, made with local timber, daub and wattle, and thatch for a roof, might go up quite quickly.

Mary Stuart had always been an enthusiastic embroiderer and would have long been accustomed to working with very valuable materials. Even while heavily engaged in the business of ruling, she also worked with her needle executing décor for her own state bed, which was to be bequeathed to her son James at her death, just as she had inherited bed hangings worked by her mother, the regent Marie de Guise. Mary signed the embroideries she sewed while imprisoned, most of which are now hanging in Oxburgh Hall in Norfolk (which was, somewhat ironically, the house of the man who had been ordered by Mary Tudor in 1554 to imprison her sister Princess Elizabeth).

One notable embroidery at Oxburgh is a design of Mary's new motto, which she'd borrowed from her mother: "In my end is my beginning." Showing an image of a phoenix rising from a funeral pyre, the impresa (as both motto and image were called) represents Mary's hope for an immortality that would last through the Stuart bloodline she had sustained by giving birth to James VI of Scotland. (Elizabeth II of the current English ruling house of Windsor is indeed directly descended from Mary's granddaughter, Elizabeth Stewart, the "Winter Queen.")

Another notable emblem is the impresa Mary sent to the Duke of Norfolk, which presents a picture of a hand reaching down from the sky, pruning off one branch of a grapevine that shows no grapes. The motto is *Virescit Vulnere Virtus*—"strength sprouts by wounding." The meaning would have been quite menacing to Elizabeth, whose barrenness could have been indicated by the branch growing only a single leaf that was in the process of being pruned. Because the hand that comes out of the sky mimics (save for its frilly Renaissance courtier's lace cuff) countless medieval manuscript depictions of God reaching into a scene to aid humankind, the image implies that such "pruning" would only be done by divine agency, thus shielding the artist from suspicion of evil intent. This piece of embroidery was, however, used as evidence against the Duke of Norfolk at his trial.

These embroideries were ultimately sewn onto a large green velvet hanging cloth to make a work of art in its own right. Now called the

"Marian Hanging," it matches two other large groupings of emblems done by Bess and her own embroiderers, the "Cavendish" and the "Shrewsbury" hangings, named for the two "houses" that Bess had married into and whose dynasties she had helped to ensure.

In their time together during the Queen of Scots' imprisonment, Bess and Mary embroidered one hundred of these emblem panels. Such a large collection suggests that Bess saw the great hanging cloths as artworks comparable to the many tapestries that decorated her houses (she owned over forty tapestries). The hangings were, however, uniquely Queen Mary's and Bess of Hardwick's original works of art, conceived and designed if not always sewn by them.

Why was there so much hanging cloth in northern houses? Art historians have suggested that tapestry—which was the most expensive form of art in the Renaissance, taking the greatest number of hours of manual labor—was northern Europe's answer to the Mediterranean art form of fresco, which mixed paint into the wet plaster that is put directly onto stone walls. A block of color in a fresco might

Mary Stuart's emblem, "Strength Sprouts by Wounding." Marian Hanging at Oxburgh Hall © *Victoria and Albert Museum, London*

take only a few minutes to paint; but to fill the same amount of space with tapestry could take hours if not days to weave, each square foot taking many passes of the weavers' hands. However, the cold stone of great house construction in the north of England would not be as suitable for plasterwork as were the walls of structures in a more temperate climate like Italy's. Also, importantly, the hanging cloths would themselves be an aid in insulating the English homes against heat loss. So the works of art were functional as well as beautiful.

In a set of hangings that has come to be called "Noble Women of the Ancient World," Mary and Bess used a different textile technique to create large hangings that included portraiture. They ordered pieces of cloth appliquéd to silk backings to create large standing figures of prominent women from history and mythology. Framed by architectural arches, the figures of Penelope, Zenobia, Artemisia, Lucretia, and Cleopatra are each flanked by two other female figures set within their own smaller arches. These supplementary figures represent allegorical virtues associated with each specific historical woman.[14] Thus Penelope stands

Lucretia wall hanging; Elizabeth Talbot and Mary Stuart, 1570. Hardwick Hall, Derbyshire, UK. *Reproduced by kind permission of the National Trust*

Mary Stuart; François Clouet, 1560. *Royal Collection Trust /
© Her Majesty Queen Elizabeth II 2020*

between Patience and Perseverance, Lucretia stands between Chastity and Liberality, Cleopatra stands between Fortitude and Justice.

Bess and Mary chose to represent not only powerful women rulers but also women who were famously loyal to their husbands (perhaps Cleopatra's official incestuous "marriages" to her two brother pharaohs were forgotten in the face of her fidelity first to Julius Caesar, then to Mark Antony).

Artemisia, flanked by Constancy and Piety, is famous not only because she built her husband Mausolus a massive monument, the *Mausoleum*, she also drank his ashes, making of her own body a living tomb. (Aside from Boccaccio's *On Famous Women*, the stories of these celebrated figures were told in the early fifteenth century by Christine de Pizan in *The Book of the City of Ladies*, printed in English in 1521.) The architectural forms framing the figures are made from ecclesiastical clothing purchased by Bess's third husband when it had become available at the dissolution of the monasteries. So valuable were these already

"Chastity," Lucretia wall hanging, Hardwick Hall, Derbyshire, UK.
*Reproduced by kind permission of the National Trust*

richly embellished damasks and silks that they were widely recycled
into new textile constructions. It is somewhat ironic that Mary used
the remnants of the destruction of the Catholic Church, for which she
thought she would—although not a martyr—die. They have become
inalienable possessions. Through the offices of Bess of Hardwick (and
now also by means of the National Trust), Mary's work remains on view
for the education of anyone interested in the history of women.

In 2010, scholar Susan Frye made a startling discovery. She
noticed that the flanking virtue of Chastity in the hanging by Mary
and Bess that centered on Lucretia bore a distinct resemblance to the
most famous portrait of Mary, Queen of Scots by François Clouet,
when Mary wore white mourning ("en deuil blanc").[15]

Clouet had drawn his famous portrait when Mary was in mourning for the death of her young husband François II. Mary's mother
and father-in-law had also died within this same year and a half, so
her mourning was especially deep. The Clouet portrait was famous,

having been copied many times and figured in poems both by Ronsard and by Mary herself.

In the panel, Chastity holds a sprig of myrtle, the symbol of innocence, and is accompanied by a unicorn, a heraldic beast that also represents sexual purity.

The figure of Penelope in the Constancy wall hanging looks a great deal like Bess of Hardwick, so it would not be all that odd for Mary Stuart to appear in a panel that the two textile artists planned and at least partly executed together. So why should the portrait of Chastity have gone so long unrecognized as an image of Mary, Queen of Scots? Frye suggests that the identification of Mary as the figure of Chastity may well have been relatively easy for those who saw it in the rooms at Chatsworth, the great house Bess had helped to build for the Shrewsburys and where Mary and Bess would have designed and had the hangings put together. The panels were then taken to Hardwick Hall when Bess finished her "prodigy house" in the late 1590s, well after Mary's death. In the context of the other surrounding portraits and belongings of Mary—including the Clouet portrait itself, with the bed of state, books, papers, and heraldic emblems on pillows—no name would have been needed to indicate the real identity of the figure of Chastity.

But the fact that the figure was "named" Chastity seems to have come up against the massive two-decades-long (and now ongoing for four centuries) propaganda machine that was continuing to grind against Mary, first by the Confederate Lords, who felt they would do a better job governing Scotland than she could have done, and then by those Englishmen who felt that attacking Mary and smearing her name (particularly by accusations of infidelity and wanton licentiousness) was a way to protect their own Queen Elizabeth against a Catholic assassination or invasion.

The unicorn in the tapestry itself should have been the signal of Mary's royal presence. While it is a traditional symbol of purity (as in the ubiquitous medieval "unicorn" tapestries, such as the seven now hanging in the Cloisters in New York City), it is also the heraldic

Gold coin of James III of Scotland,
1484–1488. *Heritage Auctions, HA.com*

beast of Scottish royalty, and has been so since the twelfth century.[16]
A gold coin from the 1480s minted for James III of Scotland displays
the unicorn, symbolizing not merely the mythological beast's purity
but also its virile aggression. The unicorn would die rather than be
captured. It is always depicted bursting its chains.

In 1603, when Mary's son James VI of Scotland ascended to the
throne as James I of England, the unicorn was added to England's
royal coat of arms opposite the English Lion and has remained a part
of it until the present day.

The four-hundred-year loss of the identification of Mary, Queen
of Scots' portrait in the figure of Chastity reveals (yet again) history's
ability not only to mischaracterize but also to utterly forget important women from the past. It may be that few visitors have paid much
attention to the sewn artifacts at Hardwick Hall. Modernity has not,
until quite recently, considered textile work an art, possibly because
it was, even when practiced by men (and most certainly as created by
women), a cooperative, often anonymous effort. It did not conform to
the Renaissance standard of Michelangelo's stamping his *Pietà* in St.

Peter's Basilica with the autograph *"Michelangelo hoc fecit."* The agony and ecstasy of a single man creating an immortal object became the epitome of "old master" art—and in many ways remains so today. Yet communally woven tapestries were infinitely more expensive to create than any other form of art in sixteenth-century Europe (save, perhaps, for monumental architecture).

As a case in point, Bess's "prodigy house" was most famous not for the remarkable woven art but for its astonishing architecture by Robert Smythson, about which someone quipped at the time (possibly William Cecil, Lord Burghley himself, who died in 1598): "Hardwick Hall. More glass than wall." To prioritize the windows, however, has been merely to see the structure from the outside, where a vast amount of glazing was beautifully arranged to form an elegant façade. According to Renaissance scholar Mark Girouard, Hardwick was the absolute pinnacle of a unique moment in Elizabethan architecture, a structure developed by Smythson in concert with Bess, who had substantial input into its design. To say so, and so the world would know, she put her initials "ES" for "Elizabeth Shrewsbury" on the top of each of the six towers.[17]

Yet on the inside, there were cloth hangings on all the walls (cloths were even draped over some of the glass in winter). And they may well have been worth the cost of the building itself (the materials being sourced locally and even the glass fabricated on site). Bess, however, never commissioned any tapestries to be made by professional outsiders. She bought tapestries from other collectors, who often sold them at below cost, and newly designed materials were made *in-house*, by the company of her own embroiderers, seamstresses, and clothworkers, and by her royal prisoner, Mary, as well by Bess herself.[18]

The appliquéd replica of Mary's "dueil blanc" portrait insists not only on Mary's status as a double queen—dowager queen of France (a status she shared with Catherine de' Medici) and formerly reigning Queen of Scots—but also on the possibility that she might well have been, like Catherine of Aragon, a virgin bride at her second marriage. Like Catherine's first husband Arthur, François II had married Mary at a very young age; he was always in quite poor health (as well as having, scholars suppose, undescended testicles), and he was dead a mere seventeen months after he was crowned. Mary wore these same white mourning clothes when she married her second husband, Henry Darnley. Their wedding entertainment involved courtiers who were allowed separately to unpin the white clothing from the bride before she withdrew to change into more celebratory and colorful garments. Mary thus created her own wedding masque out of her transformation from royal mourning widow into royal bride.

Why Bess would have condoned this virginal version of the portrait of the by then three-times-married Mary, Queen of Scots is a bit of a conundrum. Bess and Mary's friendship was rocky, and suffered real rupture in the 1580s when Bess became quite paranoid about a suspected (though highly unlikely) *amour* between her husband the Earl of Shrewsbury and their attractive prisoner, Mary Stuart. Bess and the earl were already estranged and at loggerheads. While suffering from what seems to have been an increasing dementia, the earl specifically laid claim not only to many properties Bess had inherited

Hardwick Hall, Derbyshire: west front, seen from the gatehouse.

from her second husband, the Earl of Cavendish, but also to the textiles from which Bess and Mary had created the hangings. He insisted that he had been the one who had obtained the ecclesiastical cloth that had actually come to Bess through her earlier husband Lord St. Loe and that he (the Earl of Shrewsbury) had supported the clothworkers while they had made the hangings. Queen Elizabeth herself, Lord Leicester, and Lord Burghley had to convene to help settle this controversy more than once. They found in favor of Bess each time. But Shrewsbury continued his rancor and refused ever to see his wife. The wrangle helps to suggest just how valuable that cloth had been.

It looks to be a great act of generosity for Bess to allow a portrait of Mary as "Chastity" to be created and to remain at Hardwick. Having become one of Hardwick Hall's inalienable posessions, it seems to proclaim Bess's acceptance of the innocence of Mary, Queen of Scots, even after she had been executed for treason and for allegedly consenting to the assassination of Elizabeth. But in a sense, the hanging spoke to details of Mary's earlier life, specifically her compromised sexual purity. Lucretia had, afer all, been raped by Tarquin, and many of Mary's supporters understood her true downfall to have been the result of Bothwell's abduction and probable rape of her. Perhaps Bess of Hardwick was acknowledging that it is possible for a woman to remain pure even after rape, and that she did not need to commit suicide (as Lucretia did) in order to erase the stain of the attack.[19]

Mary's supporters repeatedly put out propaganda to counter the stories circulating to smear Mary's name; one of these documents was a fake "confession" by, supposedly, the Earl of Bothwell himself, although he actually had died in 1578 in prison in Denmark—according to legend, chained to the prison wall and mad. In fact, as a nobleman, he enjoyed relatively elegant surroundings in the prison provided by his jailer. When Darnley's mother, the Countess of Lennox, read the forged "confession," she decided that Mary had been falsely accused and that she had been innocent of the murder charge all along. The countess sent Mary a letter of reconciliation and a piece of elegant lace embroidery into which she had woven strands of her own silver hair.

Margaret, the dowager countess of Lennox, would have been a family member with whom Bess of Hardwick needed to communicate when arranging the marriage of her daughter Elizabeth Cavendish to the countess's youngest son. For a mother to forgive someone who she had once supposed to have conspired to murder her oldest son (Darnley) is a strong testament to that person's innocence, even if the change of heart is based on a forgery. The countess's turnaround may have had an effect on Bess's opinion of Mary.

The fact that the most famous picture of Mary is of her in mourning garb is something she shares with her mother-in-law, Catherine de' Medici, who, as we shall see, also wore mourning throughout her entire life after the death of her husband, Henri II. Mary would have seen her mother-in-law's mourning dress daily when she was queen consort of France, married to François II for the months of his short reign; after his death, she left for Scotland. Unlike Catherine, Mary did not continue always to wear mourning, but she must have under-

Mary Queen of Scots; 1610–1640, Palace of Holyrood House.
*Royal Collection Trust / © Her Majesty Queen Elizabeth II 2020*

stood how a portrait in those clothes allowed people to remember her royal virginal widowhood. Mary wore white, while Catherine wore black, but as both of them were dowager queens of France, each was insisting on the privileged position of a king's widow through their physical representations in major works of art.

For the rest of Mary's life, even when she was not wearing full white, she had herself depicted with caps that recalled the French headdress from her "deuil blanc" portrait. Nicholas Hilliard painted a miniature portrait of Mary that copies the Clouet image when she was imprisoned at the Sheffield house, probably in 1578. It is the basis for many "Sheffield" portraits, so called because they were based on the Hilliard miniature. The Clouet portrait was thus disseminated widely and became the iconic vision of Mary, Queen of Scots.

An example of the subsequent power of this capped image of Mary is a seventeenth-century three-quarter portrait of Mary currently in Holyrood House. The vignette in the lower left corner of the painting captures the actual moment of Mary's "martyrdom" where she is shown being executed, wearing a bodice of red cloth, the color of martyrdom.

Mary's beheading was not entirely Queen Elizabeth's doing. It was the final triumphant outcome of the more than eighteen-year campaign pursued by William Cecil, 1st Baron Burghley, Elizabeth's premier counselor and secretary of state. He and his henchman entrapped Mary into leaving handwritten evidence of conspiracy—the kind of evidence that was so lacking when Queen Mary Tudor had demanded proof of Elizabeth's treason at the time of Wyatt's rebellion.

We have seen that in 1565 Ronsard (under Catherine de Medici's patronage) had conveyed to Elizabeth in exquisite humanist couplets the threat that Cecil posed to absolute monarchy. Did she take note and worry that she and her counselor had divergent views on the legitimacy of the Catholic thrones of Europe? They certainly had divergent views on one monarch. It is clear that Elizabeth hoped to be able to live in peace with her sister queen. But Cecil finally convinced her to kill Mary, Queen of Scots.

# CHAPTER SEVEN

ᔕᔑ

# A Trap for Two Queens

lthough Catherine de' Medici had early on warned Elizabeth about Cecil's program of proto-republican actions
against monarchy in Ronsard's book of poetry, La Reine
Mère never did manage to persuade Elizabeth to support Mary Stuart to the extent that she had hoped. On the contrary, Cecil made it
increasingly difficult for Elizabeth to aid her fellow female monarch
to regain her throne in Scotland by stoking her fear that Mary would
continue to endanger her own throne in England.[1]

Cecil had first tried to find material proof of Mary's collusion in
plots against Elizabeth shortly after the Queen of Scots had given
birth to Prince James in 1566. Cecil sent an agent provocateur to
Mary Stuart in the person of one Christopher Rokesby. Pretending
to be a reliable Catholic, Rokesby asked Mary to give him some token
to take back to the Catholic lords in England. Immediately seeing
through this ploy, Mary had the agent arrested while he just happened to be carrying letters from Cecil incriminating the counselor
in plotting against her. Mary then wrote to Cecil, subtly vaunting
over the failure of his plot and hinting that she could tell Elizabeth
what he had done, knowing that Elizabeth would be incensed by his
foul and underhanded dealing.[2] For some reason, she never wrote any
letter to Elizabeth (so far as we know) revealing Cecil's machinations.

The counselor's next move against Mary was not something he
actually did, but what he did *not* do. He clearly knew in advance of

the gathering plot to murder Rizzio, but he did not tell Mary about it, nor did he alert Elizabeth to the impending chaos it would cause in Mary's court. More significantly, Cecil's escalating attempt to trap Mary may have led him to scheme so that the exiled murderers were allowed return to Scotland, where they could then murder Darnley. We have seen how Cecil was part of the concerted effort to have Mary pardon the murderers of Rizzio, and how these men then promptly plotted Darnley's death.

Mary's sudden marriage to the much-suspected Bothwell mere months after Darnley's death made her catastrophically vulnerable to claims by the Earl of Moray (her illegitimate brother now acting as her son's regent) and the Earl of Morton (Moray's privy counselor) that they had "found" some of her letters to Bothwell in a silver casket marked with an "F" for Mary's first husband, François II of France. These so-called "Casket Letters" were supposed to prove that the queen had started an affair with Bothwell even while Darnley was still alive, and therefore must have known *beforehand* about Darnley's murder. She would thus have been an accessory to Darnley's murder if not an actual coconspirator. Was Morton's "discovery" of the letters part of his payback to Cecil for finagling his pardon for the Rizzio murder?

When Cecil inspected the Casket Letters prior to the "conference" called to investigate Mary's guilt held in England in 1568, he discovered that in some instances the letters seemed more likely to disprove than to prove Mary's collusion with Bothwell. So intent was Cecil on using any tool to trap the Scottish queen, he even went so far as to change a word in the description of one letter, thus making it seem to be a letter Mary had written to Bothwell *before* he had abducted her, rather than one clearly written *after* that traumatic turning point. Mary would thus appear guilty of freely conspiring with him to murder Darnley, rather than being violently forced by Bothwell to marry—or simply following his lead out of some kind of post-traumatic stress confusion.[3]

On the one hand, it was Cecil who then personally leaked the incriminating Casket Letters to a publisher, against Elizabeth's express orders that they be kept out of the public eye. He also underwrote a fake Scottish translation of George Buchanan's condemnatory Latin "Detection of the Doings of the Queen of Scots." Buchanan had written his tract to defend the Scottish noblemen's republican right to depose their queen, who had abrogated her status by her marriage to her husband's murderer. Cecil's added slanders made Mary out to be even more of a passion-driven tyrant than Buchanan had originally argued, although his characterizations had been bad enough.

On the other hand, Cecil does not appear to have played a part in conjuring up the Norfolk marriage. Nor was he part of the Ridolfi plot to have Mary freed by Spanish forces led by the Duke of Alva. When the latter plot was discovered, he found that Mary had been too wary ever to write anything explicit to Ridolfi, and so he had insufficient evidence for a trial. While much was suspected, nothing could be proved. But Elizabeth's highest counselor was far from finished.

Cecil got his next chance when another plot was discovered to put Mary on the English throne in 1583, this one named for Francis Throckmorton, a Catholic nephew of Protestant Nicholas Throckmorton (the same Ambassador Throckmorton who had waited so long to speak with the Scottish queen when she was imprisoned in Lochleven, and who had died in 1571). Francis Throckmorton's plot collapsed when, under torture, he confessed to a scheme to dethrone Elizabeth, a plot that included the Duc de Guise, that was supported by Pope Gregory XIII and by Philip II, and that had been masterminded by the Spanish ambassador Bernardino de Mendoza, who was then summarily expelled from England. This high-powered cabal was not Cecil's creation, although it made him ever more determined to compass the Scottish queen's death by some means or other. The threat she posed was clearly very real.

The following year, 1584, Cecil put forward a legal instrument that would entirely block Mary and her son James from the succession. Called the "Bond of Association," it empowered members of

Parliament to name the next ruler themselves in the event of Elizabeth's death, at the same time making it legal and *necessary* for them also to hunt down and execute anyone who would make a claim on the throne, including any next of kin of Elizabeth herself, even if the claimants could not be proved to have been personally involved in the plotting. Although the bond was advertised as a means for protecting Elizabeth from assassination, the queen well understood that it was a challenge to her sovereign authority over the choice of her successor. As John Guy puts it, "it was a quasi-republican solution to the succession issue," and as such, "in Elizabeth's view" the bond was "an almost scandalous subversion of the principles of monarchy and hereditary right."

> Cecil . . . wanted to create a radical constitutional mechanism that would automatically exclude Mary and enable a Protestant ruler to be selected by Parliament when Elizabeth died.[4]

While Elizabeth graciously accepted the bond when it was signed by three thousand loyal citizens (including Mary herself), she told Cecil to drop his plans. She proposed an entirely different bill: an "Act for the Queen's Safety." Unlike the bond, Elizabeth's law insisted that any perpetrators of a plot on her life be granted a procedure amounting to a trial. (She thus protected the concept of habeas corpus, that is, the right to a trial by a jury of peers, one of the most ancient rights of English-speaking peoples.) And finally, the verdict of such a procedure could only be officially proclaimed by royal authority. So too the next of kin to the guilty parties would *not* be hunted down and killed unless it could be proved that they were *active* conspirators. By this means Elizabeth preserved royal power in choosing an heir to the crown; such authority was not to be handed over wholesale to Parliament to do with as they pleased.

Soon afterward, Elizabeth finally recognized James VI as king of Scotland. By that decree, any plans she might once have supported to free Mary and make her co-ruler with her son were forever quashed.

When James subsequently signed a treaty with England, as Guy argues, "he made his mother's execution . . . inevitable."

Cecil's last—and finally successful—plot to entrap Mary depended upon Francis Walsingham's "genius as a spymaster." Walsingham had become secretary of state to Elizabeth after Cecil, and due to his personal experiences in Paris during the St. Bartholomew's Day Massacre, he shared the former secretary's fear of Mary Stuart as an inspiration for a Catholic revolt in England.

Walsingham had patiently recruited a Catholic refugee with connections to Mary's agents in Paris who could vouch for him. This Catholic double agent, Gilbert Gifford, became one of Mary's most trusted couriers. His use of a watertight box bearing letters in cipher, inserted through the bunghole of a beer cask, where it floated on top of the beer, was a line of communication designed for Mary's entrapment. Thinking the secret messages were safe, Mary did not know that her messages were all too easily intercepted, simply by waylaying the cask of beer. So, when Anthony Babington, a young Catholic gentleman, wrote to Mary of a plot by "six gentlemen" to assassinate the English queen and free the Scottish one, Walsingham knew immediately of the proposal. He did not, however, immediately leap in to arrest the Queen of Scots but waited for Mary to write a reply encouraging the men, thus making herself guilty of complicity in plotting Elizabeth's murder.

When Babington became momentarily paralyzed with fear over the risk he was taking, Walsingham sent his spy Gifford to buck him up. Although Babington had thought up the conspiracy on his own and was not an agent provocateur as Rokesby had been almost two decades earlier, Walsingham had Gifford nurse along the conspiracy until Mary wrote back an encouraging message to the plotters.

On the basis of such letters written to Babington, Mary was brought to answer for compassing the death of Elizabeth, and after an elaborate trial before five hundred of England's male elite, she was sentenced to die. At this point, however, Elizabeth had no intentions of officially having Mary executed.

Knowing how menaced she had become by Mary's supporters, Elizabeth finally accepted that Mary must die, but she far preferred that Mary die of natural causes, or possibly that she be assassinated by poison or some other surreptitious means as had been prescribed by the Bond of Association. As Guy puts it, "She knew that regicide authorized by a statute made in Parliament would alter the future of the monarchy in the British Isles."

Elizabeth began implying to all and sundry that she wished that someone might do away with Mary Stuart all on their own authority; in other words, she urged an undertaking for which, it must be said, the Bond of Association had already granted permission to all who had signed it. There had been, after all, *three thousand* signatories.

In a sense, by her insisting on sovereign prerogative and by substituting the formal legislative Act for the Queen's Safety in place of Cecil's ad hoc cosigned Bond of Association, Elizabeth had boxed herself in. She herself had made far less likely the possibility that someone would undertake the assassination of her prisoner. Henry IV, king of England, may well have had Richard II secretly murdered while the deposed king was imprisoned in Pontefract Castle. Henry IV's government was never charged with the death; Richard was only thirty-three years old at his demise, but he *might* have died of natural causes. In contrast to what might have been a very successful stealth murder, Elizabeth's Act made the execution of anyone who compassed the death of a sovereign entirely legal and totally official, setting clear precedent in English law; the Bond did not require the full authority of the state, merely volunteer murderers who had collectively promised each other that they would be free from any prosecution while they settled in to "elect" the next sovereign.

Elizabeth soon realized her mistake. In order to avoid the consequences of a private assassination (such as, possibly, Richard II's), Cecil had to play one last trick against Elizabeth. She had wanted the public proclamation of Mary's official guilty verdict from the trial to mention the Bond of Association, *not* the Act for the Queen's Safety, thus reminding the populace that any one of the three thousand signatories could in good conscience do the evil deed. Far better to have Mary done away with by some unofficial means, than by the official will of the state. So Cecil lied to Elizabeth and told her that there was no time to change the proclamation of Mary's guilt to mention the Bond, even though the original version had *at first* mentioned the Bond rather than the Act.[5]

For her part, Elizabeth explicitly complained to Parliament that they had put her in an excruciatingly painful position:

> You have brought me to a narrow strait that I must give direction for her death which cannot be to me but a most grievous and irksome burden.[6]

Perhaps because the proclamation had not mentioned the Bond, she herself personally and officially reminded the members of Parliament that they—and many other subjects—had taken a collective oath when they had signed that Bond of Association.

> I am mindful of your Oath made in the Association . . . entered into upon good conscience and knowledge of guilt for safety of my person.

And directly after this reminder that they had already promised to do the deed, she warned them that they should not expect her to do anything herself to execute her cousin and sister queen.

> But forasmuch as the matter is rare, weighty, and of great consequence, I think you do not look for any present resolution.

She was clearly trying to remind everyone that she had no intention of ordering the execution herself; they, however, already had the authority to kill Mary themselves—indeed they had signed an oath promising that they *would do it themselves*. Elizabeth apparently did not leave matters with these hints to Parliament, but asked Walsingham to suggest to Sir Amias Paulet, Mary's last jailer, that he murder her quietly and in secret, and spare Elizabeth the burden of ordering a sister queen's execution. The Bond of Association could be his authority. But, while Paulet was no friend to Mary and had numerous times torn down the official cloth of state she hung behind her chair or "throne" (thus denying her royal status), he refused to "make shipwreck" of his conscience by murdering her "without law or warrant."

So it still required a further trick by Cecil to get Elizabeth to sign Mary's actual death warrant. Walsingham and Cecil both told the queen that they had found evidence of yet another plot to assassinate her. But this was a lie. They used the details of a long-ago discovered and disabled plot as if it were just now about to happen. Only then did Elizabeth sign the death warrant. She told no one, however, but simply gave the document to the new undersecretary of the Privy Council and told him to keep it safe. She specifically did *not* order that the warrant be sent to Fotheringhay, the castle where Mary had been imprisoned and put on trial.

Instead, once they found out that the warrant had in fact been signed, Cecil, Walsingham, and the council arranged to have it sent immediately to Fotheringhay without Elizabeth's knowledge. They all conspired not to tell her of Mary's death until after the execution was fully accomplished.

Mary spent the day before her execution writing out her will and some letters. She willed her right to the throne of England to Philip II, and wrote to Henri III, asking him to pay her servants out of her as yet unsent French dowry money; she also asked that he pay for memorial masses to be sung for her soul. "I am to be executed like a criminal at eight in the morning," she wrote. However, just as the motto she borrowed from her mother claimed that "In my end is my beginning," Mary's dramatically tragic death was the start of a legend of sacrifice and suffering that would transfix people for centuries to come. Clearly hoping to die a Catholic martyr, she quietly prayed in Latin while a zealous Protestant in the audience yelled at her that it was not too late to convert to the Protestant faith. She rejected the offer.

When the executioner began to remove her black overgarments, she politely told him "no," and instead had her ladies take them off, to reveal a bodice and a petticoat of crimson red. Relying on French (and therefore Catholic) sources, Antonia Fraser describes the apparently startling effect of the condemned queen's dramatic staging of her sacrifice: "Stripped of her black, she stood in her red petticoat and it was seen that above it she wore a red satin bodice, trimmed with lace, the neckline cut low at the back; one of the women handed her a pair of red sleeves, and it was thus wearing all red, the color of blood, and the liturgical color of martyrdom in the Catholic Church," that the Queen of Scots was to be executed.[7] The women then put a gold-embroidered handkerchief over her eyes. She excused the axeman with real charity and put her head down on the block without flinching but with the greatest courage and quiet strength of mind. When the axeman only wounded Mary's head with the first swing of the blade, she was heard to pray out loud "Jesus!" The second swing did sever the head, but a third blow was needed to finish the cut entirely. When the clumsy axeman finally held up the head, many saw the lips continuing to move in prayer. The head itself then dropped suddenly to the floor, falling out of the red wig the executioner was holding, and revealed Mary's white hair. At that moment, one of Mary's small dogs, which had hidden within her skirts, chose to dart out into the open, covered with her blood. As people watched the dog run about in fright, they could sympathize (or not) with the horror the dog felt at the loss of his beloved mistress.

The English were careful to burn all Mary's belongings, so worried were they that any objects she possessed would become talismans of her martyred spirit and saintly relics that might inspire Catholics to worship or rebel. Usually such items were parceled out among those responsible for the execution, but here the English were unwilling to risk these traditional allowances.

When Cecil told Elizabeth that Mary had been executed, her response was perfect fury. Stephen Alford, Cecil's most recent biographer, suggests that the counselor was in no way prepared for the queen's enraged reaction. Did he think somehow he was doing her a favor by sending the death warrant without her express permission? Did he and the council finally override her sovereign will to delay further, thinking she would be relieved by rather than furious at their appropriation of her authority? They clearly knew she would countermand them had they told her the warrant had been sent—which is doubtless why they did not tell her. The simple sending of the warrant clearly expressed to the officials at Fotheringhay that Elizabeth had finally consented that Mary should be killed. However, she had never commanded that the warrant be sent.[8]

For her part, Elizabeth blamed Cecil personally for this miscarriage of her justice, and cast him into political darkness by sending him away from court, exiling him from her royal presence. Alford suggests that her punishment struck at the heart of Cecil's identity as "the great servant and counselor." Even though Elizabeth had earlier elevated him to the title of "Baron Burghley," when she banished him from her presence, he lost all his power, and as Alford points out, he thereby almost entirely lost himself. He felt that his word became no more than that of a common subject. Alford summarizes:

> So the execution of Mary, Queen of Scots was a bittersweet victory for Burghley. He had at last succeeded in obtaining one of the objectives of his career, the security of the kingdom through the death of Mary Stuart. But this achievement came at a heavy personal cost.

As testimony to the widespread public understanding of Elizabeth's personal reluctance to execute a sister queen, there is an elaborate scene in Part II of Edmund Spenser's epic, *The Faerie Queene*, that refers to the execution of Mary, Queen of Scots. Sponsored by Sir Walter Raleigh, who was at the time one of Elizabeth's favorite courtiers, Spenser had personally presented Part I of the book to the queen in 1590 and received in return the promise of a lifelong pension of £50 a year. When, later in 1596, nine years after Mary's execution, Spenser published Part II of the book, in its proem Spenser castigates a "statesman who with brave foresight" had condemned his earlier poem. Most readers assume this statesman to be William Cecil, Lord Burghley. In Book V, the Book of Justice, Spenser reveals Queen Mercilla (or "Mercy") listening to a trial that convicts another queen of capital crimes, offering remarkable contemporary witness to the queen's ambivalence in her decision to execute Mary, suggesting that her personal feelings had become well known. Spenser describes the reluctance of Queen Mercilla, or Queen Mercy, to command the execution of the Roman Catholic queen, Duessa (representing Mary, Queen of Scots).

What is singularly significant in Spenser's representation of Mercilla's decision-making is the shock and surprise most readers feel when the poem tricks them into thinking that Duessa has not, actually, been beheaded. Lulled into thinking that Mercilla has stopped justice from being done by a cleverly deceptive pun, many readers are justiably confused and even a bit angry—or at least irritated—by the trick played on them.

> But she whose Princely breast was touched nere,
> With piteous ruth of her so wretched plight,
> Though plaine she saw by all, that she did heare,
> That she of death was guiltie found by right,
> Yet would not *let* just vengeance on her light;
> But rather *let* in stead thereof to fall
> Few perling drops from her faire lampes of light;
> The which she covering with her purple pall
> Would have the passion hid, and up arose withall.
> (V.ix.442)

In this stanza, Spenser mimics the ambivalence Elizabeth clearly felt about having to sign Mary's death warrant. In one line the poet says Mercilla "would not *let* just vengeance on her light," which seems to suggest that Mercilla blocks Justice, and *instead* "lets" or "allows" to flow some tears of pity. It is thus quite a reversal for the reader when, in the next canto, Mercilla is doing obsequies for Duessa's corpse. Students of the poem always want to know, "Where did the corpse come from?!" The answer is: Mercilla executed Duessa, producing a dead body. They rightly object to this reading: "But the line says that she would '*not* let' justice be done!!" Spenser forces the reader to misread the word "let," which, in the sixteenth century, could mean either "to allow" *or* "to hinder," "to block," "to prevent." Thus the line means that Mercilla "would not prevent justice" from being done. (A "let" in tennis is when a served ball hits the net; this use goes back to the archaic meaning of "let" as "hindrance.")

Why does Spenser create such confusion? Because he wants to give the reader a sense of how conflicted Mercilla is in making this deadly decision. The reader is tricked by the uses of the word "let," with two different meanings, in two adjacent lines of verse. How does Mercy feel about letting bloody justice take its course? She does it by wanting to hinder it. In the end, however, justice is allowed to take its course. Spenser comes very close to making the reader feel the same confusion and discomfort that Elizabeth must have felt: her grieving reluctance to make the decision and her shocked response that the deed has somehow been done without her knowing it. Indeed, the execution happens somewhere in the white spaces of the pages between two cantos. It is a curious attempt to portray Queen Elizabeth's reluctance to accomplish this brute act of justice. Plato argued that poets are inspired by a divine madness that allows them to know the truth when they could not know it by any other normal human means. This may be true, but Sir Walter Raleigh, a poet who had much more intimate connections to the queen, could well have said something about her ambivalence to his close friend Spenser.

At the time, Elizabeth wrote to James VI, claiming that his mother's execution was an "accident":

> I would you knew though not felt the extreme dolor that overwhelms my mind for that miserable accident which far contrary to my meaning hath befallen.

James, for his part, at least publicly acquiesced in her claim of innocence: "I dare not wrong you so far as not to judge honorably of your unspotted part therein."[9] He had earlier written to plead his mother's case to Elizabeth, reminding her that Mary was a queen, divinely protected by God's election of her to reign. He knew how impossible it should have been for Elizabeth to consider the judicial execution of another anointed monarch. Even though James had been educated by the "atheist" republican humanist George Buchanan, who totally rejected the idea of the divine right of kings, he was himself a staunch defender of divinely bestowed royal prerogative.

> What thing, madame, can greatlier touch me in honor that is a king and a son than that my nearest neighbor, being in straitest friendship with me, shall rigorously put to death a free sovereign prince and my natural mother, alike in estate and sex to her that so uses her . . . and touching her nearly in proximity of blood?

No one, James argued, not even another sovereign, has any proper right to judge another king, all of whom God has made divine. As such, they can be subject to the "censure of none in earth, whose anointing by God cannot be defiled by man." Kings, who are "supreme and immediate lieutenants of God in heaven, cannot therefore be judged by their equals in earth." James ended the letter by ominously warning Elizabeth: " your general reputation and the universal (almost) misliking of you may dangerously peril both . . . your person and your estate."

Officially, King James VI vociferously objected to this section in

Spenser's epic whereby his mother is figured as Duessa, the Roman Catholic harlot who accompanies the seven-headed monster Hydra from Revelations. James had the book banned in Scotland, and he asked the English government to assure him that the poet would be soundly punished. (Rather than being punished, however, Spenser was promoted.)[10]

In France, soon after the guilty verdict was first reported, Catherine de' Medici expressed her fear that Elizabeth would execute Mary; she noted that on February 7, 1587, Mary "face mourir" (faces death). She sent an ambassador to ask Elizabeth for a delay of twelve days, which was granted.[11] On March 1, 1587, she asked her ambassador to check to see if what she had been told was true. It was confirmed to her that "pauvre Marie" had been executed on February 18. On March 14, Catherine wrote to Villeroy, secretary of state to her son the king.

> I assure you that there is no Catholic prince who must not resent this, and those same who are of the religion of the Queen of England, still they must have a horror of such inhumanity. . . . It will always be a cruelty without compare . . . and it must be nothing but the beginning of great difficulty for those who would reign.[12]

Catherine, for all her having supposedly hated Mary, felt deep unhappiness over the "cruel death of this poor queen," and worried that the news would further destabilize her already unstable son. Clearly "Marie" had remained very important to them both. Catherine also foresaw the "difficulty" this official act of regicide would pose for future kings.

Unlike Catherine, Elizabeth, having never agreed to meet with Mary face to face, managed to avoid loving her as a first cousin once removed (and her closest kin) or as the "sister" she always addressed her as being. But Elizabeth still did at least see herself reflected in Mary's queenship, joined by a special protected position they both shared. She had been enraged at the Scottish rebels for their refusal to recognize the divine royal nature of their queen Mary, anointed and appointed by God to rule, but instead enacting violence against the very idea of monarchy. For the same reason, Elizabeth was publicly furious that the English state had executed an anointed queen.

She blamed Cecil directly. Why had he not given in to her requests to couch the proclamation of Mary's death sentence in terms of the Bond of Association, where anyone among the three thousand signers could have killed the queen of Scotland with impunity? That choice would have, he knew, profoundly eased her soul. So, why did Cecil arrange it so that Elizabeth had to participate in a full-blown judicial execution that made regicide officially legal in English law? After all, the Bond of Association that did not require a trial and an official execution had been his own idea. Moreover, the queen had specifically hinted to all and sundry that someone should relieve her of the "burden" to be personally and legally involved as sovereign in the death of another sovereign.

Because no one undertook to execute the Bond of Association, and because Mary was judged in an official trial and beheaded in a ceremonious execution in full view of the civic leaders of the realm, it became law in England that the Parliament may legally depose and behead a divinely anointed sovereign. And members of Parliament did in fact undertake to do just that only sixty-two years later, when they voted to execute Mary Stuart's grandson, King Charles I, in 1649. England then had no king at all but a "Lord Protector" named Oliver Cromwell, a middle-class general who ruled until his death and was unsuccessfully succeeded by his son Richard. And so, pursuing his friend John Knox's idea of the nation's legal right to "unelect" an anointed monarch, to depose and execute him or her, William Cecil had made regicide not only possible but legal in England.

It was not only Elizabeth who understood what Cecil had achieved. William Camden, the first to write a history of Elizabeth's reign, quoted a sign that was put up near Mary Stuart's tomb (although soon taken down):

A princess accomplished with royal virtues and royal soul, having many times (but in vain) demanded her royal privilege, is by barbarous and tyrannical cruelty extinct . . . and by one and the same wicked sentence is both Mary, Queen of Scots doomed to a natural death, and all surviving kings, being made as common people, are subjected to a civil death. A new and unexampled kind of tomb is here extant, wherein the living are enclosed with the dead: for know, that with the sacred ashes of saint Mary here lieth violate and prostrate the majesty of all kings and princes.[13]

# PART THREE

❧

## THE MEDICI

๛

# CHAPTER EIGHT

# Catherine de' Medici

*Tolerance and Terror*

Only one of this book's quartet of sixteenth-century queens did not have the privilege of ruling as a crowned monarch in her own right. Mary Tudor, Elizabeth Tudor, and Mary Stuart were all crowned monarchs by hereditary right, but Catherine de' Medici ruled as mother of three kings. While Catherine de' Medici had noble French blood from her mother, she could never be other than La Reine Mère. Although she had turned this position into real and absolute authority, she ran the government of France because her three sons were at first too young, then too ill or incompetent, and finally too intimidated by her not to act on her decisions.

Despite the first hurtful and frustrating decade of her marriage when her husband Henri II and his astonishingly well-preserved mistress Diane de Poitiers simply ignored her, Catherine learned to work hard and well; after her husband's death, though always within the formal limitations of her carefully established motherly authority, she became the de facto ruler of one of the largest, most affluent, and most important nations in Europe.[1] Over the coming decades, like her father-in-law Francis I, she developed more projects, arranged more architectural expansions, encouraged more technological innovations (not just the merely legendary use of the sidesaddle and the fork), and gave more contributions to the arts than many earlier kings. Imbued with a sophisticated sense of culture and valuing artistic creativity from her heritage of the Italian Renaissance, she brought about and supported a renewed French culture, building new structures like the Tuileries, sponsoring new art forms like the ballet, and attempting a new practice of religious tolerance whereby people of different religions could live in the same country peaceafully together.[2]

Against the medical odds of the time, Catherine successfully gave birth to many children, and against the odds of her children's various weaknesses, she succeeded in making those who survived childhood into a powerful potential dynastic line for the houses of Valois, Bourbon, and Lorraine. Of her four sons, three became reigning kings, and through the marriages of her three daughters, two became queens and one a duchess.

In contrast, both Mary and Elizabeth Tudor were childless. Mary Stuart had one baby—James. She never saw him past his infancy, and shortly after her death he referred to her as "the defunct." At the beginning of Catherine's years as a royal wife in France, she was mocked and ignored. But by the end of her life, she was obeyed and if not always beloved, then always respected by much of her adopted country, where she inspired both admiration and fear—as if she'd become the Italian mother and La Reine Mère to all of France.

In some ways La Reine Mère was also a mother to the three "real" queens of our book. She was Mary Stuart's mother-in-law, the person with whom Mary lived from age five to eighteen. And she remained a periodic political adviser on the Catholic-Protestant divide in Mary Stuart's troubled reign in Scotland.

Earlier, she had been a supporter of Mary Tudor from the girl's birth, at which time she sent Catherine of Aragon a baptismal font for her baby daughter (as decades later she would send a sadly never-to-be-used font to Mary Tudor herself).

For Mary Tudor's half-sister Elizabeth she was a close correspondent, a negotiator on treaties, and an indefatigable marriage broker in an endless campaign to get Elizabeth to wed one of her sons. Perhaps most intensely, she advised the family-less English Protestant queen on her treatment of her first cousin Mary Stuart, specifically what to do about the now abdicated "sister queen," then living under house arrest, while all around Elizabeth's country Catholic Englishmen, and all around Europe, Catholic counter-reformationists, were plotting to put the Scottish queen back on her own throne and perhaps more threateningly, to seat her on Elizabeth's throne as well.

The threat was real. In the British Isles in 1571–72, Mary Stuart and Elizabeth Tudor were both caught up in the fallout of the failed international Ridolfi plot that had been fomented by a Florentine banker and that would eventually involve Spain, the Vatican, the Netherlands, and British Catholics in an armed conspiracy to restore Mary to the Scottish monarchy and to win for her the English throne, while deposing if not also assassinating Elizabeth. While William Cecil had no part in this particular plot, it was one of the very real Catholic threats to Elizabeth's throne.

The Ridolfi plot, like many others fomented by Mary's idolaters, was ultimately exposed, and Elizabeth survived it. She never again supported any claim of Mary's to the throne of Scotland. But the awful result of the Ridolfi plot was that Elizabeth felt forced to execute many of her own subjects, including her cousin the Duke of Norfolk as well as, perhaps more sadly, the hanging of seven hundred Catholic commoners in the north of England.

While Elizabeth was executing Catholics in England for treason, in France Catherine de' Medici was earnestly pursuing her policy of tolerance toward the Protestant Huguenots. To this end she was busy with plans to marry her Catholic daughter Marguerite de Valois to the young scion of the Protestant forces, Henri de Navarre. Eight years earlier in the children's masque by Ronsard, written to be performed at Fontainebleau on the "Queen's Day" of 1564, Marguerite may have played "Margot" (who gave the gift of a songbird to her brother, the young king Charles IX). Now she was marrying Henri de Navarre, who may have played the part of "Navarin."

Royal marriage arrangements were usually conceived years before they took place, and this marriage of the Houses of Valois and Navarre was no exception. Catherine always intently focused early and long on complex marital negotiations to ensure the longevity and the power of the Valois dynasty. As we have seen, François had been three years old when he was officially betrothed to the five-year-old Mary Stuart.

At the time of Marguerite's marriage to Henri de Navarre, the nineteen-year-old was still in love with her teenage flame, the very Catholic Henri de Guise ("Guisin" in the children's masque). But Marguerite knew she had to submit to the demands of her mother Catherine and her brother King Charles, both of whom had insisted that she marry a very different Henri, the womanizing Protestant Bourbon Huguenot prince. It was not a happy match, although from her famous *Memoirs*, Margot (as she was often called) at least seemed to enjoy the pomp and spectacle of the moment of her wedding:

> I wore a crown on my head with the . . . gown of ermine, and I blazed in diamonds. My blue-colored robe had a train to it four ells [yards] in length, which was supported by three princesses. A platform had been raised some height from the ground, which led from the Bishop's palace to the Church of Notre-Dame. It was hung with cloth of gold.[3]

The story got told that Margot was so resistant to her garlicky Bourbon groom that at the marriage altar, her brother the king had to push her head down in an affirmative "nod" in order to complete the ceremony; such a detail does not, however, appear in her own version of events and so is unlikely to be true. (Many hair-raising years later, the loveless marriage between Marguerite and Henri of Navarre was annulled due to lack of issue. Their infidelity was legendary— each had many lovers—but Marguerite was apparently infertile and never bore a child.)

Pierre de Bordeille, abbé de Brantôme, a gossipy courtier who wrote tell-all stories about the Valois court, narrates a moment when La Reine Mère, just before the wedding to Navarre, bragged about her daughter Margot to some court ladies. Margot was, she told them, not just a beautiful young girl, but a well-educated, poised, and dip-

Miniature of Henri de Navarre and Marguerite de Valois; unknown artist, 1572. From a Book of Hours belonging to Catherine de' Medici.
*Art Heritage / Alamy Stock Photo*

lomatically able speaker who could easily converse with ambassadors
in multiple languages, including Latin and Greek. Although Catherine had not allowed Margot to choose her own husband, she was still
proud of her daughter's abilities. According to Brantôme, the queen
mother told the assemblage:

> If by the abolition of the Salic law, the kingdom should come
> to my daughter in her own right, as other kingdoms have fallen
> to the distaff, certainly my daughter is as capable of reigning, or
> more so, as most men and kings whom I have known; and I think
> that her reign would be a fine one, equal to that of the king her
> grandfather and that of the king her father, for she has a great
> mind and great virtues for [ruling].[4]

Brantôme goes on for a few more pages lambasting the Salic law,
numbering the women who had ruled well and long in other coun-

tries as well as the many duchies, counties, and baronies in France governed by women.

Far from the wanton incestuous nymphomaniac popularized in the nineteenth century by Alexandre Dumas's novel *La Reine Margot* (1845), Catherine's daughter "Queen Margot" was a believer in affairs of the mind, a renowned patron of the arts, the intellectual epicenter of wherever she happened to be living. She was the first royal woman to write her memoirs. Her salons were home to preeminent philosophers, musicians, playwrights, painters, and scholars. She was a feminist long before the term was invented, famously claiming that the world is not "made for man and man for God, but rather the world is made for man, man is made for woman, and woman is made for God."

Catherine, sacrificing her brilliant daughter's desires to a state marriage, was focused on a political agenda. She had arranged to have all the most important Huguenots and Catholics assembled in Paris for the wedding. But tragically the ceremony—designed to reconcile opposing religions—would instead form the backdrop for an infamous event that would make Catherine de' Medici one of history's favorite villains, crediting her as Italian poisoner, creator of the *escadron volant*—a flying squadron of eighty beautiful women encouraged to seduce and spy on powerful men—and, most despicably, a mass murderer who had planned the St. Bartholomew's Day Massacre decades before it happened. This view of Catherine pops up century after century: In D. W. Griffith's 1916's silent masterpiece, she personifies the film's title, *Intolerance*, smiling evilly behind her fan as streets fill with the dead. The innocent hero is warned, "Medici, the old cat, is scratching out the lives of all your people."

It is strange to think that Catherine is celebrated for "intolerance" in Griffith's film, because she was, among all the rulers of the sixteenth century, the most tolerant of religious differences. Yet, in the recent past, there have been *son et lumière* performances at the huge castle of Blois, when you could hear over loudspeakers Catherine's sadistic laugh as it cackles and shrieks from high medieval parapets, from which her minions were presumably hanging her victims. At Blois you still can visit her long-popular poison collection, although authorities now concede that maybe not all the cabinets held lethal doses for "the Italian" queen's mixing. One recent visitor's comment states: "The room in question holds 237 small cabinets, hidden in the beautiful woodwork. The room was in fact associated with Catherine de' Medici, and she was certainly suspected of some heinous poison related crimes, but historians believe that the cabinets were much more likely to have held small objects d'art or confidential papers than a poison collection, which is a little bit disappointing."[5]

If mass murder is what one requires of a true villain, then Catherine is bound to disappoint.

The currently recognized facts about St. Bartholomew's Day are that her twenty-two-year-old son Charles IX had been so charmed by his friend and counselor, the Huguenot Admiral de France Gaspard de Coligny, that he fell in with that Protestant soldier's plans to go to war against Spain in the Netherlands. The result was that Catherine had lost her once unchallenged control over her volatile son. In the end, what is indisputable is that while ultimately she was one of the party responsible for all of the unintended consequences of St. Bartholomew's Day, what she had actually planned was infinitely smaller than the mass murder with which she's been charged. She apparently chose this particular moment to instigate the assassination of Coligny, war leader of the Protestant forces and himself an employer of assassins, because the attack could so easily be blamed on the de Guise family and their ongoing blood feud with Coligny.

The death of Coligny was easy to set up: all Catherine needed to do was to rescind the current royal ban against blood feuding, which had forbidden the de Guises in particular from taking revenge on Coligny for his ordering the assassination of François de Guise. Coligny had had de Guise killed in revenge for the Massacre of Vassy. Catherine genuinely believed that Coligny, as the Protestants' military leader, not only posed a threat to her power over her son Charles IX, but that he was an equally grave danger to the survival of France itself, for he had continued both to defy the commands of the royal council and to amass large numbers of soldiers close to the border with the Netherlands. If Coligny were allowed to march a French army into the Netherlands to aid the Dutch Protestants, especially if accompanied by the young French king, the sortie would provoke an outright war with Spain (the Netherlands' overlord), a war Catherine knew that France was ill-prepared to fight.

For those political reasons, just before the very public wedding, Catherine revoked the royal ban against revenge. As a result, there was a strong possibility that when Coligny turned up at the wedding of Marguerite and Henri on August 18, 1572, he would be murdered by someone, and that everyone would simply conclude that the de Guises, and no one else, had seized the opportunity to exact their revenge. As expected, the de Guises proved happy to contribute whatever they could to the destruction of Coligny. And everyone did assume exactly what Catherine had thought they would.

Such misdirection was a signal skill of politicians, as promulgated by Machiavelli, who had dedicated *The Prince* to Catherine's father, Lorenzo de' Medici. She always understood the oblique chess moves of realpolitik, and often employed them. On this occasion, she intended to hide any personal involvement of hers behind everyone else's assumption that the de Guises were the murderers of Coligny (which they were). And as odd as it is to think of a murder planned this way, Catherine's plot to have Coligny assassinated was a logical extension of her agenda to reconcile Catholics and Protestants through the harmonizing wedding of her Catholic daughter to a Protestant groom. She knew Coligny's waging a sudden war in favor of the Protestants in the Netherlands would be one more outgrowth of the Wars of Religion that had already ravaged France, and that such a new armed conflict would do the same damage again.

But her plan went awry. Three days afer the wedding, on August 21, 1572, a sniper took a shot at Coligny from a window in a house owned by the de Guises. Yet just at the moment the sniper fired, the

Protestant leader stooped down in order to fix his shoe. The bullet missed, piercing only his shoulder, causing a severe yet not immediately mortal wound. Coligny lived, but the misplaced shot let loose a riotous fusillade of killing that ended in the St. Bartholomew's Day Massacre and the deaths of twenty to thirty thousand Protestants throughout the country, with at least three thousand in Paris alone. It was the greatest slaughter in the history of France until the eighteenth-century French Revolution.

In her *Memoires* Catherine's daughter Margot subsequently provided an eyewitness account of the tense scene late into the night of the second day after the attempted assassination inside the royal palace of the Louvre. She narrated the entirely ad hoc arrangements that were quickly made to finish the job of killing Coligny and also to assassinate those Huguenot leaders who would surely rise up to avenge their leader's murder.[6] Charles IX was so horrified to learn that his own mother had been responsible for the initial attack on his favored father figure that he reportedly cried out hysterically, "Kill them all!!" by which he meant all the noblemen who had accompanied the Protestant Navarre groom to the wedding (the men most likely to take armed revenge on the king's family for the slaughter of Coligny). Charles had not meant his soldiers to target Huguenot civilians in the Parisian populace. But that is exactly what happened.

Margot goes on to tell of the moment she saved two Protestant gentlemen from the killing that had begun inside the royal apartments of the Louvre as well as outside in the streets of Paris.

> As we passed through the antechamber, all the doors of which were wide open, a gentleman . . . , pursued by archers, was run through the body with a pike, and fell dead at my feet. As if I had been killed by the same stroke, I fell. . . .
>
> As soon as I recovered . . . I went into my sister's bedchamber and was immediately followed by First Gentleman to the King my husband [Henri of Navarre] and Armagnac . . . who both

came to beg me to save their lives. I went and threw myself on my knees before the king and the Queen my mother, and obtained the lives of them both.[7]

Margot makes clear that any plan to expand the killing to include the Huguenot nobles who had accompanied her bridegroom to the royal wedding was started not by anyone's long-planned design, but by the king's ad hoc decision, shared among the members of the court party (led by Catherine) in the general panic after the failed attack on Coligny. It soon became clear that if the king did not swiftly arraign de Guise for this crime, the Huguenots were going to take their own revenge. In the end, the only actual premeditation (beyond the queen mother's unfortunate plan to use the wedding assemblage to assassinate a single enemy, Coligny) was when the king's party agreed that they should strike before the Huguenots could retaliate for their commander's assassination.

Whatever the truth, chaotic rumors spread that Catherine had deliberately hatched the idea of mass killings at her meeting with Philip II's war chief, the Duke of Alva, seven years earlier when she had met with her daughter Elisabeth de Valois, queen of Spain, during the much-admired festivities at Bayonne in 1565.[8] It is not at all true that together Catherine and the Duke of Alva planned a mass killing of Protestants to take place a number of years later. The massacre was instead the outcome of a single act of attempted assasination that went tragically awry. Her own larger plan for bringing Huguenots and Catholics together through the marriage of Margot and Henri de Navarre did, however, lie in catastrophic ruins.

A month of massive religion-based slaughter spread to other cities throughout France. Catherine was awash in congratulations from the Catholic rulers of Europe, including the pope and Philip II. With real disappointment, they learned only later that the massacre had been purely accidental, and that its origin had been practical politics rather than religious zeal.

St. Bartholomew's Day Massacre; François Dubois, 1572. *Center right:* Coligny's corpse hangs out of a window before it is thrown down to the street; *Upper left:* Catherine de' Medici in widow's black surveys the pile of dead bodies in front of the castle doors. © *Musée cantonal des Beaux-Arts de Lausanne / Nora Rupp*

Much like Mary Stuart and also like Elizabeth, Catherine de' Medici had to fight hard to defend the Valois' dynastic hold on power in France. Earlier historians have guessed that Catherine's motives were less patriotic than the other queens' defense of their blood rights to rule. As Pierre Adolphe Chéruel (a student of Jules Michelet) wrote of Catherine in 1870, "Nourished in the subtleties of Italian politics, indifferent to good and evil, without principles of religion, she only had a genius for intrigue. . . . She left the monarchy without support and France without allies."[9] A far more trustworthy—indeed eyewitness—observer, however, had an entirely different opinion: that La Reine Mère was fundamentally protecting not only her children but also the safety and peace of France. Thus when Henri de Bourbon, Catherine's son-in-law from his marriage to Margot, became the first of the Bourbons to rule after the Valois as King Henri IV, in 1589, he said of Catherine: "I ask you, what could a woman do . . .

with two [hostile] families . . . grasping [at] the crown . . . ? Was she not compelled to play strange parts . . . to guard her sons, who successively reigned through the wise conduct of that shrewd woman? I am surprised that she never did worse."[10] After having personally gone through the terror of the St. Bartholomew's Day Massacre as a Huguenot prince in the Louvre, Henri's sympathetic judgment suggests Catherine's conduct was shrewd but not diabolically evil, and her actions certainly not the Satan-inspired horrors that subsequent Protestant propaganda made them out to be.[11]

The repercussions of the massacre were, however, many and long lived; in Huguenot France Catherine's name became a byword for monstrous tyranny. Yet Catherine may have cared more, perhaps a great deal more, about the response of her sister queen Elizabeth I, with whom she had been in active negotiations for a marriage with another one of her French Catholic sons. She was eager to know how the Protestant queen would respond. Only four months after the massacre, Catherine and Charles tested the waters by writing to Elizabeth to ask her to stand as godmother to Charles's newborn daughter. Elizabeth did not reply herself, but instructed her ambassador Francis Walsingham to answer the French royals; in December of 1572, she told him to say:

> We are sorry to hear of . . . the great slaughter made in France
> of noblemen and gentlemen, unconvicted and untried. . . . They
> were not brought to answer by law and to judgment before they
> were executed.[12]

Again, Elizabeth's concern was for orderly obedience to the established laws of the realm, specifically habeas corpus, the right to a trial.

> But when more was added to the charge—that women, children,
> maids, young infants, and sucking babes were at the same time
> murdered and cast into the river, and that liberty of execution
> was given to the vilest and basest sort of the popular, without

punishment or revenge of such cruelties—this increased our grief and sorrow.

Elizabeth pointed out the hypocritical paradox in their request that she stand as godmother to Charles's infant daughter: "It must needs seem very strange, both to us and to all other, that our good brother should require us to be godmother to his dear child, we being of the religion which he doth now persecute and cannot abide within his realm."

As Elizabeth then surmised or had discovered, there had been no religious motive behind Catherine's plan to assassinate Coligny, but rather a specific effort to stop him from persuading her son the king to rush into a disastrous war. The English queen may well have grasped that it was a purely secular power play on Catherine's part, however religiously inspired the public slaughter that followed came to be. Perhaps for this reason, Elizabeth said yes to the request to stand as godmother to Charles's daughter. She always placed wise policy above religion—a priority she shared with Catherine. She even suggested that negotiations about her own marriage with a Valois son could remain open. And remain open they did, much to the subsequent horror of many members of Elizabeth's court.

Seven years after the massacre, in 1579, Elizabeth seemed to be deeply serious about marrying the youngest of Catherine's sons, François (formerly Hercule), Duc d'Alençon, whose part was "Angelot" in the long-ago *Bergerie* (his gift to the boy king had been a goat). Now Alençon was twenty-four years old, while Elizabeth was forty-six. He was Catholic, she was Protestant. The two greatest impediments to her marriage with any one of the Valois sons had always been, she had claimed to the French court, not personal but simply the unbridgeably vast differences in their ages, and their religions.

Although the twenty-two-year gap in ages was almost comically large (Elizabeth had earlier turned down Alençon's brother Charles IX when their age disparity was a mere thirteen years), the middle-aged queen seemed to care less about such proprieties as she approached

François-Hercule, Duc d'Alençon, aged eighteen. Unknown artist, 1572.
*Samuel H. Kress Collection, National Gallery of Art, Washington, D.C.*

menopause. For whatever reason, she must have been more serious than she had ever been before about a Valois suitor, despite his age, his religion, or the national disgrace of the French massacre of Protestants seven years earlier. Her fondness for her "Frog," as she dubbed François, seemed quite genuine, and was signaled by her giving him a nickname—as she had done for all her favorite counselors (Cecil was "Spirit," Dudley was "Eyes," and so forth). Moreover, Alençon was of royal blood, and at the time second in line to the throne of France. Long before, the Spanish envoy Feria had not been wrong when he had said that Elizabeth was proud and that she wanted to marry royalty.

But the English court and people responded to these marital negotiations as if they faced the greatest catastrophe; a program of resistance and critique was launched against the usually idolized queen, involving both a significant private letter and a famous published pamphlet.

The public pamphlet, titled *The discoverie of the gaping gulf where-into England is like be swallowed by an other French marriage* (1579), was authored by one John Stubbs, a Puritan lawyer and writer. Elizabeth outlawed the pamphlet and brought Stubbs, as well as his printer-publisher, to trial for "seditious" writing. Stubbs and the publisher were condemned, and while at first Elizabeth, as angry as she was, wanted them both put to death, she was persuaded that simply cutting off their right hands would be sufficient punishment. Before their public dismemberments, Stubbs wittily quipped, "Pray for me now my calamity is at hand." Despite his unjust punishment, Stubbs remained a loyal subject of Queen Elizabeth, becoming by his name something of a pun himself.

Elizabeth later repented of her excessive sentence on Stubbs and his publisher. But she never apologized for her treatment of a loyal but courageous courtier who had risked her wrath by writing a private letter warning her against any possible marriage with Catherine de' Medici's son. The author of this letter was Sir Philip Sidney, at that time the heir to his uncle Robert Dudley, Elizabeth's longest-serving favorite.

Philip Sidney was becoming a famous poet. He wrote the first ever sonnet cycle in England, setting the fashion for poetry through the last decades of the sixteenth century. (Shakespeare became his most famous imitator.) With his sister, the Countess of Pembroke, he also translated the Psalms into English verse, changing the form of English lyric for the next one hundred years. He was the paradigm of the Renaissance man—a soldier, a courtier, a poet, handsome, courteous, well educated, well traveled, much loved. (For some reason Elizabeth apparently did not share her people's admiration of him.)

Sidney had been present in Paris during the St. Bartholomew's Day Massacre and had witnessed firsthand the genocidal bloodletting that swept through the city. It was clearly this trauma that colored his response to the French marriage proposal. Risking Elizabeth's ire, he warned of the danger posed by the public horror at home should Elizabeth follow through with a marriage to a Catholic

Sir Philip Sidney; unknown artist, 1572.
© *National Portrait Gallery, London*

Valois prince like Alençon, son of the "Jezebel of our age," Catherine de' Medici.

> When they shall see you take a husband, a Frenchman and a Papist . . . the very common people well know this, that he is the son of a Jezebel of our age: that his brother made oblation of his own sister's marriage, the easier to make massacres of our brethren in belief. . . . This, I say, even at the first sight, gives occasion to all, truly religious, to abhor such a master, and consequently to diminish much of the hopeful love they have long held to you.[13]

To punish Sidney for the audacity of his chastising her, Elizabeth banished him from London (he took the occasion of his exile to write *The Arcadia*, a book from which Shakespeare would lift many of his plots). While Sidney subsequently was allowed to return to court, Elizabeth never favored him. Later, Sidney suffered a Spanish musket wound received on the battlefield of Sutphen in the Netherlands. It shattered his thigh, and he died of the abscess twenty days later. On the field of battle, he is said to have told a water carrier to give the cup of water brought him to a nearby mortally wounded common soldier. His famous words: "Thy necessity is yet greater than mine."

Elizabeth was forced to allow Sir Francis Walsingham (Sidney's father-in-law) to give him the largest state funeral ever given to a non-royal in England (until the funeral of Lady Diana Spencer in 1997), held in St. Paul's Cathedral. And in the end, Sidney's warning to his queen proved prophetic. The proposed marriage to her beloved "Frog" was demonstrably so unpopular among the English that she was finally persuaded that she could not follow through with it without damaging consequences. She broke off negotiations. And she wrote a poem, "On Monsieur's Departure," that sounds genuinely personal about her self-imposed loss:

> I do, *yet* dare *not* say I ever meant,
> I seem stark mute but inwardly do prate.
> I am and not, I freeze and yet am burned,
> Since from myself another self I turned.
>     . . .
> Let me float or sink, be high or low.
> Or let me live with some more sweet content
> Or die, and so forget what love e'er meant.

There was no similar public outcry against any of the other possible marriages that had been proposed for the Virgin Queen, and no other negotiation reached so near to a conclusion.[14] Elizabeth wrote no other such poems (that we know of) about her feelings for any other wooer (although she did write a poem about her suitors collectively). When Alençon died early at the age of twenty-six, however, Elizabeth wrote a letter to Catherine de' Medici about the loss of her Frog:

> To Madame, my good sister and the queen mother,
> If the extremity of my unhappiness had not equaled my grief

for his sake and had not rendered me inadequate to touch with pen the wound that my heart suffers, it would not be possible that I would have so forgotten myself as not to have visited you in the company that I make with you in your sorrow, which I am sure cannot be greater than my own. For inasmuch as you are his mother, so it is that there remain to you several other children. But for me, I find no consolation except death, which I hope will soon reunite us.""""15

Writing to Catherine in unusually convoluted language, Elizabeth may have been a bit vague as to how many children La Reine Mère actually had left (only two, Margot and King Henri III). The Virgin Queen would go on to say that she would use the love she still held for François (Alençon) further to bind herself to Catherine and the king, "assuring you that you will find me the most faithful daughter and sister that ever princes had." She may have known that Henri III had always hated his younger brother, and that Catherine had not supported her youngest son as well as she might have (Elizabeth suggested that if Alençon had lived longer, "you would have sent more help").

Many readers think Elizabeth's letter shows that Catherine was far more important to her than was François/Alençon himself, and that, as with all the other courtships, she was never truly serious about this marriage. But the real and vehemently expressed fears of her court that she would go through with the marriage suggest otherwise. That her advisers and courtiers were so very worried indicates how the "fires" Elizabeth claimed burned in her were at least partly real. In the letter she laid claim to a closeness to La Reine Mère that sounded like true kinship—similar to the language she always shared with Mary Stuart's son King James, with whom she did in fact share close blood ties. Just as she imagined her relationship to James VI as if he were her own son, she writes that she speaks to Catherine "as if I were your daughter born." Through her life Elizabeth had had many temporary substitutes for Anne Boleyn, the mother she'd never known, among them her older sister Mary and her father's other wives—most particularly Katherine Parr. But Catherine de' Medici was an older woman who stayed a presence longest in her life, and perhaps was the one most like her, not only in station as ruler, but in political nature. In any event, the courtship of the Duc d'Alençon, like the link of Mary Stuart, was yet another bond between Catherine and Elizabeth that served them in their shared pursuit of peace, for they continued to imagine themselves bound by family ties.

Such an intense appeal in her letter to La Reine Mère reveals how well Elizabeth understood that Catherine's fundamental identity was grounded in her successful motherhood of royal progeny. Though childless for the first unhappy decade of her marriage to Henri II, she had subsequently given birth to ten of his children; seven lived to adulthood, three of the sons becoming king. Her three female children who lived to adulthood became duchess of Lorraine, queen of France, and queen of Spain. By thinking to marry Alençon, Elizabeth was offering to become a member of a large royal family, daughter of Catherine herself, as if one "born."

Perhaps Elizabeth knew that Catherine doted on the present king Henri III, who had always been her favorite, and thus she, as would-be bride, suffered greater loneliness than the bereaved mother of the dead would-be groom. Catherine's most beloved son yet lived. Yet this sharing of grief, however unequal Elizabeth insists it was, formed still another link between the two queens.

༺࿔

# CHAPTER NINE

# Eight Valois Tapestries

*Catherine de' Medici's Inalienable Possessions*

lizabeth's allegedly unintended "miserable accident" of executing Catholic Mary, Queen of Scots in 1587 left England catastrophically vulnerable to a counterattack by Catholic Philip II of Spain. Similarly, when Catherine de' Medici's instigation of the assassination of Coligny ended in the accidentally botched murder attempt and the subsequent massacres throughout France, the Valois suffered a massive stain to their honor as responsible governors of the realm. Queen Catherine was blamed, and the massacre haunted the Valois dynasty for decades to come.

The elimination of seventy thousand Protestants by such massacres did so please the pope, however, that he had a medal cast in celebration of them, to match the one he had cast the year before in 1571 for the victory of the Battle of Lepanto over the Ottoman Empire. Clearly, in the pope's mind, the death of so many French Protestants equaled the historical victory over Muslim Turks; both Protestants and Turks were, equally, "infidels." Although briefly celebrated by Catholic Europe, Catherine understood how great the threat to the reputation of the Valois monarchy such a spectacular failure of law and order posed, and it may be for this reason that she thought of conjuring an immense face-saving project to try to recover the family's name. It seems to have been only a few years after the massacre that she began to conceive her plan to create the Valois tapestries.

These eight enormous woven artworks, as large as twelve and a half feet tall by twenty feet wide, may act as the Rosetta Stone on which we may now read what Catherine de' Medici chose to say about her long, productive life, what she valued. Just as we know Elizabeth through her brilliant speeches, her acts of courage, her letters, her poems, her creation of herself as a spectacularly successful Gloriana, a courageous woman ruler and England's Virgin Queen, for Catherine de' Medici it is these tapestries, representing her projects and productions—her buildings, parks, masques, concerts, ballets—that tell us who she was. We have only just begun to study these mute (and neglected) artworks, only now able to translate them into legible evidence of Catherine's most triumphant achievements—her royal children and their performances in her spectacular "magnificences."

The dissemination of Mary Stuart's multiple portraits, all echoing Clouet's vision of her in white mourning, were an effective signal of the purity of her double widowhood and contributed to a powerful and lasting image of the Queen of Scots as a beautiful, romantic heroine who died a sacrificial death. Her execution was a drama that allowed her to triumph over the tragedy of a ruined reputation to become the sainted founder of a royal bloodline that lasts to this day.

Mary Tudor courageously became the queen her mother always knew she could be. While she was prevented from fulfilling the promise of a Tudor-Hapsburg Catholic dynasty by her barrenness, and was unable to turn back the tide of change her father had so abruptly let loose upon the English people, she was, by becoming (and remaining) the first independent queen to rule England, something more than the shallow synopsis by which history has named her, "Bloody Mary." For she also taught her sister how to be a queen, and not merely by negative example, but by deploying a rhetoric of independent queenship that many have taken to be original to Elizabeth but which was Mary's best gift to her sister: mother to her people, gallant orator in a crisis, a woman wedded to the realm with her coronation ring.

Like "Bloody" Mary, Catherine de' Medici has been one of history's favorite villains. Both were bloodied by their real and imagined religious hatred of Protestants. Both owed much of their scandalous public reputations to the urgent polemical need in Protestant propaganda to move culture off its traditional foundations into a new understanding of the signal importance of the individual, as opposed to a collective, conscience. Catherine's Valois tapestries display with exquisite mannerist skill La Reine Mère's vision of a peaceful France, one not violently divided—as both Mary Tudor's England and Catherine's France had been—between Catholics and Protestants.

Although earlier scholarship assumed that the tapestries were given as a gift to Catherine de' Medici by William of Orange, more recent research has tied the origin of the tapestries directly to her as the patron who almost certainly commissioned and provided the designs for them. No longer the mere recipient of a man's gift, Catherine is now recognized as the creator of these immense works of art, as well as of the spectacles they celebrate. We now understand that they may have been designed to be a gift to a granddaughter and thus were, from their inception, slated to be inalienable possessions of the Medici family.

Catherine's creation of the Valois tapestries sprang from the same motives that had previously caused her back in the 1560s to create her "magnificences," those extravagant public spectacles in which she persuaded both Catholic and Protestant courtiers to participate in feats of physical prowess, providing means by which they could display their martial skills, but by making art, not war. Catherine organized the violence that was the *métier* of the military classes, and elevated it into a form of art. She then celebrated and archived it in yet another form of art. The tapestries, woven a decade after the magnificences, were reminders of an earlier harmony that had been destroyed by the massacre. Having been a supporter of her son's Peace Edict of 1576, which ended the fifth war of religion, Catherine used the tapestry series to display what France looked like when Catholic and Protestant were not at war.[1]

The series of eight massive weavings in sumptuous wool, silk, silver, and gold-wrapped thread supply portraits of many individuals in

Valois tapestry "Tournament," unknown atelier, 1570s. Catherine de' Medici is flanked by Henri de Navarre and Margot on the left; on the right, Henri III of France is in profile, while his wife, Louise de Vaudément, faces the viewer.
*Gallerie degli Uffizi, Florence*

the Valois Court, standing in the foreground of the designs, dressed in the style of the 1570s. These include both prominent Catholics (members of the de Guise family) and, most importantly, Henri de Navarre, the leader of the Huguenots and at that moment husband of Marguerite.

Catherine de' Medici herself appears in seven of the eight tapestries, where she is always clothed in heavy black mourning, which makes her stand out among the other generally pastel costumes. All but one of the eight tapestries juxtapose two different time frames. The foreground in each presents the current members of the family as they looked around 1576, when the tapestries were doubtless woven. Many of these people look directly at the viewer, and most of them are distinctly identifiable. In the middle ground of seven of the tapestries, we see the various magnificences and jousting performances that were presented in the 1560s.

*Top:* Valois tapestry "Journey," unknown atelier, 1576. Catherine is the small figure being carried in a litter close to the center of the scene.

*Bottom:* Detail of "Journey." Catherine in a litter with Henri III on horseback. He looks directly at the viewer. *Gallerie degli Uffizi, Florence*

Yet it is only in the "Tournament" tapestry that the queen is shown as a dominant personage, and even then she is near the left margin of the frame.[2] In all other panels, Catherine is a smaller black-clad figure who occupies the midground or deep background and is sometimes quite difficult to find, as in the "Journey" panel. Locating her feels like something of a game, almost as if she had designed her various places in the tapestries to allow for children to seek out and find her. Grandchildren perhaps?

The "Tournament" design does *not* show two men running at each other on horseback, brandishing level lances as in a jousting tournament, but instead seems to show a mêlée, a tag-like mock battle where the greatest danger comes from the fireballs thrown among the horses' hooves. For the most part the almost symmetrical arrangements of the opposing forces look more like a work of art than a bloody battle—such as the kind of *ballet de cour* that formed set pieces in many of Catherine's magnificences, for which she was often the choreographer. Catherine had outlawed actual jousting when she came to power, still mourning her husband Henri, who had died after the wound to his eye received in a joust.[3]

The matched pair of married couples framing the complex composition in the "Tournament" form a quartet, emphasizing the fecund possibilities for the future of two different dynasties, Valois and Bourbon (neither of which were to come to fruition).

On the left, one of Catherine's court dwarves stands in for a yet unborn male grandson and heir. The designer of this panel has copied a drawing by Antoine Caron for a text by Nicolas Houel, the story of Artemisia, a widow famous for honoring her husband Mausolus

"Tournament," detail. The two carts in the upper corners and the two white horses entering the field just below the carts suggest a very loose kind of artful symmetry. *Gallerie degli Uffizi, Florence*

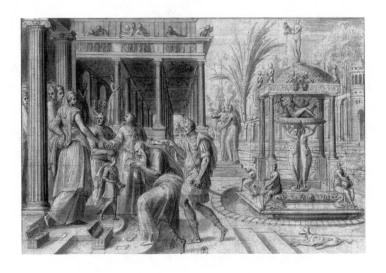

*The Story of Queen Artemisia*; Antoine Caron, 1563–1570. Source: *gallica. bnf.fr / Bibliothèque nationale de France*

with an immense tomb, the Mausoleum. Caron's design was never woven into a tapestry series for Catherine, but one was commissioned by Henri IV for his queen Marie de' Medici. Henri intended the hangings as a record of a prince's education. However ironically, the series became more fully appropriate for the widowed Marie when Henri IV was assassinated, so that she too served as regent for her son, Louis XII.[4]

The cartoon drawn for this panel in the Artemisia story by Caron not only presents the arrangement of mother and "son" as in "Tournament," but also makes a very witty comment on the imagined "revenge" that Catherine might have taken on Diane de Poitiers, her husband's former mistress of many years.

On the left Artemisia presents her son to some aged nobles, while on the right a small domed temple structure cramps down on (and so reduces the top of) a fountain that includes a very recognizable statue of Diana the huntress, the Roman goddess who frequently served as a representation of Diane de Poitiers. This image is of a famous marble carving of Diana and Actaeon (transformed into a stag), formerly thought to

Diana with Stag; unknown artist, sixteenth century.
Located in the Louvre Museum, Paris.

be by Germain Pilon, which had long graced Diane de Poitiers's Anet, a chateau given her by Henri II. The statue is currently in the Louvre.

Anet was a beautiful example of the best of sixteenth-century architecture and so it was chosen, along with Fontainebleau, as one of the two chateaux to be honored in the Valois series.

Catherine's supposed ill treatment of her husband's former long-time mistress is always alleged as proof of a jealous Italian queen's notorious vengefulness, but it has always struck me that the facts do not necessarily support that view. Catherine did not simply confiscate the exquisite chateau Chenonceau, another of Diane's favored places of retreat in the Loire Valley. Instead she proposed a swap, giving Diane the chateau Chaumont in exchange for Chenonceau. Only seventeen miles south of Chenonceau, Chaumont is a beautiful and grand chateau. It retains its characteristic thick, round medieval towers. It was at the time larger than Chenonceau and might have been considered more valuable as real estate, although—depending on one's taste—it could also be considered less elegant.

Detail B, Valois tapestry "Journey," detail. Chateau of Anet.
*Gallerie degli Uffizi, Florence*

At Chenonceau, Diane had had a bridge built spanning the Cher River; Catherine emphasized the extension by adding two stories to the bridge, thereby creating a long gallery stretching the entire breadth of the water. A decade earlier in Catherine's native Florence, Giorgio Vasari had built a strikingly similar long corridor that spanned the Arno River. Had Catherine received word, or seen drawings, of this structure in Florence and copied the idea?

In 1560 Vasari had begun the structure known as the Uffizi for Cosimo I, Grand Duke of Florence, only the second Medici to rule Florence by hereditary right after the Republic was reconquered by Medici forces. The corridor he designed allowed the Medici family to pass from the Uffizi to the Pitti Palace without encountering any former, possibly hostile citizens of the conquered republic. It also became a place to display some of the many masterpieces of portraiture that the Medici were then amassing. The corridor still forms the top floor of the Ponte Vecchio. Even today it houses a special collection of artists' self-portraits.

The only one of the Valois tapestries that does not split the foreground from the background into two separate temporal frames is "The Polish Ambassadors." The tapestry displays the celebrations

Chateau de Chenonceau, spanning the Cher River,
Indre-et-Loire, France.

that were put on when the Polish ambassadors came to take Henri,
at the time Duc d'Anjou, to Poland to become their king, as he had
been elected to the position when the former Polish dynasty had
died out.

The election had been dicey because the Poles practiced freedom
of religion in their country, and the St. Bartholomew's Day Massacre in France had given them pause. But Charles IX, who was

Ponte Vecchio and the Vasari Corridor over the Arno River, Florence.

eager to have his brother Henri out of France at any cost, spent an immense amount of money on the Polish election, going so far as to promise to build a Polish navy while also offering other largesse. Energetic diplomacy promised that religious toleration would be guaranteed.

Capturing the Polish crown was a coup for the Valois—and may have helped to recoup the family's prior fame for toleration. The "Polish Ambassadors" tapestry beautifully captures the elaborate festivities with which the French welcomed the exotically and sumptuously dressed ambassadors who came to escort their king back to his kingdom. The tapestry also depicts one of Catherine's more famous creations, the Tuileries Gardens in Paris. In addition to the park and other legendary contributions to her adopted culture, the queen had in fact introduced France to the ballet. The panel shows off not only the park, but a multiday fete that culminated in an elegant ballet danced by courtiers and some of the most beautiful and distinguished women of northern Europe, who formed elaborate martially

Valois tapestry "The Polish Ambassadors," 1576. The setting for the dance is the Tuileries, the gardens Catherine had built to the west of the Louvre. *Gallerie degli Uffizi, Florence*

inspired geometric sequences based on the "games" in Book V of Virgil's *Aeneid*. By such references, the tapestry celebrates the Valois' increased and long-lived empire (implying a lineal connection to the Roman Empire), now enlarged by its addition of Poland.

The French nobleman who stands with the ambassadors on the left of this panel is not Henri de Valois, the new King of the Poles, but Henri de Guise (the heartthrob of the teenaged Margot), who apparently underwrote the festival depicted in the panel. Henri de Guise was also the leader of the Catholic faction, pitted against the Huguenots; Catherine was careful to include representatives of both faiths. In this tapestry, unlike others in the series, there is no temporal distance between the foreground and background of the picture planes. All figures occupying the space are alive at the same time and harmoniously dance together, with Catherine again in a secondary position, though still placed in the center. Both contending houses, Catholic de Guise and Huguenot Bourbon, find their places in the Valois series; their purpose is together to depict a peaceful France no longer torn apart by faction. (A further reason for depicting the two families may well have been that the granddaughter to whom Catherine would ultimately gift the tapestries was a member of the de Guise family; the tapestries thus also celebrate her specific lineage.)

No family member who had died before the 1570s appears in the tapestries, their place being taken by a living member. Thus, although Charles IX was the actual ruler at the time of the royal tour's 1564 departure from Anet, his place on the white horse at the center of the tapestry is taken by the then living King Henri III. Time is not so much stopped as past and present are woven together to forecast a happy future for the dynasty. The inclusion of members of both the de Guise and Bourbon families repeatedly insists on Catherine's program of rapprochement between opposing forces.

The truth was not so harmonious: Henri was king of Poland for only one brief year; after his older brother Charles IX's death, he returned to France to ascend the throne as Henri III. His departure from Poland was as furtive, ad hoc, and rapacious as his departure from France had been ceremonious, elegant, and generous. He left in the dark of night, absconding with all the Polish jewels his men and he could carry.

"Journey" again presents a de Guise, alongside another figure who gives a hint of one reason for including the Catholic family in the mix. The man standing at foreground on the right has been identified as Charles III, Duke of Lorraine, Catherine's favorite son-in-law, who had been the husband of Catherine's already deceased favorite daughter Claude. Christina of Lorraine, their daughter, was Catherine's favorite granddaughter. Lurking behind is Charles de Guise, the Duke of Mayenne.

Charles is present in another tapestry panel, "Barriers," accompanied by his two sons. François-Hercule, Duc d'Anjou, formerly d'Alençon—Elizabeth's "Frog"—stands on the right with a lance, while Charles III of Lorraine speaks with one of his two young sons, the other son facing away.

Charles's daughter Christina is nowhere to be found in any of the Valois tapestries. While it is easy to recognize so many of the portraits in the tapestries, it is not possible to discern in any panel the features of this woman—or girl rather, for Christina would have been only eleven or twelve years old in 1576. Catherine was close to her favorite grandchild, who had her own separate apartments with her at the Hôtel de la Reine in Paris. Because her own mother Claude had died at the young age of twenty-seven, Christina lived with Catherine much longer than usually was the case with royal grandchildren. But while the cart in the upper right of the picture carries an important unidentifiable female, it is most probably not Christina but Louise de Lorraine-Vaudément—who is following after her husband Henri III in the middle of the tapestry and preceding her mother-in-law, as precedent would require. Henri III had met Louise at the home of his brother-in-law, Christina's father, on his way to Poland to be crowned king.[5]

Caron's cartoon for the event depicted in "Journey" shows the figure of a minstrel leading a bear in the first line of travelers, the rest of which is made up of a random troupe of entertainers: ani-

*The Chateau of Anet*; Antoine Caron, 1565–1574.

mal handlers, bear trainers, bird carriers, dog walkers. In contrast to the cartoon, the finished Valois tapestry has figures from this motley gathering of entertainers coming *after* the mounted figures, who are an entirely different sort of entourage.

In the tapestry, conversely, a first group of elegantly dressed men and women ride on prancing horses, with Henri III centered among them on a beautiful white horse. Behind him, Queen Catherine comes in her litter, a cart ferries another elegant woman, and pages and guards walk in front of and beside their masters.

While individual portraiture was itself a great and favored art form of the Florentine Medici, they also commissioned family group portraits. One of the most famous frescoes in Florence is *Journey of the Magi* by Benito Gozzoli, a group portrait of the Medici family making an equestrian journey that slowly winds through the entire picture frame, as the riders move in serried rows away from what appears to be their castle home. The fresco is spread across three walls in a small chapel in the Palazzo Medici Riccardi, where Catherine might have seen it many times as a child.

Scholars have identified the figure of Caspar, the youngest of the

Valois tapestry "Barriers," 1576, Catherine is seated on the dais in the background, beneath the high canopy, watching her son, her son-in-law Charles, and her grandsons prepare to perform. *Gallerie degli Uffizi, Florence*

Magi, as representing Lorenzo "Il Magnifico," who was born in 1449 and so was still a boy when the fresco was completed. Closely following Caspar are the contemporary head of the family, Lorenzo's

Charles III de Lorraine et Bar; François Clouet, sixteenth century.

father Piero, on a white horse, and the devout founder of the family, Cosimo de' Medici, on a humble donkey. I would like to suggest that the Valois tapestry "Journey" seems artfully to recall Gozzoli's fresco group portrait. There is nothing in the fresco to make clear which family member was standing in for which historical or biblical character; this understanding would have been supplied by contemporaneous viewers. The same is true of the "Journey" as well as all the other Valois tapestries; viwers have to supply the identification out of their own knowledge and wit. While the *Journey of the Magi* is a fresco, immovably displayed on the walls of the Medici Palace, where identification would naturally begin with the family, the Valois tapestries lost history's knowledge of the figures celebrated in them when they were moved to the Pitti Palace, and then to the Uffizi.

Yet the direct reference in "Journey" to the one-hundred-year-old fresco (if indeed it is a reference) may have been an effort to keep the meanings of "Journey" readable after the tapestries left France; the figures would still refer to members of the Medici family, also members of the French royal family, the Valois. The reference also forces a logical question: if Catherine suggested to the designers of the "Journey" tapestry that they make the specific changes they should make in the Caron drawing in order to make it recall the Gozzoli fresco (whether consciously or out of some vague memory), had she already planned to send these tapestries to Florence? We now may well suppose that she had always intended to give the tapestries to her granddaughter Christina, but how long had she known Christina would be going to Florence in particular?[6] Catherine only managed their removal to her birthplace fairly late in her life by giving them to Christina, whose marriage by proxy to Ferdinando de' Medici, Third Grand Duke of Tuscany, was celebrated in France on December 8, 1588. This proxy ceremony occurred a little less than a month before Catherine de' Medici died on January 5, 1589. With her always indomitable will, Catherine, on the edge of death, still managed to attend this momentous occasion. But it took place just barely in time. She had been explicitly urging the marriage for two full years, using

Benito Gozzoli, *The Journey of the Magi*, 1459–1462,
Palazzo Medici-Riccardi, Florence.

it to settle some long-term problems with the considerable property
she still owned in Tuscany.

She willed her property in Italy to Christina, along with what she
stated should be one-half of her movables from the Hôtel de la Reine,
her main residence in Paris. Originally intended to copy some ele-
ments of the Uffizi, her mansion contained the earliest known chamber lined with Venetian mirror glass. (Catherine's taste would exert a
centuries-long history of influence in France, Versailles's hall of mir-
rors perhaps being a descendant of her first lavishly mirrored room.)
She also bequeathed to Christina a dowry of fifty thousand scudi (at
one assessment, a million dollars in today's money). Shortly after her
grandmother's death, Christina had to send an agent to the Hôtel de
la Reine to gather the objects of her inheritance, as the residence had
been taken over by Charles de Guise.[7] The inventory made for Christina listed four hundred fifty items, some of the most coveted being
pieces of porcelain china and elaborately engraved rock crystal vases,
goblets, and statues set with precious metals. An earlier inventory had

listed five thousand precious objects, so clearly some items had gone missing when the Hôtel de la Reine fell into de Guise hands. But what Christina did manage to take with her to Florence clearly established her special position there, as it was intended to do. And indeed the richness of the movables given by Catherine to Christina was one reason the latter's marriage to the grand duke did not fall through when it became clear the Valois dynasty was close to collapse. (The Grand Duke of Tuscany was a great collector of rock crystal; Catherine's collection was famous, having been begun with wedding gifts from her uncle Pope Clement.)

Christina brought from France a pearl-embroidered set of royal state bed hangings and more than two thousand meters of luxurious textiles. And she brought the Valois tapestries. When displayed in the bride's apartments in the Pitti Palace, the artworks would have demonstrated, as her grandmother would have wished them to do, her wealth, lineage, and royal dynastic connections.

Christina de Lorraine, Grand Duchess of Tuscany;
Scipione Pulzone, 1590.

Orazio Scaribelli, 1589, "Naumachia." Naumachia in the Court of
Palazzo Pitti, from an Album with Plates documenting the Festivities of
the 1589 Wedding of Arch Duke Ferdinand I de' Medici and Christine
of Lorraine. *Metropolitan Museum of Art, New York*

A second wedding ceremony for Christina and the grand duke
was performed in Florence with great pomp and circumstance, public parties, parades, masques, drama, and an amazing naumachia
worthy of Catherine de' Medici herself. Staged in the rear courtyard of the Pitti Palace, which had been flooded with water to make
a "sea," the entertainment was a battle between forty galleons. The
aristocratic audience watched the fireworks and combat from the bal-
conies of the palazzo.

Christina lived up to this auspicious beginning when she showed
her intelligence by hiring Galileo Galilei as a tutor for her son. The
astronomer wrote a famous letter to her, outlining the differences in
the knowledge bases for theology and science and how it is best to
consider them separately. Galileo wrote to the grand duchess not just
because she was his patron but because the subject had come up at
one of her dinner parties and it had been made public that she had

subsequently asked for more information. Known to be both curious about science and also devout, she was an excellent choice to represent the lay audience who could usefully be informed about this central controversy involving the earth's relation to the solar system.[8] In her, Galileo had found an ideal interlocutor. Christina of Lorraine, Grand Duchess of Tuscany, was, in short, a worthy heir to her grandmother. She subsequently ruled Florence as co-regent with her daughter-in-law, and as such, patronized scientists, philosophers, and theologians, founded monasteries, and supported the arts. She was the perfect family member to inherit Catherine's most prized inalienable possessions, the Valois tapestries.

# PART FOUR

❧

## THE HAPSBURGS

☜

# CHAPTER TEN

# Philip II

*The Bridegroom Returns*

hortly before her execution, Mary, Queen of Scots had made out a will that bequeathed to Philip II of Spain her claim to the English throne. She had specifically rejected her son James VI of Scotland as her heir, unless he converted to Roman Catholicism. The very Protestant Henri IV of France, formerly the Protestant leader Henri de Navarre, *would* convert to Catholicism within the next decade, suggesting that in this period such a change was entirely possible. Henri IV is said to have stated, "Paris vaut bien une messe" ("Paris is well worth a Mass"), but this excuse for his conversion may be apocryphal. There had been a number of plans afoot to help James convert and achieve a pro-Catholic plan for the restoration of a Catholic Scottish monarchy—and Elizabeth was very worried about them. But James remained staunchly Protestant. Mary rightly feared he would never convert.

James's loyalty to the creed he had been taught as a child under the brutal tutelage of George Buchanan—and thus his rejection of his mother's faith—cleared the way for the Catholic Philip II to make a claim on *both* the Scottish and English thrones. For England, he did so by tracing his lineage back to the Plantagenet kings (the bloodline he shared with Catherine of Aragon, his great-aunt); he thus made a case for the legitimacy of Mary Stuart's naming him to be her heir. Philip could also, at the same time, assert title to the French throne by claiming it for his daughter Clara Isabella Euge-

nia, who had been born to his third wife, Elisabeth de Valois, eldest
daughter of Henry II of France and Catherine de' Medici; Clara Isabella was thus half Valois and was of the royal French bloodline.
Unfortunately, as Catherine de' Medici had often lamented, the Salic
law made it illegal for a woman to rule France. It is interesting how
uniquely free of misogyny Philip could be, at least where females in
his own family were concerned. He fought the Salic law fiercely for
his daughter so Clara Isabella could succeed to the throne as queen of
France; but when Henri IV converted to Catholicism, this possibility became moot, for France could thereby properly acquire a legitimate Catholic sovereign who was male. When, with the defeat of the
Armada, Philip also failed to clear the way for his daughter to replace
Elizabeth in England, Philip II had finally to make Clara Isabella a
co-ruler (with her Hapsburg husband) of the Spanish Netherlands
(essentially, modern Belgium). With Queen Isabella of Castile for
his great-grandmother; with Mary of Hungary, Beatrice of Portugal,
and Mary, Catherine, and Isabella of Austria for his aunts; with Margaret of Parma and Maria and Johanna of Austria for his sisters, it
is no wonder how fundamentally Philip II of Spain understood that
women were capable of ruling and ruling well.

Philip II was in his own right a Renaissance prince of magnificent achievements. He was also Mary Tudor's husband, Catherine
de Medici's son-in-law, Elizabeth Tudor's suitor and then great foe,
and Mary, Queen of Scots' declared heir and would-be avenger. Yet
in none of many hundreds of previous versions written of this inter-
woven history of four queens and a world-dominating king (at least
in those tales told in English), Philip II is never once the hero of the
story. He is not depicted as a powerful leader—though he expanded
Spain and the Hapsburg Empire into global greatness. He was not
seen as a conquering warrior—though he financed, helped organize,
and was victorious in many major military battles, such as the defeat
of the Ottoman Turks at Lepanto, the defeat of the French at St.
Quentin, and the annexing of vast sections of the Americas. He is not
presented as a Renaissance patron of the arts—though it was during

Philip's reign that Spain's golden age of literature, drama, and painting and architecture began. Most commonly, he is, like his wife Mary
Tudor, reduced by English-speaking historians to a Catholic zealot
who persecuted Protestants, and as the man who was defeated by
Elizabeth when he sought to invade England with a titanic Armada
of one hundred thirty ships and close to twenty-eight thousand soldiers and sailors.

But there was always much more to Philip than zealotry and failure. Philip trusted that women could govern countries. And along
with his third wife, Elisabeth de Valois, daughter of a Medici, he
was the original patron of the woman painter Sofonisba Anguissola,
who finally—after some centuries—now ranks among the greatest
of Renaissance grand masters. In art as in government, Philip was no
misogynist.

He even gallantly accepted part of the responsibility for Mary
Tudor's barrenness, saying to his cousin and brother-in-law Maximil-
ian that "the queen's pregnancy turns out not to have been as certain

Philip II of Spain; Sofonisba Anguissola, 1565, 1575.
*© Museo Nacional del Prado, Madrid*

as we thought. Your Highness and my sister manage it better than the queen and I do."

But however often he wooed and married, he has never been remembered as a figure of romance, like Sir Philip Sidney (who was, in fact, named in his honor), or a figure of epic victory like his opponent in the Armada battle, Francis Drake. In his youth he had a reputation as a womanizer, but he gave over this behavior after marriage in 1559 to the fourteen-year-old Elisabeth de Valois, whom he personally—and quite unusually for a husband and a king—nursed through smallpox. Elisabeth was the mother of his favorite daughter, Clara Isabella Eugenia, who would in turn nurse him through his own death. When Elisabeth died after a miscarriage at age twenty-three, leaving him with two small daughters, her mother Catherine de' Medici suggested that Philip marry Marguerite de Valois ("Margot"), Elisabeth's younger sister. However, Philip refused, claiming that he did not want to marry two sisters, although a decade earlier he had proposed to Elizabeth after Mary Tudor's death. (Margot, alas, ultimately married Henri Navarre instead, just days before the St. Bartholomew's Day Massacre.)

Since Philip's eldest son, the mad and tragic Don Carlos, had died at age twenty-three, Philip needed another male heir for the Spanish throne, but now only had daughters. In rejecting the idea of marrying Margot, he may well have remembered Elizabeth Tudor's claim to have rejected his suit on the grounds that he had formerly been married to her sister; or Henry VIII's belief that God had punished him for his incest with his brother's wife by giving him only daughters. In 1570, the forty-three-year-old king instead married Anna of Austria, his twenty-one-year-old niece, with whom he was truly happy and who gave him two sons, one of whom survived to reign as Philip III.

In 1587, Mary Stuart was executed. In 1588, Mary Tudor's former husband Philip II sent his Armada against his wife's sister Elizabeth to retaliate for that execution. On January 5, 1589, in France, Catherine de' Medici, Mary Stuart's *and* Philip II's former mother-in-law, died in her bed.

According to Honoré de Balzac, who wrote a biography of Catherine, her final words on her deathbed were her advice to her son Henri III after hearing of his using a squad of guards to slaughter various members of the de Guise family, "Enough cut off, my son, now piece together." She was savvy enough to know that her son's recent killings might well lead to his own assassination, and that his death would bring an end to the Valois dynasty. In August, only seven months later, Henri III was murdered.

By 1588, the memorable year that fell between the deaths of Elizabeth I's two "sister" queens—Mary, Queen of Scots and Catherine de' Medici—the Virgin Queen herself, last of the Tudor line, was in the thirtieth year of what would be a long and glorious forty-five-year reign. But her story would have been very different if a much anticipated British defeat by the Armada in 1588 had ended the Elizabethan Age (in which case, this book might have been written in Spanish, if at all).

In May 1588, Elizabeth's regime was threatened with catastrophic collapse as massed galleons of the Spanish Armada fast approached the English shore. Spain was a much more powerful nation than England, much wealthier, with a hugely superior navy and army. Philip was now the ruler of much of the New World, as well as much of Europe. He had not once returned to England since before Mary's death three decades earlier in 1558. He had first arrived in England as a bridegroom. Now he returned, not in person, but through the formidable launching of a large flotilla of huge, heavily armed Spanish ships carrying 2,500 cannons, 8,000 seamen, and 20,000 soldiers, all sent to avenge Mary Stuart's sacrilegious execution. He reportedly shed tears when he heard of Mary Stuart's death and ordered an immense Requiem Mass to be said for her soul. He was sending the Armada to defeat England, to depose its queen, to seize the crown that he had refused for so long to agree belonged to Mary Stuart (until she willed it to him). He proposed to give Elizabeth's throne to his daughter Clara Isabella.

It is perhaps surprising that I take this time to address the subject

of Philip II of Spain at the close of the story of four women who ruled
Europe during the sixteenth century. I do so not only because Philip
truly did rule the *world*. Mary I and Elizabeth I ruled the southern
end of a small island; Mary, Queen of Scots ruled the northern end
of the same island. As ruler of France, Catherine de' Medici oversaw
one of the richest parts of Europe, which would soon become even
more powerful in the seventeenth century under Louis XIV, the Sun
King, descended from another branch of the Medici family. But the
Spanish Empire would for centuries continue to stretch from Italy
to the Netherlands and all the way to the islands of the Philippines,
which were in fact named for him. King Philip also named Cuba and
its capital city Havana; he took the names from the language of the
Taíno, the native tribe there—one that quickly became extinct. The
Spanish Empire was not conquered by English-speaking forces until
1898, when Teddy Roosevelt, scrambling up San Juan Hill (actually
"Kettle Hill," a less imperially resonant name), conquered Cuba for
the United States, while Commodore Perry bested the Spanish navy
in Manila Bay in the Philippines. Between Philip's death and Teddy
Roosevelt's victory stretched three full centuries of Spanish rule over
an empire upon which the sun never set.

For this long while, it seems, English-speaking modernity simply forgot that Spain was a part of Europe. The index of the pivotal volume of
essays *Rewriting the Renaissance: The Discourses of Sexual Difference in
Early Modern Europe* most embarrassingly contains no entry for Spain or
indeed "Spanish" *anything*. The denigration of Spain in most Renaissance
Anglophone scholarship has many causes and is, I think, fundamentally
racially biased—for as some Frenchman once said, "Africa begins at the
Pyrenees." This denigration is literal, and a journalist in the twentieth
century gave it a name—"The Black Legend." The legend—or propa-
gandistic disinformation—is that Spain's destruction of New World
populations was infinitely worse than any other European nation's.[1] It
was not. Indeed, judging from the amount of native DNA still present in
the different regions after much European-caused population collapse,
the peoples of Central and South America have far more indigenous

genes than the peoples in North America, where, in contrast to South America, native racial inheritance has been almost entirely obliterated.

In the United States, Spain's negative reputation also depends, more hauntingly, on the fact that the part-indigenous peoples of South and Central America—those living embodiments of the populations that were far more rigorously eradicated in the north—speak Spanish.[2] In startling contrast to North America, there was so much intermarriage between Europeans and (to use the apt Canadian term) "first peoples" in South and Central America that at least in Mexico the blends were codified into elaborate fractions, presented often in remarkable portraits of individuals.[3] In the New World the English continued the practice of exclusion begun in Ireland, where the lands of rebellious native Irish were confiscated and the "savage" inhabitants moved to the west country; they outlawed marriage with Irish natives in their first "overseas" Atlantic colony. (Currently, the native American population in the US is a little over two percent.) The Spanish, however, ultimately did not see the indigenous people as a separate race, to be cordoned off into reservations. The Valley of Mexico finally recovered precontact levels of population in the late twentieth century. Mexico City is now finally again the most populous city in the Americas, just as it had been when Hernán Cortés first saw it; today its population is ninety percent part or full Amerindian.[4]

Philip and the overseas empire he helped to expand is an important part of the story of western global domination. But because of the historic defeat of the Armada, English-speaking history has allowed itself to ignore subsequent Spanish imperial activity. The bad weather that was ultimately responsible for the defeat was itself enlisted in the narrative of God's preference for the Protestant nation's survival, a narrative continued into the nineteenth century with America's white supremacist idea of "Manifest Destiny"; it included the continued appropriation of Spanish and indigenous lands in the western United States. Just as the exact nature of European women's exercise of political power in the sixteenth century has been forgotten or merely misremembered, the importance of Spain's lasting influence on European globalization has been similarly waived aside. This forgetting, I would like to argue, began with the Elizabethan era.

The bulk of the Armada's loss of ships occurred not in battle, but when the primal forces of a great storm forced its retreat north around the tip of Scotland and then into the North and Irish Seas. Of course, brilliant English tactics by smaller forces—sending fireships into the Spanish fleet at anchor off Calais to break up the formidable crescent-shaped formation of the Armada, deploying superior experience in heavy seas in the Battle of Gravelines—forestalled any immediate landing of Spanish soldiers on English soil. But the loss of so many ships to the storm made Spain's attempts at redeployment far more difficult than they otherwise would have been. Elizabeth's navy did not bring on the stormy weather, but the nation assumed with gratitude that God had assured them of the victory.

There may have been yet another factor contributing to the Spanish defeat, having to do with the very different arrangements of the chains of command. Neither Philip nor Elizabeth actually stood at a helm or led a battalion; yet it was their very different styles of administration and their differing management of warfare that may well have helped to shape the final outcome. Elizabeth made the decision to relinquish any superior authority she might have wanted to hold in formulating strategy, turning all decision-making over to her commanders Sir Francis Drake and Lord Charles Howard. In contrast, Philip insisted on being in absolute charge of his navy, micromanaging even small details of the Armada's maneuvers from Madrid, more than nine hundred miles overland from Calais.

Philip's detailed plan was for the Armada to sail from Spain to Flanders and make safe the route across the Channel for a second flank of barges carrying thirty thousand additional soldiers under the command of the Duke of Parma. Reaching the English coast together, the united flanks would only then join forces to launch a land invasion of fifty thousand men. The land soldiers, especially those from the Netherlands, were the most experienced and preeminently successful of Spanish troops, triumphant in past battles in the Low Countries and in urban battlespaces. For years, Philip's army had been in almost constant warfare in Italy, the Netherlands, and the Americas. During the sixteenth century it numbered as many as three hundred thousand men. In 1571 his navy had soundly defeated the Ottoman Empire at Lepanto near the shores of western Greece. The Spanish military was a formidable force.

Despite endless battles, Philip insisted he did not fight wars of aggression but only defended what already belonged to Spain. The conquests of the Aztec and Inca empires had occurred during the reign of his bellicose father Charles, the Holy Roman Emperor; Philip could claim he was merely keeping what his father had already won. And indeed the whole New World belonged to Spain; by the Treaty of Tordesillas, Pope Alexander VI had partitioned the western hemisphere, giving Spain the entire world to the west of a boundary that was set at 46°30'W, on a line from pole to pole drawn 1,185 miles west of the Cape Verde Islands; Portugal was given everything to the east. Thus, save for that part jutting east into the Atlantic which became Portuguese Brazil, the rest of South America, all of Central America, and all of North America "belonged" to Spain.

Philip's soldiers often fought different wars on different fronts simultaneously. During his forty-two-year reign, the Spanish Empire was at peace for a mere six months. So expensive was this constant warfare that Spain went bankrupt at least three times during his reign, even with the enormous and constant inflows of New World gold and silver. Philip II was sovereign over fifty million human souls spread across the globe on three continents. He was understandably increasingly overwhelmed.[5]

In contrast, there were the occasions when Philip did delegate responsibility, and he was then often astonishingly successful. For example, his field of operations in America was so much farther away than anywhere in Europe that he could not exercise the degree of supervision he could (and did) at least attempt on the continent. During the reign of his father much of the conquest of the New World had been led not by the Emperor Charles himself but by a talented collection of very individualistic entrepreneurs, professional explorer-conquistadors like Cortés, who ignored all orders from the governor of Cuba and forged ahead on his own into Mexico, where he conquered the Aztec Empire (with massive aid from indigenous tribes rebelling against their Aztec overlords). Only after Cortés's victory was he rewarded by Charles V for what had been his quite independent actions.

Another such go-it-alone general, Francisco Pizarro (distantly related to Cortés), also ignored a governor's orders when he persisted in a plan to conquer the Incas in Peru. Unlike Cortés, he then returned to Spain to receive express permission from Charles V to pursue this conquest further. Back in South America, Pizarro, an illiterate, tricked the Inca emperor, Atahualpa, by handing him a Bible that, he said, could speak to him. When Atahualpa listened to the silent book and, hearing nothing from it, threw it down in frustration, Pizarro's men at that anticipated signal attacked the unarmed Inca assembly and captured the emperor. Perhaps the illiterate Pizarro's own inability to read made him predict that the native ruler would respond to the mute book with anger. It was in any case a bold and successful strategy, unapproved by any distant authority.[6]

By the time Philip succeeded to his father's throne, the administration of the now vast American colonies required, he believed, a restructuring beyond his personal capacity, so he assigned to a large committee, the "Junta Magna," the responsibility for coming up with plans to reorganize the region. They did an excellent job. As Philip's biographer Geoffrey Parker argues, "These initiatives cemented Madrid's control over the American continent from the Rio Grande in northern Mexico to the Bio Bio in Chile, while the religious, political and economic initiatives proposed by the Junta and endorsed by the king ensured that South and Central America would remain Spanish until the nineteenth century and Catholic to this day. It forms Philip's greatest achievement and his most lasting legacy."[7]

What we now might call Philip's obsessive-compulsive nature

stood him in good stead when, rather than organizing every minute detail of his foreign settlements, he began designing and building various country houses at home in Spain. Like Catherine de' Medici, he had both a talent for architecture and the means to build. One of his most impressive building projects is his Escorial, a monastery and royal home for king and family. Like Fontainebleau for the Valois, Hampton Court for the Tudors, and Stirling for the Stuarts, the Escorial was one of Philip's favorite places of retreat and respite from the busyness of court, the place where he could get the most work done. Situated close to Madrid, the Escorial is also one of his architectural triumphs. Known for the monumental severity of its architecture and its exquisite uniformity of finish, the building owes much of its beauty to Philip's detailed supervision.[8] He hired Juan Bautista de Toledo, who had worked with Michelangelo, as his royal architect. But as he did not trust Toledo, he often intervened in his work. When Toledo died, Philip did not replace him but instead used a talented draughtsman whom he could supervise even more closely.

Parker notes that "the pharaonic splendor of the Escorial impressed everyone." Ultimately covering thirty acres of buildings and gardens and including not only a monastery and basilica but also a training school for priests as well as a mausoleum for all of Philip's ancestors, it also housed a huge library of fourteen thousand books plus a royal apartment off the basilica. The Escorial was built to specifications down to the sixteenth part of a foot.[9]

Yet the obsessive micromanagement that served Philip well as an architect and builder utterly disabled him as a long-distance military commander. While he owed many of his early victories not only to his wealth but also to his own presence on the field of battle, and while the tactical brilliance of his illegitimate half-brother Juan as direct commander of the galleys in the Mediterranean had ensured the triumph at Lepanto over the Ottomans, the enterprise of invading England, thirty years in the formulation, collapsed in part because of Philip's over-elaborate plan of attack. (There was also, of course, the

Philip II, Monastery of San Lorenzo de El Escorial,
sixteenth century, Madrid.

huge storm that blew his ships off course, driven by winds that much of Europe considered to be sent by God.)

In contrast, for years Philip's archenemy Queen Elizabeth had been making capitalistic investments in voyages (some to the New World, some in European waters) both to attack and to plunder Spanish ships. Raids were carried out by various highly skilled sea captains ("privateers" or, in fact, pirates). She maintained complete deniability about their lucrative exploits, honestly claiming to know nothing of their whereabouts or their activities while they were at sea. They usually returned with enormous booty—most of it stolen from Spanish ships and colonial ports. The queen gave her "Sea Dogs" (most notably Drake, John Hawkins, and Walter Raleigh) freedom to command and loot, and in return they gave her a share of their booty.[10]

The greatest mistake King Philip made in planning for the Armada, according to many of his biographers, was his decision to refuse to allow the Armada ships to sail directly to and land on the coast of England (or Catholic Ireland), so that the soldiers could then immediately begin a series of invasions that would set up forward bases of operation. The English were not trained or ready to repel any such unpredictable invasion of land forces (much less multiple invasions at multiple unknown landing points) along their coast. But instead, Philip ordered all ships to sail along the Channel, near but not landing on England's shore until the meeting with Parma's forces in the Netherlands. The plan was for the Armada ships to provide cover for the twenty thousand men in barges who would be loaded in Belgium. Only after that maneuver would the Armada ships and Parma's barges together land their soldiers, who would then march together on London.

Historian David Howarth asks a good question: why did the Armada sail up the English side of the Channel? If they had followed the French shore, they might have made it to Dover (just below London) before the English ever saw them. "But to sail along the English coast as they did, past each of its harbors, gave the English every possible advantage. The answer to this question, as to so much else, is that the king had given the order."[11]

The fundamental problem of Philip's strategy was that his two commanders, the Duke of Parma in the Netherlands and the Duke of Medina Sidonia on a ship in the Armada, could not easily communicate with each other from opposite ends of the Channel. Thus Parma did not learn that the Armada had even arrived in the Channel until after the English had already set fire to empty ships that then floated down on the Spanish galleons, forcing the Spanish to cut anchors and scatter away from their protective crescent-shaped formation, far easier prey for the English guns. The orders Philip had given each commander never addressed the crucial problem of communication or how, tactically, the Duke of Parma, the general of the land forces, and the Duke of Medina Sedonia, the admiral in charge of the Armada, were to join forces. Parker pointedly argues that at just the moment in the final written orders Philip sent where tactics would normally be addressed, the king instead gave specific detailed commands as to how all the fighting men must be kept to highest standards of spiritual purity in so godly an enterprise. No blasphemy, no gambling, cursing, fighting, drinking, sodomy, and so on. Nothing about tactical specifics.

For his part, the Duke of Parma, ordered by Philip to be entirely deceitful in negotiations with the English and to go through the motions merely in order to allow time for the Armada to arrive, had come to realize that negotiations with the English could in fact succeed and that no attack was necessary to achieve what he had been told was the putative purpose of the foray, to block English aid to the Dutch rebels and to stop attacks on Spanish shipping in the Caribbean. Of course, that would not achieve the conquest of Protestantism in England and the kingdom's return to the Catholic Church. According to Howarth, Philip's nephew Parma was somewhat disgusted by his uncle's designs. Parma (who was Italian, a Farnese) lost faith in the entire military enterprise, and even when he did receive multiple messages from the other end of the Channel (all of which, despite their time of dispatch, arrived at about the same moment, due to the shortening distance that each subsequent letter had to travel), he did not reply to any of them.

The Vatican had been the first to command that Philip take on this crusade against England, a command Philip had at the beginning resisted, but the king had finally complied. Ultimately, he accepted the pope's order, at least in part because he realized that Drake was causing such damage to his Spanish treasure fleets that it might be more efficient for the Spanish to take the war to the pirate's home base than to chase him all around the Caribbean. Philip also anticipated a wonderful, easy victory over England's Protestant heretics. He had taken pride in the fact that "God has already granted that by my intervention and by my hand that kingdom was previously returned to the Catholic Church." God clearly would grant such a boon again. God would take England from Elizabeth and join it (and Scotland) to the Catholic Spanish Empire.

But because of the great storm that gave the final blow to the Armada fleet, scattering it irrevocably, every good Catholic began to wonder why God had chosen to provide a miracle to help the

English rather than the Spanish. Admiral Howard noted that the weather had been unusually rough and stormy at the time; if even for him, accustomed to the Channel, the seas were worthy of comment, how much more terrifying would the weather have been for Spanish sailors used to sailing on the Mediterranean and on the tropical Atlantic tradewinds that blew smoothly (save for the occasional hurricane) from east to west across the sea to the New World. Even the papal nuncio in Madrid wondered whether "these impediments . . . might be a sign that 'God does not approve of the enterprise.' "[12] All of Spain went into abject mourning, their honor lost, their service to God unaccepted. Philip, devastated, thought it would be better to be dead himself. He lived another ten years. He sent other armadas. They, too, failed.

He died with his daughter the Infanta Clara Isabella Eugenia beside him. He loved his daughters, as he loved his sisters and at least two of his wives, one of whom (Elisabeth de Valois) he shamelessly spoiled. On his deathbed, he asked for his parents' crucifix to kiss. And he laughed softly when it was obvious that all the counselors and priests surrounding his bed had assumed that he had already died. Few had seen this humorous streak beyond his immediate family, but it was there at the end, along with his immense faith in God.

Elizabeth's military decisions tended not to be predicated on an appetite for the glory of conquest, but for simple profit. She was famously furious with her beloved Robert Dudley, Earl of Leicester, for accepting the governorship of the United Provinces of the Netherlands when she had only allowed him to take an army there to help protect Protestants against Spain's military might. Elizabeth didn't want to expand England's territory but to make her country rich by engaging in what we would call "public-private" enterprises. And these enterprises tended to be successful. When she commanded Sir Francis Drake to attack the preparations for the Armada that had begun in the Spanish port city of Cadiz, she stipulated to him that she would get fifty percent of any treasure he seized because she was lending his expedition four ships for the attack. Many other ships on the adventure against the Armada were funded by other, private groups of stockholders who expected to make tidy returns on their investments.

Tilbury sat at the mouth of the river Thames, where it was feared that Parma's army, loaded into barges, might still mount a land attack aimed at London. But at the moment when Elizabeth is said to have made her famous speech there to the troops about defending their country against the Armada (a speech reproduced in countless books, in films, and on other screens), history now knows that the present danger had already passed. The Spanish were rounding the northern tip of Scotland, battered and smashing up in a great storm in the North Sea, as the huge ships desperately tried to maneuver their way back to Spain.

Wearing decorative armor and seated on a burly muscled war-horse, the queen spoke to her troops. She called attention to the odd fit between her gender and the military threat of the moment. "I have the body of a weak, and feeble woman; but I have the heart and stomach of a king, and of a King of England too."[13] The horse was led by a page, and she was flanked by her two favorite masters of the horse, Robert Dudley, Earl of Leicester, and Dudley's nephew, Robert Devereux, Earl of Essex. It was Dudley who had planned on Elizabeth's speech being what biographer Sarah Gristwood calls "an iconic publicity coup." While Elizabeth wrote the speech herself, it was Dudley who arranged to have it circulated immediately afterward.[14]

Although Elizabeth claimed that she had come to Tilbury "in the heat and dust of battle to live and die among" her people, and "to lay down for my God and my kingdom mine honor and my blood even in the dust," she also offered them the military guidance of Dudley, her lieutenant general, "in my stead." Elizabeth thus delegated her authority right in front of her troops, just as she had done with Drake, Hawkins, Frobisher, and Howard, when, after first countermanding many of her own orders, she finally just charged her admiral, Lord Howard, "to use his own judgment, subject only to the advice of his council of war" (that is, the other sea captains, Drake, Hawkins, Martin Frobisher, and George Fenner). Her gender doubtless made this handoff easier for her to do than it would have been for Philip. It was a capacity to trust and to delegate authority that Philip II usually chose not to practice.

Very sadly, Elizabeth was unable to triumph with any joy in her great victory over the Spanish because only a few weeks after their glorious triumph together at Tilbury, Robert Dudley, her "Robin" since their youth together, died suddenly. As biographer Gristwood puts it, "Elizabeth was condemned to an extraordinary conjunction of public rejoicing and private agony."[15] Her people were wildly celebrating the defeat of Spain, but she was anguished by the loss of her devoted and beloved friend. She withdrew from the court and shut herself in her room for days, and when she returned, looked, according to the Venetian ambassador, "aged and spent." Until her death, she kept Dudley's final note to her in a box labeled "His last letter." However sad this knowledge, it is good to learn that by her sorrow the Virgin Queen proved that she had loved, and had been loved, not just by the people of England as their queen, but as a woman by a man she had known since childhood, the friend who had, like her, also once feared a death sentence from her sister Mary.

There is no doubt that Good Queen Bess did indeed love her people. In her speech closing Parliament in 1593, five years after the Armada, she again insisted on her womanly care of the people she ruled:

> It may be thought simplicity in me that all this time of my reign I have not sought to advance my territories and enlarge my dominions. . . . I acknowledge my womanhood and weakness in that respect . . . only my mind was never to invade my neighbors nor to usurp upon any, only contented to reign over my own and to rule as a just prince.

Again she drew a pointed contrast between herself and King Philip:

Yet the King of Spain doth challenge me to be the beginning of
this quarrel and the cause of all the wars—that I have sought to
injure him in many actions. But in saying that I have wronged
him . . . he doth me the greatest wars that may be.[16]

Elizabeth here appears to be making an argument similar to the one
Ronsard had made thirty-nine years earlier about the peace treaty that
the queen of England had negotiated with Catherine de' Medici—
that their womanly rule tended toward peace rather than war. In
declaring her innocent desire for peace and her distaste for war, Elizabeth conveniently forgot the activities of her pirates, a strategy as
illegal as—and rather more sucessful than—Catherine de' Medici's
planned murder of Coligny. Doubtless Philip's complaint about her
"many actions" referred to these "private" depredations.

Like Catherine de' Medici, like Mary Stuart, and unlike her sister Mary Tudor (with whom Philip once shared in the credit for
burning Protestant heretics alive in England), Elizabeth believed in
religious toleration. She only prosecuted those Catholics who were
agents of the pope, after the pope had excommunicated her and
had publicly authorized a violent mission to overthrow her hereti-
cal regime—and to assassinate her. Otherwise she would "not make
windows into" men's souls. She even, in a late speech, made her
peace with Philip II, implying that if she had not forgiven him, she
did not condemn him for his Catholicism. She guessed and hoped
that "his soul be now in heaven."

# The Gifts They Gave

*hen Women Ruled the World* has centered its story on a quartet of Renaissance queens whose crowded lives were intertwined by complex blood and marriage ties, by changing allegiances and the fractures of religion, by their premier places in the world of a few dozen European monarchs, and by the great worlds that those neighboring monarchs ruled, worlds both Old and New. We have traced their giving of gifts as a means for understanding their attempts to cement familial bonds of peace among themselves and their realms.

As we have seen, Catherine de' Medici presented Elizabeth I with the text of Ronsard's volume of poetry, containing masques, praise, and subtle words of warning. (She additionally offered Elizabeth two of her four sons to marry.) Catherine gave to Mary, Queen of Scots one son, François II, and a collection of pearls from her own wedding (a gift from her uncle the pope), which Mary was allowed to take to Scotland with her when she assumed her throne there. After Mary bolted to England, the "Medici pearls" were put up for sale by her half-brother, Moray. Catherine tried to recover them by purchase. However, they went instead to Elizabeth I, who in a secret transaction paid twelve thousand ecus ($360,000 in today's money) for them. Elizabeth said that she would wear the pearls in honor of her dead sister queen Mary Stuart for the rest of her life.

At least four of these pearls have, it is said, now descended to

Elizabeth Stuart, "The Winter Queen," Queen of Bohemia; unknown artist, 1613. The pearls sewn on her clothing and hairpiece and the multi-strand necklace may well include the "Medici" pearls.

Queen Elizabeth II and currently grace the imperial crown. Most people seeing the crown would not know the provenance of the four pearls, that they were first given to Catherine de' Medici by her uncle the pope, then given to Mary, Queen of Scots as a wedding present, had been purchased by Elizabeth Tudor, and then descended to the "Winter Queen," Elizabeth Stuart, the daughter of James I, on her marriage to the Prince of Bohemia.

Elizabeth Stuart gave them to her daughter when she married the elector of Hanover; in such a way they escaped destruction during the Commonwealth period. With the Hanovers, the pearls came back to England and passed into the collection of crown jewels through Victoria to Elizabeth II, a branch member of the Hanovers, renamed Windsors. Even without knowing the details of the history, people who see the crown may still sense the immense weight of generations of inheritance carried within those pearls, feeling the jewels' expression of royal female authority handed down through five centuries.

Catherine had also given to Elizabeth's older sister Mary a silver gilt baptismal font after Mary Tudor announced her pregnancy. Sadly, Mary did not get a chance to use it. The font was elaborately chased with both Tudor roses and pomegranates (the emblem of Granada) in honor, as we have seen, of both Mary's mother Catherine of Aragon and her husband Philip II of Spain. Long after Mary's death, the font was finally put into service when James I and Anne of Denmark had their last child, Charles I, in England. The font was then melted down to defend against Parliament's army in the English Civil War. Charles I was deposed and beheaded. Elizabeth had, of course, given to Mary Stuart another (solid) gold font, also melted down to defend against another "parliamentary" army in Scotland.

Over the years, Mary Stuart gave a number of gifts to Elizabeth Tudor, in particular, presents of her fine embroidery. One notable item was a petticoat of "crimson satin," with red taffeta underskirt, the material for which she asked the French ambassador to procure "in fifteen days" if he could, along with one pound of double silver thread. She embroidered it herself. The red satin skirt was duly delivered to Elizabeth, also by the French ambassador, who wrote to King Charles IX that his former sister-in-law's gift was very "agreeable" to the English queen, who "prized it much" and who seemed to the ambassador to be "much softened" toward Mary.[1] A piece of this precious embroidered red satin skirt is said still to exist in a private collection; it is unlikely that the piece of silk in question is indeed the gift sewn by Mary, who used silver thread for the embroidery, while the cloth is a *mille fleur* pattern in which silver does not dominate. The material may indeed have been saved—or simply conjured; but it expresses the wish that such a thing might exist as an actual inalienable possession with the power to connect not only Mary to Elizabeth but also the two queens to us.[2]

The evidence allows there to be no doubt that a red silk petticoat, embroidered by Mary Stuart's own hands, was in fact given to Elizabeth. Elizabeth's red silk undergarment takes on an eerie significance when we remember another red silk petticoat of Mary's. This second one provided the famous shocking scene Mary orchestrated at the ceremony of her beheading. Stopping the executioner from removing the black outer garments she had worn to the scaffold, Mary had her ladies-in-waiting remove her black gown to reveal beneath a dark red petticoat.

Wearing the liturgical color of martyrdom in the Catholic Church, the queen of Scots bent her neck to the block.[3] Clearly transforming her execution for treason into a saintly martyrdom for her faith, Mary turned her own red petticoat and sleeves into a drama that enforced a very different story than the one the English preferred. Two red petticoats: one given as a gift pleading for friendship and a grant of freedom that never came, the other a signal of Mary's power to take control of her own narrative to the very end.

In her last decades Elizabeth's wardrobe was vast—with two thousand dresses, two thousand pairs of gloves, hundreds of wigs, and around eight hundred pieces of jewelry. Most of these had been gifts to her. In the lists of New Year's Day gifts to Elizabeth (the official day for gift-giving in England), items of cloth (napkins, handkerchiefs, pillow covers, sleeves, petticoats, and personal clothing) made up approximately ninety percent of the gifts given to the queen by women; even the gifts of money (from men) were bestowed in purses made of precious cloths, the materials of which are carefully specified: satin, silk, velvet, linen; embroidered, embellished with lace, bound with silver or gold strings. Many of these gifts were then passed along to lady courtiers or regifted to foreign visitors. The clothes were often repurposed into new designs to be worn again in public. As I have noted, Renaissance Europe was a "cloth culture," in which this most important material served many profound purposes. It was both the most valuable capitalist commodity of the era, underpinning England's growing trade economy, and also the repository of hugely affective identities created by one's membership in key familial "houses," with their elite standing and prestige, their names proudly anounced by the color of their servants' livery. Also, as Elizabeth well knew, "We princes are set upon stages in sight and view of the world." And costume counted for a lot.[4]

THE STORY IS TOLD that as she was dying, Mary Tudor lamented that people would find after her death the word "Calais" engraved on her heart. She had lost the last English outpost in France for her husband Philip's sake, and she knew that the defeat had cost her her people's love. She had enjoyed that love from her childhood through her ascension to the throne, but lost it when she married a Catholic Spaniard and started burning commoners for heresy.

In a last speech to Parliament, Elizabeth said that her greatest gift from God was that the English people had never stopped loving her. She said their love was what had always been written on *her* heart. They were her spouse, her children, her all.

> My care was ever by proceeding justly and uprightly to conserve my people's love, which I account as a gift of God not to be marshaled in the lowest part of my mind, but written in the deepest of my heart, because without that above all, other favors were of little price with me, though they were infinite.[5]

She won the loyalty of the British people, however, not by gifts to them of colonies, not by bread and circuses, not by palaces and pageants, but by her own constancy (*Semper eadem*—"Always the same"), by her bravery, her intelligence, and frankly, by the beautiful delivery, the wit, the Good Queen Bess simplicity and honesty and soaring style of her speeches.

Judging by Elizabeth I's final "Golden" speech to Parliament, we should perhaps think of her addresses to her countrymen as *her* Valois tapestries, her Escorial, her own version of inalienably enduring art, her heir as much as Mary Stuart's son James would be.

For myself I was never so much enticed with the glorious name of a King or royal authority of a Queen as delighted that God hath made me his instrument to maintain his truth and glory and to defend his kingdom as I said from peril, dishonour, tyranny and oppression.

She had a marriage with her people; not a political contract, but a relationship saturated with a sacramental sense of divine love.

And though you have had, and may have, many princes more mighty and wise sitting in this seat, yet you never had nor shall have, any that will be more careful and loving.

Elizabeth was laid to rest in the tomb of her grandfather Henry VII. Later her coffin was placed on top of that of her sister Mary Tudor. Her successor James I of England erected a monument with an elegant effigy of Elizabeth lying in state, in all her regal splendor, wearing her crown and holding her orb and scepter. King James also had a monument made for his mother's tomb, placed in the same Chapel as Elizabeth's. Mary, Queen of Scots's tomb is taller than Elizabeth's, although it is not possible to see the difference as they are on different aisles of the Chapel. The effigy of James's mother does not wear a crown but the lace cape of her mourning costume; perhaps serving as an avatar of a crown, the cap memorialized by Clouet, then worn at her marriage to his father Lord Darnley, also resembled the lace handkerchief placed on her head at her execution.

James supplied an elaborate epitaph for the glorious Elizabeth in which her manifold virtues are eloquently described. Beneath is a simple inscription left over from the tomb of Mary and Elizabeth Tudor, buried together.

PARTNERS BOTH IN THRONE AND GRAVE, HERE REST WE TWO SISTERS, ELIZABETH AND MARY, IN THE HOPE OF THE RESURRECTION.

Mary Tudor's body is still there, but unremarked, hidden from the attention of visitors by the more famous standoff between Elizabeth and the other Mary, the Queen of Scotland, the two "sister" cousin queens, whose rivalry history has so loved to tell and retell.

But if, following the old epitaph, we say that the "sister" queens buried in that same chapel shared the same hope of resurrection, finally refusing to see the difference religion made among them, the inscription may also refer to Mary Stuart as well as to Mary Tudor. Mary Stuart and Elizabeth both aimed at toleration in an intolerant age, in the same ways that Catherine de' Medici, the mother-in-law of one and the almost mother-in-law of another English queen, labored her whole life to heal the rift between Catholic and Protestant in France. All three of these queens worked as diligently and as astutely as they might to restrain the fratricidal wars of Christian against Christian. What they had to hold up against that violent seismic shift in human sensibility was the orderly traditions of monarchy. If they did not ultimately succeed, they slowed and tempered the disorder and violence. They failed no more than Philip himself when he could not return England to Catholicism and when he lost the Protestant Netherlands, which became, in his own lifetime, a Protestant Republic.

These women shared the rule of the world of western Europe in a period we will doubtless always call the Renaissance. And if major forces of the Reformation weighed against them, they proved they could rule as well as any man—just as Ronsard had so early and so certainly written in the book Catherine assigned him to dedicate and send to Elizabeth I. And perhaps, as he also claimed, so far as peace was concerned, these women ruled just a bit better.

# ACKNOWLEDGMENTS

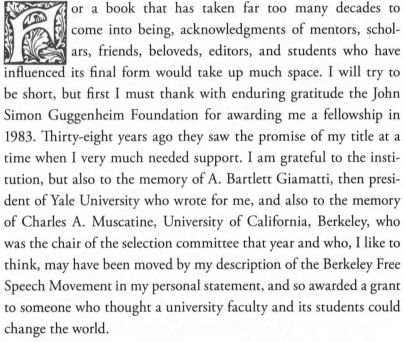

For a book that has taken far too many decades to come into being, acknowledgments of mentors, scholars, friends, beloveds, editors, and students who have influenced its final form would take up much space. I will try to be short, but first I must thank with enduring gratitude the John Simon Guggenheim Foundation for awarding me a fellowship in 1983. Thirty-eight years ago they saw the promise of my title at a time when I very much needed support. I am grateful to the institution, but also to the memory of A. Bartlett Giamatti, then president of Yale University who wrote for me, and also to the memory of Charles A. Muscatine, University of California, Berkeley, who was the chair of the selection committee that year and who, I like to think, may have been moved by my description of the Berkeley Free Speech Movement in my personal statement, and so awarded a grant to someone who thought a university faculty and its students could change the world.

Michael Malone, novelist, screenwriter, and also my husband, has been a heroic guardian spirit sacrificing much of his own time for writing to support mine, a very bad trade for American fiction, which needs all of his paragraphs and words to make a claim for greatness in the twenty-first century. If there are any sentences in the present book that give real pleasure, they are, I assure you, his.

My extremely patient and believing agent, Charlotte Sheedy, who kept saying "I love this book!" for all the years it had not yet been written. I hope in the end she is pleased with this one, difficult as it has been to bring to completion.

My editor at Liveright, Robert Weil, valiantly tried to make me write a better, more enjoyable book by encouraging me to focus on dramatic, colorful stories instead of passages of dry theory. He is a brilliant editor, scribbling correction and encouragement in margins and across the pages, probably the only one left in the business who works with a real pen and paper, doing line-by-line, thorough, and thoughtful work. His insights were invaluable and I have put almost all of them to use. He tried to make me a historian, and although I tried to become one, I was too old to change (I was already teaching English at Yale when he was a freshman history major there). I am also profoundly indebted to Haley Bracken, assistant editor at Liveright, who had to field my uncoordinated attempts to keep track of permissions and high-resolution images when I had actually managed to download them from the internet. She was graciousness itself in the face of my ineptitude and Luddite rage, and I can here witness that she is a true saint. I also wish to thank project editor Rebecca Munro and production manager Beth Steidle, who so beautifully arranged the images on the pages of this book that they convey its argument better than my own words.

I owe profound debts of gratitude to two friends and colleagues: Nancy J. Vickers, former president of Bryn Mawr College, and Margreta de Grazia, distinguished professor emerita at the University of Pennsylvania. Nancy was part of the germinal (as well as decades more) conversations that first hatched the idea for a conference on Renaissance women in 1983, and also the idea, if only the title, for this book. Margreta owned the copy of Annette Weiner's book on "inalienable possessions" that I borrowed and first read (and believe I have never given back), and her own achingly precise thought and efficiently elegant writing clearly inspired me to pay better attention to all the objects so central to my argument. The informed and intelligent friendship offered by both these women has mattered to me more than I can say.

I must also thank Deborah Jacobs, the brilliant and humane chief librarian at Duke University, first for ordering Early English Books Online when I first arrived at Duke, and second for ordering a vast digital archive of all the old books and monographs I could no longer access during COVID when I was revising my book and checking footnotes. Although she didn't do it just for me, but, rather, for the whole Duke community, I am personally grateful. It would have been absolutely impossible for me to do this work without that archive. Let me also thank once more Martin Kaufman, keeper of Western manuscripts at Duke Humfrey's Library at the Bodleian in the University of Oxford. He allowed me to view in very close detail Princess Elizabeth's embroidered book and even lightly to touch it. I will never forget that moment—so digital in the fleshly sense—the winter-pale English sun streaming in through the windows, lighting up the rustling tissue paper in which the book had been wrapped. The small volume has become more and more significant in my scholarship, especially as an object in and of itself, and I will always be grateful for Mr. Kaufman's kind generosity.

I must also thank the many librarians and curators at the large group of European, UK, and American libraries and museums who have helped in my collecting the large number of images I felt it was important to include in this volume. Gathering the high-resolution images and the permissions has been a more than usually complicated task during COVID, and while some of the processes could be done almost automatically, there were others where I was at the mercy of the kindness of many strangers who went way out of their way to help me, digital Luddite that I am.

I also wish to thank the students who took my many undergraduate and graduate seminars over the years at Yale, Penn, Duke, and Cornell that focused on the political power women wielded in the Renaissance: Bruce Boehrer, Wendy Wall, Juliet Fleming, Katherine Crawford, Karen Rabe, Rayna Kalas, Julie

Crawford, Kim Hall, Kent Lehnhof, Whitney Trettien, and many other of the myriad souls who taught me far more than I ever taught them.

I have dedicated this book to my daughter Maggie Malone, and her daughter, Maisie Malone Shakman, the first for her patience with the long writing of this book, and the second for letting me off one more game of hide and seek so I could write these acknowledgments.

# NOTES

༄

## INTRODUCTION: INALIENABLE
## POSSESSIONS AND FEMALE POWER

1     The entire works of John Knox are available in a six-volume collection edited by David Laing, *The Works of John Knox* (Woodrow Society, 1846–64). A more streamlined edition including *The First Blast of the Trumpet against the Monstrous Regiment of Women* along with other writings on similar topics, is *John Knox: On Rebellion*, ed. Roger A. Mason (Cambridge University Press, 1994). In "A Letter to the Regent" (1556), addressed to Marie de Guise, Mary Stuart's mother, Knox reveals the fundamental nature of his attack not merely on women, but on the idea of social hierarchy itself—and therefore on monarchy, which rests upon that hierarchy. His ostentatiously and perhaps mockingly obsequious indication of his lower social position in relation to hers as a ruling woman underscores the compelling difference in class status between them. It is this very hierarchical status that his theology would erase, placing him on a equal (if not superior) footing with her. The difference in their social standings can be overcome only by Knox's personal sense of a crisis in Christianity. He also insists that it is her very hierarchical position over him (a high-status woman over a lower-status man) that poses the fundamental problem: "Superfluous and foolish it shall appear to many that I, a man of base estate and condition, dare enterprise to admonish a princess so honourable, endued with wisdom and graces singular. . . . But when I consider . . . the troublesome estate of Christ's true religion . . . I am compelled to say that this preeminence wherin ye are placed shall be your dejection." Mason, *John Knox: On Rebellion*, 55. In one paragraph we can see the Reformation's assumptions about the evils of worldly hierarchy, the very basis of kingship, and therefore of high status women's inherited authority to rule over men.

2     This accounting of at least sixteen women who had real executive power in sixteenth-century Europe has already been brilliantly begun. In *Game of Queens: The Women Who Made Sixteenth-Century Europe* (New York: Basic Books, 2016), Sarah Gristwood deftly interweaves the histories of sixteen women who exercised a remarkable amount of political and cultural power in the sixteenth century and

who indeed "made" Renaissance Europe. They often knew each other quite well (as elites often do), and they exercised their authority with a distinct awareness of the work they had done as a *group* of women who had achieved lasting impact on the culture of their times. I am everywhere indebted to Gristwood's pioneering work uncovering the central importance of so many ruling women in the culture and politics of the sixteenth century. She asks a very interesting question at the end of her book: why did subsequent centuries have fewer powerful ruling women than the European sixteenth century? I suggest it might have something to do with the advance of the Reformation and its attendant republican policies. After the Commonwealth period, the Stuart monarchs were beholden to Parliament, and in 1688, Catholic James II was deposed in favor of his daughter Mary, and her powerful Protestant husband, the Dutch Prince William of Orange. Once Parliament had obtained the power to choose the ruler they wanted (and to unelect the one the didn't) it did not matter if that ruler were a woman. Thus came the last of the Stewart queens, Mary and then her sister Anne.

3    In "Catherine de Medici: The Legend of the Wicked Italian Queen," N. M. Sutherland traces the changing views of Catherine from the earliest laudatory accounts by people who actually knew her, to the Protestant propaganda mythology about her as poisoner, necromancer, and diabolical mastermind of the St. Bartholomew's Day Massacre; *Sixteenth Century Journal* 9 (1978): 45–56. In these Protestant accounts, Catherine, in particular, was filled with Medicean cruelty, foolish ambition, and envy of every throne; an avowed anti-Catholic, Michelet imagines that "Day and night with her astrologers, from her turret . . . she surveys the stars and sees that she and her sons will be masters of Europe." Mary Stuart fares little better: "One guesses in her divine portrait the tragic violence which avenged itself so cruelly on Darnley for his offence against her royalty and which, without scruple, accepted the murder of Elizabeth." Jules Michelet, *L'Histoire de France*, vol. 12, Project Gutenberg, https://www.gutenberg.org/files /39335/39335-h/39335-h.htm.

4    For one of the early first steps in this generational project, see Margaret Ferguson, Maureen Quilligan, and Nancy Vickers, eds., *Rewriting the Renaissance: The Discourses of Sexual Difference in Early Modern Europe* (University of Chicago Press, 1986).

5    Annette Weiner, *Inalienable Possessions: The Paradox of Keeping-While-Giving* (Berkeley: University of California Press, 1992), makes a paradigm-shifting argument about the nature of the "gift" in twentieth-century anthropological theory by going back to the Trobriand Islands, the site where Marcel Mauss first theorized the importance of the gift. In *The Gift: The Form and Reason for Exchange in Archaic Societies* (1925; rpt. Norton, 2000); Mauss's main point is that each gift *forces a gift in return*. The repeated reciprocities ensure the continuation of connections between groups that constitute society. The most important subsequent development of Mauss's argument, which argues that women are the most precious kind of gift that can be given between men, is Claude Lévi-Strauss's *Elementary Structures of Kinship* (1949; rpt. Beacon Press, 1969). Lévi-Strauss's argument in particular denies women any distinct agency in the creation of cul-

ture; he argues they are merely passive gifts given and received in return among separate groups (clans, tribes) of men, which "traffic in women" constitutes the fundamental foundation of civilization. His theory has been contested by many feminist theorists, among them Gayle Rubin, Marilyn Strathern, Nancy Chodorow, and Kaja Silverman. Perhaps more importantly, Annette Weiner went into the field to discover the overlooked giving of gifts among women; she thus adds substantive weight to the theoretical critiques of other feminist thinkers with data drawn from the same sites in which Mauss himself worked.

6    For a discussion of this "book," see my "Elizabeth's Embroidery" in *Shakespeare Studies* 28 (2000): 208–14. For further discussion of the *Glass of the Sinful Soul* as an inalienable possession and its decades-long life as a book in print, see my *Incest and Agency in Elizabeth's England* (Philadelphia: University of Pennsylvania Press, 2005); the poem by Queen Marguerite de Navarre, sister of François II, that Elizabeth translated from the French, *Le Miroir de l'Âme Pécheresse*, uses the traditional medieval metaphor of the soul's relation to God as "Holy Incest" in which the soul (Latin *anima*) is wife, sister, and daughter to God (Christ). In a most provocative way, this metaphor speaks to the fundamental endogamy of the "giving" of inalienable possessions; the female soul is never traded out of the holy "family."

7    For a detailed discussion of the tapestries as expressions of Catherine's political agenda, see Elizabeth Cleland and Marjorie E. Wieseman, *Renaissance Splendor: Catherine de' Medici's Valois Tapestries* (Cleveland Museum of Art, Yale University Press, 2018). A catalogue of the exhibition of six recently restored (out of eight) Valois tapestries, the book strengthens the arguments of Uffizi curators and scholars that Catherine was the commissioner of the weavings. See also Ewa Kociszewska, "Woven Bloodlines: The Valois Tapestries in the Trousseau of Christine de Lorraine, Grand Duchess of Tuscany," *Artibus et Historiae* 37 (2016): 335–63. An earlier groundbreaking study of the tapestries, which the more recent investigations are correcting in profoundly new ways, is Frances Yates, *The Valois Tapestries* (London: Courtauld Institute, 1959).

8    In the "Summary of the Second Blast," also published in 1558 (Mason, 128–29), Knox further argued against the central driver of kingship (and queenship): "It is not birth only nor propinquity [nearness] of blood that maketh a king lawfully to rule over a people." Knox thinks that not only should women *never* rule, but also that only male rulers who have exclusively received and maintained the affirmation of the men of the country are eligible to hold such office. Indeed, men of the realm "may . . . depose and punish him that unadvisedly they did before nominate, appoint, and elect." In a sense Knox's misogynist attack was merely a first sally in his attack on monarchy itself, which is based firmly on "propinquity of blood."

9    *Elegies, Mascarades et Bergerie*, Pierre de Ronsard, *Oeuvres Complètes*, ed. Paul Laumonier (Paris, 1948), volume 13. Only the first edition of the book published in 1565 makes clear that Ronsard's political commentary is a nuanced critique of Cecil's republican sympathies; because Ronsard revised all of his works throughout his life, the poem to Cecil changes radically in response to the poet's ever more darkening view of Elizabeth's secretary. In *Renaissance*

*Studies: Articles 1966–1994*, Malcolm Smith discusses the *Bergerie* poems and traces Ronsard's continuous revisions of its contents. In the end, Ronsard entirely erases Cecil and any mention of England from the "Elegie" originally addressed to him. Instead, the "Cecil" of the poem in 1584 is merely a man living in Sicily and thus a subject of King Philip II of Spain. It is perhaps possible to see some lurking irony in Ronsard's transformation of the very Protestant Cecil figure into a loyal subject of a *Catholic* king, who was one of the most energetically focused on rooting out Protestant heresy in Europe. Ronsard died in 1585, two years before his beloved Marie, La Reine d'Écosse, was executed by the government of Elizabeth I of England.

10    John Guy, *My Heart Is My Own, The Life of Mary, Queen of Scots* (London: Fourth Estate, 2004). The book is also published under the title *Mary, Queen of Scots: the True Life of Mary Stuart*. I have found Guy's argument to be of inestimable support to me in making my own argument, that ultimately it was Cecil's machinations—and not Elizabeth's jealousy—that led to the execution of Mary Stuart. Because I had first, before reading Guy, understood how Ronsard and Catherine had *literally named Cecil* the anti-monarchal threat at the time, I was all the more convinced that Guy's argument was right. While Guy does not argue that Elizabeth and Mary were sisters in arms fighting a patriarchal Protestant reformation that threatened the very idea of monarchy, I have very heavily relied on his archival research, of the sort I could never do by using primarily digitized documents. I do not, however, quote chapter and verse for every instance of my reliance on Guy, thereby preventing a forest of endnotes, but I do signal the few moments when I have found it necessary to disagree with him.

## CHAPTER ONE: THE DEVICE FOR SUCCESSION

1    An excellent recent biography of Mary I of England is Linda Porter, *The Myth of "Bloody Mary": A Biography of Queen Mary I of England*, Kindle Edition (New York: St. Martin's, 2009). Porter makes a most persuasive argument that Edward VI's "Device for Succession" was his own independent idea, not something conjured up to make it possible for his Protector, Lord Northumberland, to continue in power, as has been the received opinion for quite some time. She also stresses that the teenaged king disinherited *both* of his sisters, including the Protestant Elizabeth, and thus it must have been something other than Mary's Catholicism that disabled the sisters in Edward's eyes.

2    All quotations from Elizabeth's letters are from *Elizabeth I: The Collected Works*, ed. Leah Marcus, Janel Mueller, and Mary Beth Rose (Chicago: Chicago University Press, 2002), 46. This scholarly edition is the first in history to collect and print all of Elizabeth I's letters, poems, and speeches; it has taken one year short of three centuries to make Elizabeth I's work as an author accessible to the greater public.

3    Mary's second signal speech rallying men to risk their lives for her queenship at the Guildhall opened up many of the centrally important themes her younger sister would use throughout her own reign. The full text of Mary's speech taken from *Holinshed's Chronicles* may be found at https://thehistoryofengland.co.uk/resource/speech-of-mary-i-1554.

4     The text (modernized) is taken from the database Early English Books Online (EEBO, https://eebo.chadwyck.com/), which presents digital copies of virtually every page printed in the first two centuries of printing in England.

5     As reported by George Cavendish in *The negotiations of Thomas Woolsey, the great Cardinall of England containing his life and death. . .* (London: William Sheares, 1641). The words do match what the French ambassador wrote of the scene to King François I: "Finally, she fell on her knees before him, begging him to consider her honor, her daughter's, and his; that he should not be displeased at her defending it, and should consider the reputation of her nation and relatives, who will be seriously offended." https://www.british-history.ac.uk/letters-papers -hen8/vol4/pp2523-2531. Shakespeare put Cavendish's words into verse in *The History of the Life of King Henry VIII.*

6     Porter, *The Myth of "Bloody Mary,"* 90; Kindle Edition, loc. 1577.

7     Henry's liaison with Mary Boleyn may have produced living children, perhaps adding to Henry's hopes for Anne's fertility. In *Mary Boleyn: The Mistress of Kings* (New York: Random House, 2011), Kindle Edition loc. 3241, Alison Weir concludes that while Mary's son Henry Carey was *not* fathered by Henry VIII, her daughter Katherine may well have been. Katherine was the grandmother of Lettice Knollys, whom Robert Dudley, Elizabeth's favorite, secretly married, earning them Elizabeth's lasting anger. Elizabeth thus "lost" Dudley to her first cousin once removed. Lettice was also the mother of Robert Devereux, Earl of Essex, her son from a prior marriage, upon whom Elizabeth doted after Robert Dudley died.

8     Porter, *The Myth of "Bloody Mary,"* Kindle Edition, loc. 3724. Porter cites the Proclamation itself: "Oxburgh Hall: *Bedingfeld MS,* proclamation of 18 July 1553." Henry Bedingfeld was clearly a longtime loyal servant of Catholic Mary as queen; she had appointed him to be Elizabeth's jailer in Woodstock for two years after her release from the Tower. Elizabeth remembered him fondly, but he found his job as her jailer onerous. He remained Roman Catholic until he died. It is thus not surprising that a copy of Mary's Proclamation has remained safely in the possession of the Bedingfelds for over four hundred years.

9     Raphael Holingshed, *The first and second volumes of Chronicles. [vol. 3 (i.e., The Third Volume of Chronicles)] comprising 1 The description and historie of England, 2 The description and historie of Ireland, 3 The description and historie of Scotland: first collected and published by Raphaell Holinshed, William Harrison, and others: now newlie augmented and continued (with manifold matters of singular note and worthie memorie) to the yeare 1586. by Iohn Hooker aliàs Vowell Gent and others. With conuenient tables at the end of these volumes* (London: Henry Denham, 1587), 1091. Early English Books Online, https://quod .lib.umich.edu/e/eebo/A68202.0001.001/1:200?rgn=div1;submit=Go;subview =detail;type=simple;view=fulltext;q1=Mary+I.

10    October 8, 1553. I cite the letter as it appears in *The Calendar of State Papers, Spain*, vol. 11, *1553. The Calendar* comprises the official archive of British governmental papers from the reigns of all the rulers of England up to the present day; the earlier manuscript books were printed in multiple volumes throughout

the nineteenth and twentieth centuries, and have now been digitized. The digital copies are available at British History Online, http//:www.british-history.ac .uk/cal-state-papers. For the material dealing with Mary's reign, I have consulted *CSP, Spain, 1553*, ed. Royall Tyler (London, 1916); *CSP, Spain (Simancas), 1558– 1567*, ed. Martin S. A. Hume (London, 1892). I cite specific entries in the body of the text by date. The narrative the entries present reads like a novel, although often interrupted by mundane government housekeeping (budget payments, recommendations of servants, notice of minor litigations, payments to soldiers, etc.), all of which reveal the creation of history in the daily immediacy of the moment.

11    The poem is so famous one can Google it with merely the first four words:

> Whoso lists [desires] to hunt, I know where is an hind [female deer],
> But as for me, *hélas*, I may no more.
> The vain travail hath wearied me so sore,
> I am of them that farthest cometh behind.
> Yet may I by no means my wearied mind
> Draw from the deer, but as she fleeth afore
> Fainting I follow. I leave off therefore,
> Sithens [since] in a net I seek to hold the wind.
>
> Who list her hunt, I put him out of doubt,
> As well as I may spend his time in vain.
> And graven with diamonds in letters plain
> There is written, her fair neck round about:
> *Noli me tangere*, for Caesar's I am,
> And wild for to hold, though I seem tame.

12    Porter, *The Myth of "Bloody Mary,"* Kindle Edition, loc. 2190.

13    The letters concerning Philip's worries for Elizabeth and possible marriage with her were sent and received between March 1557 and December 1558, and are accessible in *CSP, Spain,* https://www-british-history-ac-uk.cal-state-papers /spain/vol13/pp394.

## CHAPTER TWO: THE MARY TUDOR PEARL

1     The editor's comments on Elizabeth's reluctance to marry Philip can be found in the introduction to *Calendar of State Papers, Spain (Simancas)*, volume 1, *1558– 1567*, ed. Martin A. Hume, History Online, https://www.british-history.ac.uk/cal -state-papers/simancas/vol1/i-lxiii. Count Feria wrote to Philip specifically spelling out Elizabeth's objections: "The impediment she discovered in the fact of your Majesty having married her sister, and after that she denied point-blank the Pope's power, which she had previously only pointed out indirectly" (February 29, 1559).

2     When Emperor Charles asked the Pope for a dispensation for incest in his son Philip's first marriage to a Portuguese princess, he listed four instances of forbidden kinship relations; there were, however, so many other instances of interdicted affinity due to the many royal intermarriages on the Iberian Peninsula, that he simply opted for a blanket dispensation that would cover any additional

cases that he might have overlooked. Geoffrey Parker, *Emperor: A New Life of Charles V* (New Haven, CT: Yale University Press, 2019, plate 28). Strange to say, though not surprising in this story of powerful families marrying among themselves to increase political power and status, Charles V himself had first been proposed as a possible groom for his niece Mary Tudor when her father Henry VIII was still alive. And indeed when first proposing much later that Queen Mary should marry a Hapsburg prince, Charles put forth himself again, only soon to switch to his son Philip. Perhaps in memory of this earlier engagement, Charles V also sent Mary a second table diamond for her wedding to his son.

For a fascinating discussion of the possible purposes of the elaborate rules against incest formulated by the Church in the Middle Ages, see Jack Goody, *The Development of the Family and Marriage in Europe* (Cambridge: Cambridge University Press, 1983). In brief, Goody argues that the incest rules were designed to make it difficult for a family to pass down its property among kin, so that the property was more likely to be granted to the Church. See also my *Incest and Agency in Elizabeth's England*, introduction.

3  This bond of extended family connections has remained constant into modern times for British royalty. Victoria and Albert were first cousins. Elizabeth II and Prince Philip were second cousins. More remotely, Prince Charles and the late Princess Diana are descended from two different sisters of Henry VIII, Charles from Henry's elder sister Margaret Tudor, and Diana from Mary Tudor, his younger sister. Prince William has broken this tradition by marrying Kate Middleton, a proper commoner with no blood connections to her husband's family.

4  In her will Mary does not mention any pearls attached to the diamonds Philip and his father gave her: "And I do humbly beseech my saide most dearest lorde and husbande to accepte of my bequest and to keep for a memory of me one jewell being a table diamond which the [e]mperours Majesty, his and my most honourable Father, sent unto me by the Contdegment, at the insurance of my sayde lorde and husbande and also one other table dyamonde whiche his Majesty sent unto me by the marques de les Nanes." A copy of Mary Tudor's will can be found at https://tudorhistory.org/primary/will.html.

5  David Starkey, ed., *The Inventory of King Henry VIII: The Transcript* (Harvey Miller Publishers for the Society of Antiquaries of London, 1998), 77, item 2619.

6  The medal was one with a matching profile of Philip, both clearly struck to celebrate the wedding of the two monarchs (https://www.coingallery.de/KarlV/Engl2_E .htm). For more information on the medal, see S. K. Scher, ed., *The Currency of Fame: Portrait Medals of the Renaissance* (New York: Thames and Hudson, 1994).

7  Painted by an unknown artist in 1590 copying an earlier portrait, the painting shows a more rounded gold medallion as pendant on the sitter's necklace and a different, sharper-cornered diamond and drop pearl on a pendant hanging from an elaborate gold, pearl, and diamond chain attached to the sitter's bodice. The identification of the sitter as Jane Grey is controversial. See Cynthia Zarin, "Teen Queen: The Search for Lady Jane Grey," *New Yorker* (October 15, 2007). See also Janel Mueller, ed., *Katherine Parr: Complete Works and Correspondence* (Chicago: Chicago University Press, 2011). Mueller argues that "Lady Jane Grey's Prayer-

book" had in fact belonged to Katherine Parr, who had written it in her own hand, taking prayers from many places and also composing her own. Mueller suggests that Parr gave it to Jane Grey, who carried it to the scaffold where she was finally executed. Alternatively, because the portrait was painted posthumously, it may simply give to the sitter Queen Katherine Parr's—that is, "Mary Tudor's Pearl"—familiar-looking brooch, as an added proof of Jane's viability as Queen.

8     In *The Book of the Pearl: The History, Art, Science and Industry of the Queen of Gems* (1908), George Frederick Kunz repeats the legend about the origins of "La Peregrina": "Garcilasso de la Vega. . . says that he saw it at Seville in 1597, this was found at Panama in 1560 by a negro who was rewarded with his liberty." He notes the pearl went into the Spanish crown jewels.

      The long-lived misapprehension that this gem entered the Spanish crown jewels *before* Philip's marriage to Mary in 1554 may derive from the appearance of a large pear-shaped pearl in a portrait of Philip's mother, the Empress Isabella, painted by Titian in 1548. Done after the empress had already died, Titian copied a painting done from life by a Flemish artist. When asked by the emperor to copy this earlier portrait of the empress, Titian expanded a small jewel, fabulously enlarging it in his version into a distinctive drop pearl. While Isabella does wear a necklace with a pearl in the earlier portrait, it is quite tiny and unimposing. See Georg Gronau, "Titian's Portraits of the Empress Isabella," *Burlington Magazine* 2 (August 1903): 281–85. In a stunning portrait of Elisabeth de Valois, Philip's third wife, Sofonisba Anguissola gives the queen a jewel very similar to the empress's; an actual jewel may have been created to refer to the empress's, or Anguissola may have simply copied Titian's. The sequence in which the pearl appears in royal Spanish portraits may have strengthened the myth that the made-up pearl enlarged by Titian had entered the Spanish crown jewels by the time of Philip's mother, the empress, so he could give it to Mary Tudor.

9     For a recent foray into the confusions between Mary Tudor's pearl and the Spanish "La Peregrina," see https://eragem.com/news/a-tale-of-two-pearls-tracing-la -peregrina-mary-tudors-pearl-through-portraits/.

10    Louis Montrose, in *The Subject of Elizabeth: Authority, Gender, and Representation* (Chicago: University of Chicago Press, 2006), may be the first scholar to argue for the importance of the bow and pearl in the Armada portrait and its relationship to Holbein's famous picture of Henry VIII. No one that I know of has yet commented on the jewel to which the bow is attached, and on its similarity to the Mary Tudor Pearl or indeed to the gem worn in earlier portraits (or later, as in the Ditchley Portrait of 1592). One of the first scholars to study all the portraits in detail is Roy Strong, *Gloriana: The Portraits of Elizabeth I* (New York: Thames and Hudson, 1987). He does not, however, mention the jewel.

11    A new group biography of Elizabeth Stuart and her daughters offers an engrossing and fascinating study of the way such women allowed the Stuart dynasty to endure: Nancy Goldstone, *The Daughters of the Winter Queen: Four Remarkable Sisters, the Crown of Bohemia, and the Enduring Legacy of Mary, Queen of Scots* (New York: Little, Brown, 2018).

## CHAPTER THREE: THREE QUEENS, ONE POET, AND THE REPUBLICAN COUNSELOR

1   Kate Williams, *The Betrayal of Mary, Queen of Scots: Elizabeth and Her Greatest Rival* (New York: Hutchinson, 2018), 41. Apple iBooks. My claim is not that there was never animosity between Mary Stuart and Elizabeth, simply that the chasm that they tried to bridge was not something for which either was personally responsible. At the very least, Elizabeth's poem "The Doubt of Future Foes" testifies to Elizabeth's joy-destroying worries about the sedition that Mary, whom she termed "the daughter of debate," could arouse in her otherwise peaceful land.

2   Pierre Adolphe Chéruel, *Marie Stuart et Catherine de Médicis: Étude historique sur les relations de la France et de l'Écosse dans la seconde moitié du 16e siècle* (Paris, 1858), 17n. Chéruel prints the Italian sentence in a footnote, but does not mention that the Pope to whom the letter was addressed was Giovanni Angelo de' Medici, who, being a proud member of the Medici family (although not of the Florentine branch), may well have appreciated the gossip in a more personal manner than most. Doubtless, his Nuncio only chose to report this otherwise trivial remark because of the personal connection. The Medici were bankers, not merchants (or doctors). At random, two recent scholars who repeat the anecdote include: Jane Dunn, *Elizabeth and Mary: Cousins, Rivals, Queens* (New York: Vintage, 2005), 173, and Leoni Frieda, *Catherine de Medici: Renaissance Queen of France* (London, 2003), 127.

3   *The Memoires of Sir James Melvil of Hal-hill, containing an impartial account of the most remarkable affairs of state during the last age, not mentioned by other historians: more particularly relating to the Kingdoms of England and Scotland, under the reigns of Queen Elizabeth, Mary, Queen of Scots, and King James. In all which transactions the author was personally and publicly concerned* (London, 1683), 29.

4   The "Medici pearls" were said at the time to be worth "a kingdom," though subsequently it was discovered that they had been bought from a jeweler in Lyons. See Frieda, *Catherine de Medici*, 42. When Mary bolted to England, Catherine made efforts to purchase the pearls she had given to Mary, but had to give up the attempt when she learned that Elizabeth had already bought them for twelve thousand ecus (*Lettres de Catherine de Médicis*, vol. 3, 142n). They perhaps figure in images of the many pearls Elizabeth wore in all of her portraits. (She had said she would wear the pearls she purchased to honor the memory of Mary Stuart.) This jewelry was subsequently inherited by James I, who gave them to his daughter Elizabeth Stuart; she took them with her to Bohemia where she became queen. She then gave the pearls to her daughter Sophia, who married into the German Hanover family. At the demise of the Stuart dynasty in 1714, Sophia's son became George I of England, over which the Hanovers ruled throughout the eighteenth century. Queen Victoria inherited what remained of the collection from her uncle, George IV. Through his father Prince Albert, Victoria's son was a member of the House of Saxe-Coburg; the current royal dynasty changed their family name to Windsor during World War II. Four pearls, said to be from the

Medici collection, currently grace the top of Elizabeth II's imperial crown. In essence, the pearls follow the Stuart DNA as it has passed down the centuries tracking the descent of female agency.

5    David Hume, *The History of England, under the House of Tudor: Comprehending the Reigns of K. Henry VII. K. Henry VIII. K Edward VI. Q. Mary, and Q. Elizabeth* (London, 1759).

6    James Anthony Froude, *History of England from the Fall of Wolsey to the Death of Elizabeth*, vol. 8 (New York: Scribner and Sons, 1856), 3, https://www.google .com/books/edition/History_of_England_from_the_Fall_of_Wols/AWMN AAAAIAAJ?hl=en://._

7    The first edition of *Elegies, Mascarades et Bergerie* (1565) can be found in Pierre de Ronsard, *Oeuvres Complètes*, ed. Paul Laumonier (Paris: Didier, 1948), vol. 13; https://gallica.bnf.fr/ark:/12148/. All translations are my own.

Very little has been written about this volume. The single scholarly book dedicated to the *Mascarades et Bergerie* is by Virginia Sturm-Scott and Sarah Maddox, *Performance, Politics, and Poetry on the Queen's Day* (Farnham, UK: Ashgate, 2007). Scott and Maddox primarily deal with the *Bergerie* in its context within French performance culture; in a "Postscript" they deal briefly with the part that the drama plays in Ronsard's book as it was sent to Elizabeth, but make no comment on its possible political message beyond its praise of rule by women.

8    Robert Dudley had employed Edmund Spenser, premier nondramatic poet of the age, as his secretary. He early on supported the growth of the Elizabethan theater with his own troupe, Lord Leicester's Men, to whom he offered legal protection and license to present plays throughout England. The ties were not financial (in either direction), but they set the model for the development of all the future troupes that formed under the protection of various noblemen, including the Lord Chamberlain's Men, Shakespeare's acting company.

9    Frederick Chamberlin, *Elizabeth and Lycester* (New York: Dodd, Mead, 1939), 40; Chamberlin was greatly exercised when later historians followed Bohun's lead in slandering Dudley: "Would you hang a dog on such evidence?" https:// babel.hathitrust.org/cgi/pt?id=inu.32000001826165&view=1up&seq=52&q1= Hang%20a%20dog.

10   Alison Weir, *Elizabeth, the Queen* (New York: Vintage, 2009), 108. Quadra's letter can be found at *CSP, Spain, (Simancas)*, September 11, 1560.

11   For a clear discussion of all the ins and outs of this scandal, which has remained a mystery for centuries, see Sarah Gristwood, *Elizabeth and Leicester: Power, Passion, Politics* (London: Penguin, 2007), 99–12. Gristwood assesses the possibility of Cecil's guilt as murderer because "he had the best motive" (119). Quadra was right that Cecil had been sidelined in favor of Dudley at this juncture, so any jolt to his reputation could right the balance between the two counselors. Gristwood also entertains Elizabeth's possible interest in a scandalous death for Dudley's wife, which would make it impossible for her to marry him but at the same time allow her to keep him as her beloved favorite. Gristwood, however, favors the idea that Robsart may have committed suicide, as there is evidence from the testimony of servants that she was deeply depressed at

this time. Although Gristwood's book was published in 2007, a year before the discovery of the missing coroner's report in 2008, the report does not provide certainty among the possibilities of accident, murder, or suicide, as the newly discovered head wounds might arguably be caused not only by being attacked with a blunt instrument, but also by falling down a flight of stairs, whatever the cause of the fall: an accidental slip, a push, or a determined leap to death. The true cause of Amy's death must remain a mystery.

12    Guy, *My Heart Is My Own.* According to Guy, Cecil launched a decades-long campaign against Mary's queenship. He makes a very persuasive case for Cecil's ultimately successful entrapment of Mary—and also of Elizabeth—by forcing Elizabeth officially to execute Mary, thus setting the precedent that made regicide legitimate. As early as 1560, before Mary returned to her homeland, Cecil argued that Scotland should be ruled by a group of nobles.

13    In the introduction to *John Knox: On Rebellion*, John Mason notes that when Knox was in Geneva trying to convince John Calvin of the need for a more aggressive response to the persecution of the godly, Calvin did not agree, the argument being that, because humankind was naturally evil, the "greatest danger was that baser motives would masquerade under the cloak of religious zeal" (xii). See also Gary Z. Cole, "John Calvin and Civil Government," *WRS Journal* 16:2 (August 2009): 18–23. Cole summarizes, "Calvin thought it safer for government to be in the hands of many than in the hands of one, maintaining that monarchies are generally unable or unwilling to regulate themselves. Calvin vehemently opposed the theory that the Pope, or any king, should be able to claim absolute power." However, Calvin in no way agreed with Knox that the faithful might legitimately turn to violence to protect their religious rights. Interestingly, Calvin uses the same formulation as Mary Stuart when remarking on the danger that religion might provide a "cloak" for baser motives of political ambition.

14    The official Pléiade edition does not print the earliest version of the poem that dedicates the poem about "Sicily" to Cecil, so it is only by looking at Laumonier's edition, or having access to the original book or to a facsimile (or digital copy) of it, that it becomes possible to understand this (very subtle) warning.

15    *Lettres de Catherine de Médicis*, vol. 3. Catherine wrote another letter the next year, on December 27, 1569, slightly more irritated with Elizabeth for not doing what she had promised: "We pray you to put the said queen of Scotland in liberty and ready what aid and support that you are able, in order to replace her in her realm with all the authority and obedience which are due her from her subjects" (*Lettres*, 3:289).

Susan Doran summarizes the diplomatic relations between Catherine and Elizabeth: "Despite their mutual suspicion and religious differences, the two queens proved able to set aside traditional . . . rivalries and to keep the amity professed at Troyes in 1564." Doran then adds a notable caution: "Their rapprochement owed nothing to their gender. . . . Rather, pragmatic considerations and diplomatic practices kept them on a peaceful track." Susan Doran, "Elizabeth I and Catherine de' Medici," in *"The Contending Kingdoms": France and England*

*1420–1700*, ed. Glenn Richardson (London: Routledge, 2008). Kindle Edition, loc. 3753. Such an argument does not, however, take into account the understanding Catherine expressed to Elizabeth in her handwritten postscript about Mary Stuart, that the support a sovereign offers another sovereign in repressing rebellion is especially important in the case of princesses, that is, women rulers. This is not the womanly softheartedness that Doran perhaps rightly dismisses, but hardheaded pragmatic politics that, at least according to Catherine and her poet, has everything to do with gender.

## CHAPTER FOUR: "SISTER" QUEENS, MARY STUART AND ELIZABETH TUDOR

1   *The Memoires of Sir James Melvil of Hal-hill*, 131.
2   James Anthony Froude, *History of England from the Fall of Wolsey to the Death of Elizabeth*, vol. 8 (Scribner and Sons, 1856), 256, https://babel.hathitrust.org/cgi/pt?id=ucl.b3884223&view=1up&seq=296&q1.
3   James Emerson Phillips, *Images of a Queen: Mary Stuart in Sixteenth-Century Literature* (Berkeley: University of California Press, 1964), 34–35.
4   Few historians note more than the existence of the font, but Guy acknowledges its impressive weight. *My Heart Is My Own*, 273.
5   William Camden, *Annals, or, the historie of the most renovvned and victorious princesse elizabeth, late queen of england containing all the important and remarkable passages of state both at home and abroad, during her long and prosperous reigne* (London: Thomas Harper, for Benjamin Fisher, 1607), 71.
6   The Venetian ambassador's description of the gold baptismal font can be found in *CSP, Venice*, vol. 7, *1558–1580*, ed. Rawdon Brown and G. Cavendish Bentinck (London, 1890), 386–87, British History Online, http://www.british-history.ac.uk/cal-state-papers/venice/vol7/pp386-387.
7   In 1555 Catherine de' Medici had sent to Mary Tudor a silver gilt font, chased with roses and pomegranates (for which Granada, original seat of Mary's mother's and her husband Philip's family, had been named); it also included Mary's motto "Truth, the Daughter of Time" in Latin. Although Mary Tudor, sadly, never had use for it, the font may have served for James I's English-born child, Charles (it was he who was beheaded in 1649). A. Jeffrey Collins, ed., *Jewels and Plate of Queen Elizabeth I: The Inventory of 1574* (British Museum, 1955), 310.
8   Elizabeth wrote a letter in the same vein:

> You knowe, my deare brother, that, sins you first brethed, I regarded alwais to conserue hit as my womb hit had bine you bare. [You know, my dear brother, that, since you first breathed, I have always seen to consider it to have been my womb that bore you.] (January 1592 )

> In another letter, James responded with the same language of connection between them, thanking her for her maternal care of him "as a louing mother wold use hir naturall and deuoted chylde." John Bruce, ed., *Letters of Queen Elizabeth and King James VI of Scotland* (London: Camden Society, 1849). https://search-alexanderstreet.com.

9    "Commère" in French translates as "gossip," but in the sixteenth century, "gossip" meant "god-sib," that is, a relative linked by a sacramental ceremony (such as baptism); it was, however, far more powerful than our current sense of "godparent." It was, for example, considered incest to marry a "god-sib."

10   *Lettres de Catherine de Médicis*, ed. Hector de la Ferrière (Paris, 1887), vol. 3, 289.

11   George Buchanan, *Opera Omnia*, vol. 2 (1725), 399–405. Translations from the Latin are my own.

12   Michael Lynch, "Queen Mary's Triumph: The Baptismal Celebrations at Stirling in December 1566," *Scottish History Review* 69 (April 1990), 1–21; Lynch argues that "at the time the birth and baptism were envisaged as accelerating the process of internal reconciliation, both of Mary with her errant nobles and of Protestants with Catholics" (4).

## CHAPTER FIVE: REGICIDE, REPUBLICANISM, AND THE DEATH OF DARNLEY

1    *Mémoires de messire Michel de Castelnau, seigneur de Mauvissière* (Paris, 1823), in volume 2 of Alexandre Teulet, *Relations politiques de la France et de l'Espagne avec l'Écosse* (Paris: Librarie de la Société Histoire, 1862), 152; Teulet prints political documents covering the years 1559–73. Because Castelnau had been charged with making peace between Mary and her barons, he ignored Mary's adamant insistence on how anti-monarchal she considered the rebel lords to be; he decided that hers was a profoundly immature political analysis. Yet Elizabeth's own moral outrage at these same rebels' affronts to monarchal principles, when, two years later, they refused to obey *her* commands to release their anointed queen from prison, suggests that Mary was simply being clear-sighted rather than naïve and saw earlier what Elizabeth learned only later. Mary was neither stupid nor ill-educated. She knew what she was talking about. See also Chéruel, *Marie Stuart et Catherine de Médicis*, 43.

2    Guy, *My Heart Is My Own*, 226, 303. Guy understands that George Buchanan had a fully articulated theory of republican government but does not seem to think that his views would have been known to Mary, or that they would have informed her opinion of the barons' political attitudes. Knox had certainly made no bones about his rejection of the divine right of kings. Guy shows how Buchanan, like Knox, thought that "rulers were chosen by the people"; if the rulers failed in government then "the people had the right to depose them"—again, a Knoxian precept. Buchanan approved of Mary's forced abdication, "which he regarded as one of the best practical illustrations of his theory of royal accountability in eight hundred years of Scottish history" (375).

3    Guy, *My Heart Is My Own*. Mary argued that the rebels "were outright 'republicans'—she used the word—set on destroying the 'ancient monarchy.' The rebels would depose and kill her and Darnley, and then create a 'republic' in which sovereignty was vested in the nobles" (263, Kindle Edition, loc. 4010). Mary read Livy with her Latin secretary, George Buchanan, who had of course an even more radical notion of government power than Knox, which he held flowed not from God, but only and fundamentally from the people. Livy's description of the tran-

sition of Rome from a kingdom to a republic, instigated by the rape and suicide of Lucretia, was a story she would have known well.

4       *CSP, Scotland, Elizabeth*, February 27, 1560; Article Berwick, *CSP, Scotland, Elizabeth*, August 1559.

5       The declaration by Mary and François II can be found in Jean Joseph François Poujoulat, *Nouvelle collection des memoires pour servir à l'histoire de France* (Paris: Guyot Frères, 1851), 451.

6       From his sermon on Isaiah 26. The entire works of John Knox are available in the six-volume edition edited by David Laing, *The Works of John Knox* (Woodrow Society, 1846–64); this sermon can be accessed digitally at http://biblehub.com/library/knox/the_pulpit_of_the_reformation_nos_1_2_and_3_/a_sermon_on_isaiah_xxvi.htm.

7       The Elizabethan Homily on Obedience 1.10.2.158 can be found at http://www.library.utoronto.ca/utel/ret/homilies/bk1hom10.html. Because the Reformed Church in England had turned from emphasizing Communion as the center of worship to the preaching of the word during the sermon, and few ministers were schooled in the changed doctrines, the government provided printed volumes of ready-made "homilies" for them to use. Titled "Certain Sermons or Homilies Appointed to Be Read in Churches," the first version offered thirty-three separate sermons on different topics. The importance of preaching the word to active listeners, rather than offering a visual drama in a foreign language, made the Homilies central to educating the people in the new religion. Cranmer's first book, printed in 1547, included a sermon on obedience. The expanded "Second Book" by John Jewel, published in 1571, added a new sermon, "An Homily against Disobedience and Willful Rebellion." It makes explicit the danger faced by woman rulers: "What an unworthy matter were it then to make the naughtiest subjects, and most inclined to rebellion and all evil, judges over their Princes . . . specially if they be young in age, women in sex, or gentle and courteous in government, as trusting by their wicked boldness, easily to overthrow their weakness and gentleness, or at the least so to fear the minds of such Princes, that they may have impunity of their mischievous doings." Internet Shakespeare Editions, ed. Michael Best and Rosemary Gaby, https://internetshakespeare.uvic.ca/doc/Homilies_2-21_M/index.html.

8       George Buchanan, *Opera Omnia*, vol. 2 (1725), 399–405; translations from the Latin are my own.

9       Titus Livius, *The History of Rome*, trans. Rev. Canon Roberts (London, 1905), Book I, Chapter 59, http://mcadams.posc.mu.edu/txt/ah/Livy/Livy01.html.

10      Guy, *My Heart Is My Own*, 203, 227.

11      *Elizabeth I: Collected Works*, ed. Marcus, Mueller, and Rose, 116.

12      The details are from Mary's letter to James Beaton, Archbishop of Glasgow, April 2, 1566, in Alexandre Labanoff, ed., *Lettres, instructions et mémoires de Marie Stuart* (London: Dolman, 1844), vol. 1. See also Guy, *My Heart Is My Own*, 596–97.

13      Felix Pryor, *Elizabeth I: Her Life in Letters* (British Library, 2003), 49, https://www.google.com/books/edition/Elizabeth_I/Nre2VCIIUxcC?hl=en&gbpv=1&bsq=March%2015,%201566.

14   *Elizabeth I: Collected Works*, 115. Elizabeth clearly knew that Darnley was unbalanced when she called him "mad."

15   Guy, *My Heart Is My Own*, 350.

16   Melville, *Memoires*, 177.

17   Guy, *My Heart Is My Own*, 275.

18   Labanoff, *Lettres, instructions et mémoires de Marie Stuart*. A digital version of this edition of Mary's letters can be accessed at https://catalog.hathitrust.org/Record/000111814.

19   *CSP, Elizabeth*, Scotland, July 17, 1657.

20   Elizabeth's letter of July 14, 1567. Alan Stewart, *The Cradle King: The Life of James VI and I, the First Monarch of a United Great Britain* (New York: St. Martin's Press, 2003), 27.

## CHAPTER SIX: MARY, QUEEN OF SCOTS

1   The letter itself can be found in *Lettres de Catherine de Médicis*, vol. 3, 143–44. The translation here is mine.

2   *CSP, Scotland*, vol. 2, *1563–69*, item 697. The Queen Mother of France to Elizabeth (May 26, 1568).

3   *Lettres de Catherine de Médicis*, 144.

4   Frieda, *Catherine de Medici*, 60.

5   Marguerite makes Catherine an important member of the select party of courtiers whose salon first proposed the game that becomes the frame for Marguerite's famed *Heptaméron*, a collection of seventy-two stories by design based on recent fact rather than old tales or fictions. Printed in 1558, the collection provides a French challenge to Boccaccio's *Decameron* (or one hundred stories). One story in particular describes a tragic assault on a highborn woman by a longtime friend of her family, thus suggesting that such outrages were not unknown among the French upper class. Some have suggested that Marguerite was writing about her own experience of rape. See Patricia Cholakian, *Rape and Writing in the Heptaméron of Marguerite de Navarre* (Carbondale: Southern Illinois University Press, 1991).

6   Frieda, *Catherine de Medici*, 60.

7   I have followed Guy's sleuthing in *My Heart Is My Own* through the *Calendar of State Papers* in making the argument that Cecil was responsible for Morton's pardon. Cecil, of course, could not be certain that returning Morton to Scotland would *guarantee* Darnley's death, but it turned out to be a useful risk to take.

8   *CSP, Scotland, Elizabeth*, item 458; emphasis added.

9   *Lettres de Catherine de Médicis*, ed. Ferrière, vol. 3, 316.

10   Mary S. Lovell, *Bess of Hardwick: Empire Builder* (New York: W. W. Norton, 2006). Bess made certain that she was never forgotten, taking care to erect her initials on the tops of the six towers built at Hardwick Hall. A distinguished monument of Elizabethan architecture, sporting the six "ES's" for "Elizabeth Shrewsbury," Hardwick Hall would stand as stone and glass testimony to Bess's indomitable will and architectural good taste.

Lovell traces Bess's astute financial dealings beginning, at the death of her second husband William Cavendish, with her fight against Parliament's decision to seize much of her (and her children's) property for debt. Having weathered this storm, with the help of the noblemen from the Grey-Dudley family who were close friends of hers, she went from one financial success to another, prospering by intelligent frugality and wise risk-taking. A third marriage to another well-placed courtier in Princess Elizabeth's entourage, William St. Loe, left her with even more wealth, including valuable ecclesiastical cloth. Her final marriage to George Talbot, Earl of Shrewsbury, brought her the presence of Mary, Queen of Scots, as prisoner in her household.

11    Santina M. Levey, *An Elizabethan Inheritance: The Hardwick Hall Textiles* (Swindon, UK: National Trust, 1998). Levey explains that the needlework at Hardwick Hall was done by a mixed group of embroiderers, servants of both genders, and aristocratic daughters and granddaughters, as well as Bess and Mary Stuart. But the greater part was done by professional male embroiderers, itinerant craftsmen who went from great house to great house working as day laborers. The appliqué work, however, was "always" the purview of professional male embroiderers, including particular persons hired from London who became long-serving members of the household.

12    In *Renaissance Clothing and the Materials of Memory* (Cambridge: Cambridge University Press, 2000), Ann Rosalind Jones and Peter Stallybrass discuss the many ways in which Renaissance Europe was a "cloth culture," where cloth was the most valuable commodity throughout all the realms. The importance of clothing and costume, Jones and Stallybrass point out, can be seen in the fact that a sitter's face would be copied by the artist in one or two sessions with the portraitist; but the sitter's clothes would be sent to the studio, where the artist would painstakingly paint the minute textures of the velvet, the satin, the lace that the sitter had worn. The clothes of the sitter were far more valuable than the portrait the artist painted, which was, after all, only daubs of color applied to a fairly coarse woven backing. Indeed, one could say that the portrait was about the costume perhaps even more than about the sitter.

In the Shakespeare Birthday Lecture at the Folger Library in 1992, Stallybrass floated a provocative theory, that the English stage was enabled in part by the circulation of "old" clothes. Because sumptuary laws made it impossible for anyone who was not noble to wear a nobleman's clothes, the theater, with its actors who could wear such outfits as theatrical costumes with far less risk than other citizens, provided a market for recycling the very expensive suits worn by the sixteenth-century elite. For a more fully developed discussion of the relationship between the theater and discarded clothes, see Chapter 7 of *Renaissance Clothing*, "The Circulation of Clothes and the Making of the English Theater," especially 187–90.

13    In *The Culture of Cloth in Early Modern England* (London: Routledge, 2006), Roze Hentschell argues that wool cloth was a fundamental part of England's identity as a nation, and constructed social as well as individual identity.

14    In medieval portraits of the Virtues, personifications are central, while the individual historical instances are subsidiary. In the Ancient Women hangings the

reverse is true, showing just how precisely balanced these hangings are on the sixteenth-century cusp of the change in allegorical technique from medieval to Renaissance. For discussion of the fabulously vexed question of why personifications of abstractions (Chastity, Holy Church, Reason, Lady Philosophy) should bear the female gender, see Gordon Teskey, *Allegory and Violence* (Ithaca, NY: Cornell University Press, 1997). See also my "Allegory and Female Agency," in Brenda Machovsky, ed., *Thinking Allegory Otherwise* (Stanford, CA: Stanford University Press, 2009).

15  Susan Frye, *Pens and Needles: Women's Textualities in Early Modern England* (Philadelphia: University of Pennsylvania Press, 2010), 46–65. I myself have stood in front of the "Lucretia" hanging impressed by its beauty, but utterly blind to the—in this case—self-portrait of Mary Stuart. Susan Frye discusses Mary's prior use of her mourning garment–wedding dress in a marriage masque she created when she married Darnley, by which she established a lasting identity for herself as the mourning wife–virgin bride. Frye has put color, wit, and clothes on Weiner's idea about inalienable possessions, embedding her overall argument about royal Mary Stuart in an archivally vast analysis of the cooperative (and of course often anonymous) textile art of a multitude of other women of all classes. While Mary's embroidery was not unique, the royal use to which she put it is: in some sense she accomplished for herself, alone and in prison, what Queen Elizabeth I managed with an entire regime arguing for the imperial power of her virginity; Mary's veil forever floats in the air as she is transformed from widow to bride. I am everywhere indebted to Susan Frye for the arguments and details of my discussion of the Marian hangings.

16  An inventory of King James V of Scotland lists a "unicorn" tapestry among the many he owned. Based on this item, Historic Scotland has had the set in New York copied and woven anew (2001) in a sixteenth-century handmade manner. They are presently displayed at Stirling Castle in rooms decorated as they would have appeared during Marie de Guise's residency. The New York series were used as model for the tapestries at Stirling, as there is a so far unproven theory that a set of unicorn tapestries might have been brought by Madeleine de Valois from France on the occasion of her marriage to James V. The French set at the Cluny Museum of the Middle Ages in France, "The Lady and the Unicorn," is a very different series. A recent monograph traces the remarkable number of interpretations of this "allegorical" series: Patrice Foutakis, *De "La Dame à la licorne"* (Paris: Editions L'Harmattan, 2019), showing a brief connection to Scotland.

17  Mark Girouard, *Robert Smythson and the Elizabethan Country House* (New Haven, CT: Yale University Press, 1983). Girouard deals with Hardwick Hall in Chapter 4. Bess was renovating the "Old Hall" until she decided to build an entirely new structure when she was in her early sixties. According to Girouard, Bess liked symmetry, height, light, and squareness, which Smythson supplied with "square towers, great windows with grids of transoms and mullions" recalling the British style of Gothic Perpendicular, "stripped of. . . detail." The style of the Elizabethan prodigy house was "of the greatest daring and beauty." Girouard emphasizes that this style was quite "unique to England" (161–62).

18    Margaret Ellis, "The Hardwick Wall Hangings: An Unusual Collaboration in English Sixteenth-Century Embroidery," *Renaissance Studies* 10 (1996): 280–300. Ellis argues that Mary, with a far better education than Bess's, would have been the partner who thought up the design details for the portraits of the classical women, and their virtues. At her death, Bess owned a mere four books; in Mary's case, the Earl of Shrewsbury complained constantly of the expense of transporting Mary's extensive library. Mary was moved forty-seven times during her captivity (not all, but most of these moves were under the aegis—and at the expense—of the Shrewsburys).

19    Mary may have known Christine de Pizan's treatment of Lucretia. Christine de Pizan's version of the story of Lucrece is contextualized by the simple question, do women enjoy being raped? Christine's Lucrece, like Livy's Lucretia, at first fights off King Tarquin's son's attempt to assault her. When he realizes she will not give in even to save her life, the rapist says that he will lie about her to the world, claiming that he found her making love with a servant. It is to save her honor and not her own life that Lucrece ceases fighting. The next day she summons her family and other aristocrats and tells them what has happened, slaying herself with a sword hidden in her clothes; henceforth women can invoke her as an example of the seriousness with which women will protect their honor. Lucrece's relatives begin a rebellion against the king's autocratic power, and the Republic of Rome is born. More importantly and uniquely in Christine's version, the people institute a law that makes rape a capital crime, and the punishment for it, death. As evidence that Christine's work was known to many elite sixteenth-century women, either in print or manuscript form, see the sleuthing work of Susan Groag Bell, *The Lost Tapestries of the City of Ladies: Christine de Pizan's Renaissance Legacy* (Berkeley: University of California Press, 2004).

## CHAPTER SEVEN: A TRAP FOR TWO QUEENS

1    Stephen Alford, *Burghley: William Cecil at the Court of Elizabeth I* (New Haven, CT: Yale University Press, 2008), 95. Alford, a student of John Guy's, accepts Guy's argument that Cecil was against Mary Stuart from the very beginning but is much more tempered in his judgment about Cecil's motives, stressing Cecil's sense of the strength of England's Catholic enemies and how imperiled Elizabeth's government was. Alford does not posit that Cecil was in any way critical of monarchy, nor that he was aiming to use Mary as a means for placing limitations on that form of government.

2    Mary wrote to Cecil on October 5, 1566, as reported in the *CSP*, vol. 8, *1566–68*: she had "Always had a good opinion of him that he at all times did the duty of a faithful minister in the entertaining of mutual intelligence between her and the Queen of England until the strange dealings of Rokesby. [She] [u]nderstands by Melville's report that he is nothing altered from his former good inclination. [She] [i]s of the same goodwill towards him as she was before."

3    I here rely on John Guy's brilliantly careful scrutiny of the archival evidence. Guy argues that Cecil's clerk, who translated one of Mary's French letters to Bothwell, honestly described it as being written *after* her "ravissement" by him, thus

denying the claim of the lords that it implicated her in a *willing* abduction. Guy argues that Cecil quickly realized that the clerk's honest notation undermined the whole case against Mary's active collusion with Bothwell—which, the lords hoped to prove, demonstrated her fully consensual (and lustful) acceptance of their marriage as well as her prior consent and indeed conspiracy in the murder of her husband. Realizing this danger, Cecil scratched out the clerk's "after" in his own "inimitable scrawl," as Guy terms it, and himself wrote "afore." Although he did not change the verb tenses within the letter itself, it was thus headed "Copie from Sterling *afore* the Ravissement." Cecil's doctoring of the record in this way was, according to Guy, "the most important single word . . . in any document connected with Mary, Queen of Scots" (*My Heart Is My Own*, 414).

4    Guy, *My Heart Is My Own*, 461.

5    Guy, *My Heart Is My Own*, 479.

6    For this statement to Parliament, see *Elizabeth I: Collected Works*, ed. Marcus, Mueller, and Rose, 195.

7    Antonia Fraser, *Mary, Queen of Scots* (1969; rpt. New York: Weidenfeld and Nicolson, 1993), 681.

8    Alford, *Burghley*.

9    Marcus, *Elizabeth I: Collected Works*, 296–97.

10   The letter describing James VI's objections is quoted in Jonathan Goldberg, *James I and the Politics of Literature* (Baltimore: Johns Hopkins University Press, 1983). Goldberg offers a fascinating discussion of James's concern for the relations between poetic and sovereign authority (1–17). Spenser was granted the office of sheriff of the County of Cork sometime after this, so it is clear there was no punishment.

11   Frieda, *Catherine de Medici*, 361.

12   Ferrière, *Lettres de Catherine de Médicis*, 194; my translation.

13   Cited by A. N. McLaren, *Political Culture in the Reign of Elizabeth: Queen and Commonwealth 1558–1585* (Cambridge: Cambridge University Press, 1998), 296. A similar set of political sentiments was gathering in France as well. In *Francogallia* (1573) the Calvinist writer François Hotman examined the history of the French monarchy, concluding that its present absolutism was a far cry from the original form where the monarch was elected by the National Assembly or Parlement. Hotman also denounced the rule of women (Frieda, *Catherine de' Medici*, 295).

## CHAPTER EIGHT: CATHERINE DE' MEDICI

1    Katherine Crawford, *Perilous Performances: Gender and Regency in Early Modern France* (Cambridge: Harvard University Press, 2004), traces the careful maneuverings by which Catherine, at the first *lit de justice* during Charles IX's reign, managed to turn her regency into something more powerful and permanent, summed up in the new title created for her, "La Reine Mère." Crawford also considers Catherine de' Medici's ability to strengthen her regency into something more durable: "Catherine de Medicis and the Performance of Political Motherhood," *Sixteenth Century Journal* 31 (2000): 643–73. The various regencies of

Louise de Savoy for François I were important models, but as a woman who was not a queen (being only a duchess), she never appropriated the king's authority as Catherine did with her sons' powers.

2    The Tuileries, built on land Catherine had had cleared of tileworks and where monarchs from Henri IV to Napoleon III lived, was both a palace and a large garden. Catherine had turned the garden itself into a public space.

3    Marguerite de Valois, *Mémoirs of Marguerite de Valois, Queen of Navarre, Written by Herself: Being Historic Memoirs of the Courts of France and Navarre* (Boston: L. C. Page, 1899), Letter IV, http://www.gutenberg.org/files/3841/3841 -h/3841-h.htm. Margot's *Mémoirs* were not published until 1628, some years after her death in 1615.

4    Pierre de Bourdeille, Abbé de Brantôme, *The Book of the Illustrious Dames* (New York: Versailles Historical Society, 1899), Kindle Edition, loc. 2283. The Salic law was first formulated during the reign of Clovis I, the first king of the Franks, in 507 CE. It organized many rules for the structure of society, including taxation, justice (which included trial by jury—half a century before England recognized the fundamental right of habeas corpus), and fines to be levied in recompense for injury to property. But its most famous stipulation was the law about "agnatic succession," by which women were barred from inheriting any throne or fief, which must, by law, pass to the closest male relative of the ruling man: son, brother, or even a very distant cousin. The line may also not pass *through* a female, but must maintain an unbroken succession from one male successor to the next. In the case of the Valois, the sons of Catherine's favorite daughter Claude de Valois, sister of the three Valois kings, Francis II, Charles IX, and Henri III, and married to Charles duc de Lorraine, could not inherit the throne because the right to the crown could not pass through their mother. François I had inherited his throne when one branch of the Valois died out. Directly descended from Philip III's son, François I took precedence over any Bourbon male because the Bourbon-Navarre family descended from Philip III's *younger* brother and was only in line for the throne after all of François's male grandsons had died. In modern England, some of the same rules apply to succession: Prince Harry Windsor will inherit the throne only if all the children and grandchildren of Prince William, his older brother, have died. However, Charlotte, Prince William's second child, would be able to inherit if her older brother George dies without issue, because there is no Salic law in England preventing female succession; had she been born first, she would have become the direct heir to her father. The law that for centuries made it impossible for females to inherit before males, even before younger brothers (as with Mary and Elizabeth Tudor), was changed only shortly before William was born.

5    https://www.atlasobscura.com/places/catherine-de-medicis-chamber-secrets.

6    A fine examination of the complicated rhetorical effects of Margot's prose in creating her own subjectivity in contrast to Brantôme's idealized portrait is Caroline Trotot, "The *Mémoirs* of Marguerite de Valois: Experience of Knowledge, Knowledge of Experience," *Arts et Savoirs* 6 (2016); https://journals.openedition .org/aes/728.

7    Marguerite de Valois, *Memoirs*, 27.

8        Probably published in Geneva in 1575, only three years after the massacre, the
         pamphlet by an anonymous writer (perhaps Henri Estienne) was the first of a
         vast number of attacks on Catherine for the massacre, and the first to offer the
         theory about Catherine's conspiracy wth Alva. See the *Discours Merveilleux de
         la Vie, actions, et les deportements de Catherine de Médicis la Royne Mère: Auquel
         sont recitez les moyens q'elle a tenu pour ursurper le gouvernemement du royaume
         de France, & reuiner l'estat d'icelui* (Paris, 1649). The argument is that the royal
         tour's stop at Bayonne was not a means to introduce the young king to his realm,
         but a chance for Catherine to speak to Catholic nobles about the planned *"exter-
         mination des Huguenaux"* and to consult with the Duc d'Albe about ways to
         "trouble the realm" (p. 29). Nine editions were published between 1575 and
         1579. https://www.e-rara.ch/bau_1/content/zoom/8652779.

9        Chéruel, *Marie Stuart et Catherine de Médicis*, 27–28.

10       The quotation comes from Brantôme, *The Book of Illustrious Dames* (www.Gutenberg
         .org), https://www.gutenberg.org/files/42515/42515-h/42515-h.htm#page_085.

11       Nancy Goldstone, *The Rival Queens: Catherine de' Medici, Her Daughter Mar-
         guerite de Valois, and the Betrayal That Ignited a Kingdom* (Boston: Little, Brown,
         2015). While Goldstone is often careful to note the moments when Catherine
         appeared to be on her daughter's side in the endemic eruptions at the Valois court
         and the subsequent violent wars, as her title suggests she sees the major issue to
         be a rivalry between mother and daughter. The fundamental tragedy of Margot's
         life, however, was the conflict between her brothers, exacerbated by Catherine de'
         Medici's marked preference for her third son, Henri III. Margot's barrenness also
         denied her one of the safeguards against women's vulnerability, just as her moth-
         er's late-appearing fecundity had saved her marriage and also her place in society.
         The propaganda campaign against Margot's supposedly monstrous licentious-
         ness began in earnest when it became clear that her husband Henri de Navarre,
         who, after Henri III died in 1589 and he finally converted from Protestantism to
         Catholicism, became King Henri IV of France. As king he badly needed an heir.
         The result was the annulment ten years later of their Catholic marriage, granted
         by the pope in 1599, due to Margot's barrenness. So long as her husband settled
         on her sufficient support for her to continue her privileged life in Paris, Margot
         made no problems with the annulment.When Henri married Marie de' Medici, a
         quite distant relation of her mother, Margot happily attended their wedding and
         became something of a confidante of the new queen. The marriage between Mar-
         guerite de Valois and Henri de Navarre, which had begun in such catastrophic
         bloodshed, in the end turned into an amicable friendship.

12       Marcus, *Collected Works*, 116.

13       Philip Sidney, "Sir Philip Sidney to Queen Elizabeth, Anno 1580, Dissuading
         her from Marrying the Duke of Anjou," http://www.luminarium.org/editions/
         sidneyeliza.htm.

14       Susan Doran, *Monarchy and Matrimony: The Courtships of Elizabeth I* (London:
         Routledge, 2002); Kindle Edition. Doran points out that "there is little sign
         of the elusiveness and prevarication with which she is said to have dazzled and
         bewildered her suitors" (217); she was far more "straightforward and direct with

those who wooed her." While Elizabeth herself had of course said she would
never marry, Doran notes that the creation of her public image of chastity was in
part "imposed upon her by writers, painters and their patrons during the Anjou
matrimonial negotiations."

15    Marcus, *Elizabeth I: Collected Works*, 261.

## CHAPTER NINE: EIGHT VALOIS TAPESTRIES

1    One of the first scholars to study the tapestries in detail, Frances Yates was a
twentieth-century art historian who understood the tapestries to be serious
works of high Renaissance art; while she argued that Catherine had not commissioned their creation, she did acknowledge the great artistry that went into
Catherine's designs for the pageants (*The Valois Tapestries*). Following earlier
work by Uffizi curators, Pascal François Bertrand's early twenty-first-century
study puts Catherine firmly in charge of the creation of the tapestries. "A New
Method of Interpreting the Valois Tapestries, Through a History of Catherine
de Médicis," *Studies in the Decorative Arts* 14, no. 1 (2006–7): 27–52, http://
www.jstor.org/stable/40663287.

2    Sheila Ffolliott, "Catherine de' Medici as Artemisia: Figuring the Powerful
Widow," in *Rewriting the Renaissance: The Discourses of Sexual Difference in Early
Modern Europe*, ed. M. Ferguson, M. Quilligan, and N. J. Vickers (Chicago:
University of Chicago Press, 1986), 227–41. Ffolliott traces the indebtedness
of the design of this Valois tapestry to a drawing by Antoine Caron for the narrative of *Artemisia* by Nicholas Houel, written for Catherine. Ffolliott long ago
brilliantly pointed out the important placement of the figure of Catherine, copying Caron's off-center placement of Artemisia in the Caron drawing. I am also
indebted to Ffolliott for pointing out the fountain's joke on Diane de Poitiers.

3    For a diametrically opposed argument about the meaning of the Valois tapestries, see Lisa Jardine and Jeremy Brotton, *Global Interests: Renaissance Art
Between East and West* (Ithaca, NY: Cornell University Press, 2000). Jardine and
Brotton locate the significance of the Valois panels in light of the grand tradition
of tapestries celebrating heroic military battles between Renaissance European
armies and an equally grand and related tradition of prototypic battles between
Roman armies and Rome's non-European adversaries. They roundly reject Frances Yates's argument that the Valois tapestries depict a peaceful France where
Huguenot and Catholic forces are in harmony and religious toleration is the
theme of the day. Instead they understand, for example, that the costumed Turks
in the "Tournament" and other panels are representations of France's internal
infidels, the Huguenots, and that the battles displayed are therefore images of
actual violence aimed at military intimidation, thus fulfilling the traditional purpose of the majority of earlier tapestry series (122–31). While they praise the level
of artistry in the Valois tapestries, they do ignore Catherine's unarmed, pleasure-
seeking, and slyly ubiquitous presence in the tapestries and the fact that, while
a shield has fallen in the foreground of the battle represented in "Tournament,"
there are no bodies fallen to the ground nor indeed any weapons making visible
wounds. This bloodless treatment is quite different from wounded soldiers prone

on the ground, some clearly dying, vividly detailed in earlier tapestry series that depict the effects of war's violence on human bodies.

4    For a useful review of an exhibition at the Uffizi in 2008 of the Artemisia tapestries, see "In Praise of Powerful Women," *The Economist*, October 30, 2008, https://www.economist.com/books-and-arts/2008/10/30/in-praise-of-powerful -women. Although the unsigned review concerns the tapestry series Marie commissioned from Peter Paul Rubens, an uncanny remark ending the essay calls attention to the inalienable function of tapestry art: "Maria de' Medici is said to have had few gifts for ruling but she certainly had a genius for inheritance planning." Catherine de' Medici, her distant relative, had both in abundance— possibly because for a woman ruler, they are connected.

5    For an archivally rich reading of the various interlinked festivals for the Polish ambassadors, see Ewa Kociszewska, "War and Seduction in Cybele's Garden: Contextualizing the *Ballet des Polonais*," *Renaissance Quarterly* 65, no. 3 (2012): 809–63, www.jstor.org/stable/10.1086/668302. Avoiding any comment about religious reconciliation, the events focused on the ballet's ability to mime martial order in the service of a new Valois empire, nurtured by a dominant Trojan-Roman Cybele, figured as Catherine de' Medici, who indeed served as regent while Henri was king in Poland (and also while he was taking an entirely too leisurely return trip back to France through the pleasure gardens of Italy). Catherine as the mother goddess Cybele had been celebrated in Ronsard's ill-timed epic, *La Franciade*, published the month after the St. Bartholomew's Day Massacre. Ronsard never finished the poem, but clearly Catherine retained an interest in seeing herself figured as Cybele.

6    In "Woven Bloodlines," Ewa Kociszewska argues that Catherine may have planned from the very beginning to give the tapestries to Christina to take with her to whatever court she ultimately married into. A portrait of Christina is notably absent from the tapestries even though she was often shown very prominently in contemporaneous paintings of the Valois court. Kociszewska suggests this very absence may indicate that Christina was always slated to inherit the tapestries, it being indecorous for a young bride to display her own portrait, although displaying portraits of her family members would have been entirely appropriate as a way to demonstrate the excellence of her lineage. The central importance of Christina of Lorraine to the conception of the tapestries' designs may also help to explain the prominence of the hated de Guise family members among the portraits, for the de Guises (however much Catherine mistrusted them) were a cadet branch of the august Lorraine family, who claimed descent from Charlemagne. On the basis of these connections, a portrait of James VI of Scotland, the son of Mary Stuart and a grandson of Marie de Guise, also appears in the tapestry series, even though he never visited France. The tapestries celebrate not only the Valois but also the specific blend of Christina's heritage. The tapestries are an almost textbook definition of what makes a textile an "inalienable possession."

7    Charles de Guise, the Duke of Mayenne, a member of the Catholic League, had taken possession of Catherine's house and so Christina had to apply to have him

vacate. The seizure of the house by a de Guise reveals how far the Valois had fallen. See Frieda, *Catherine de Medici*, 383.

8       Jean Dietz Moss, "Galileo's Letter to Christina: Some Rhetorical Considerations," *Renaissance Quarterly* 36, no. 4 (Winter 1983): 547–76, http://www.jstor.org/stable/2860733.

## CHAPTER TEN: PHILIP II

1       Margaret Greer, Walter Mignolo, and Maureen Quilligan, eds., *Rereading the Black Legend: The Discourses of Religious and Racial Difference in the Renaissance Empires* (Chicago: Chicago University Press, 2007), introduction. This "black" legend may well have been begun by the most influential Renaissance collection of visual images depicting European "discoveries" of the "New World" in the Americas—and also the old worlds of Africa and Asia. Theodor de Bry and others published a lavishly illustrated thirteen-volume collection of European travelers' voyages to America, Africa, and Asia, titled *Collectiones peregrinationum in Indiam orientalem et Indiam occidentalem, XIII partibus comprehenso a Theodoro, Joan-Theodoro de Bry, et a Matheo Merian publicatae* (Frankfurt, 1590–1634). The de Brys' collection, taken all together, not only showed Spanish and Portuguese treatment of American natives in worse lights than the Anglophone North American colonization, it also tended to strip old-world cultures (China and India) of their clear achievement of civilization. Chinese and Indian elite figures were endowed with the feathers of unlettered Algonquin chiefs and were often shown wearing far less clothing than they would normally have worn, and which had in fact been pictured in the original drawings from which the de Brys made their engravings. For a collection of essays about these seminal volumes, see Maureen Quilligan, ed., "Theodor de Bry's Voyages to the Old and New Worlds," *Journal of Medieval and Early Modern Studies* 41 (2011).

2       David E. Stannard, *American Holocaust: The Conquest of the New World* (Oxford: Oxford University Press, 1993), tracks the staggering collapse of population in the Americas with the arrival of Europeans and their germs and violence. At least 90 percent of the population died after contact; that is three times more than the number of Europeans slain by the bubonic plague, which depleted the European population by a mere 30 percent. Not all deaths were due to disease, as Europeans also engaged in wholesale population clearance, or what we might call genocide.

3       Called "casta" paintings, they usually depict the generations of a single family, but some reveal, as if in graphic terms, the variations throughout the color spectrum. They are for the most part Mexican eighteenth-century paintings, revealing idealized images of a diverse and prosperous society. See Ilona Katzew, *Casta Painting: Images of Race in Eighteenth-Century Mexico* (New Haven, CT: Yale University Press, 2005).

4       In 2012 Mexico City demographics were mestizo (Amerindian-Spanish), 62 percent; predominantly Amerindian, 21 percent; "pure" Amerindian, 7 percent; other (mostly European), 10 percent (https://www.worldatlas.com/articles

/largest-ethnic-groups-in-mexico.html). In contrast, Native Americans, mixed or pure blooded, comprise a little over 2 percent of the current population of the United States (https://en.wikipedia.org/wiki/Modern_social_statistics_of_Native_Americans).

5    Geoffrey Parker, *Imprudent King: A New Life of Philip II* (New Haven, CT: Yale University Press, 2014), 239. As his title suggests, Parker's main point is that Philip was not as prudent as many historians have celebrated him for being, because his very prudence, his attention to detail and his concern to keep all things in his personal control, made him lose sight of the more important chores to which he should have attended, not delegating to others the less important. Instead he micromanaged everything, assuming that God would supply a miracle should he make a mistake.

6    In "Of Books, Popes, and *Huaca*," an essay in *Rereading the Black Legend*, Gonzalo Lamana analyzes the many different retellings of this famous moment between Atahualpa and Pizarro, a signal pivot point in Spanish colonial history.

7    Parker, *Imprudent King*, 239. Of course, Protestant evangelical religions have made some inroads into this historical hegemony, South America remaining 70 percent Catholic, while now 19 percent of Brazil and 40 percent of Central America embrace Protestantism.

8    Henry Kamen, *The Escorial: Art and Power in the Renaissance* (New Haven, CT: Yale University Press, 2010).

9    Parker, *Imprudent King*, 143. In contrast, the immense stones of the Inca Empire, still standing after centuries of earthquakes along the "rim of fire" on the Pacific coast of South America, are honed to the depth of a micrometer. It is impossible to slip the smallest penknife between the slabs. Peruvian silver mines paid for much of Spain's Renaissance splendor; one wonders if Philip knew about the precision of Inca building techniques.

10   Susan Ronald, *Queen Elizabeth I, Her Pirate Adventurers, and the Dawn of Empire* (New York: HarperCollins, 2019).

11   David Howarth, *The Voyage of the Armada: The Spanish Story* (New York: Penguin, 1982), 110.

12   Parker, *Imprudent King*, 362.

13   Parker, *Imprudent King*, 361–62.

14   Gristwood, *Elizabeth and Leicester*, 328.

15   Gristwood, *Elizabeth and Leicester*, 334.

16   Susan Frye, "The Myth of Elizabeth at Tilbury," *Sixteenth Century Journal* 23, no. 1 (1992): 95–114, doi:10.2307/2542066. Frye cautions scholars about the foggy provenance of the speech. I quote it here in its canonical form because it has become an indelible part of the story, and it is at least certain that Elizabeth made a rousing speech to her soldiers on that day, even if we do not have the exact words she said.

## EPILOGUE

1    Janet Arnold, *Queen Elizabeth's Wardrobe Unlock'd: The Inventories of the Wardrobe prepared in Juy 1600, edited from Stowe MS 557 in the British Library, MS LR*

*1/21 in the Public Records Office, London, and MS V.b.72 in the Folger Shakespeare Library, Washington, DC* (Leeds: Maney and Sons, 1988), 94.

2    A picture of the cloth is held by Bridgeman Images, number CH1767229: "Detail of an important skirt or petticoat of crimson silk said to have been embroidered by Mary, Queen of Scots for Queen Elizabeth I while she was captive at Hardwick (silk)." https://www.bridgemanimages.us/en-US/asset/1767229. Mary never lived at Hardwick, having died before Bess built it. But the Marian hangings are still there.

3    Fraser, *Mary, Queen of Scots*, 680–81. Fraser cites *The letter books of Sir Amias Paulet, Keeper of Mary, Queen of Scots*, ed. John Morris (London, 1874). The official report does not mention the red undergarments, but the French reports do; Morris gives a list of them (378). Morris tracks the inventories of Mary's clothes before and after the execution. A reddish brown dress is mentioned in the first but is missing in the second.

4    Jones and Stallybrass, *Renaissance Clothing and the Materials of Memory*. Costume was fundamental to Renaissance ideals of social identity. Polonius was not lying when he said, "Apparel oft proclaims the man."

5    Marcus, *Elizabeth I: Collected Works*, 347.

# BIBLIOGRAPHY

༚

## PRIMARY SOURCES

d'Angoulême, Marguerite. *Le Miroir de l'Âme Pécheresse*. Paris, 1533.

Anonymous (possibly Henri Estienne). *Discours Merveilleux de la Vie, actions, et les deportements de Catherine de Médicis, Royne Mère: Auquel sont recitez les moyens q'elle a tenu pour vsurper le gouvernemement du royaume de France et ruiner l'estate d'icelluy.* Paris, 1649. https://www.google.com/books/edition/Discours_merveilleux_de_la _vie_actions.

Arnold, Janet. *Queen Elizabeth's Wardrobe Unlock'd: The Inventories of the Wardrobe prepared in July 1600, edited from Stowe MS 557 in the British Library, MS LR 1/21 in the Public Records Office, London, and MS V.b.72 in the Folger Shakespeare Library, Washington, DC.* Leeds: Maney and Sons, 1988.

de Brantôme, Pierre de Bourdeille, Abbé. *The Book of Illustrious Dames.* New York: Versailles Historical Society, 1899. Project Gutenberg. https://www.gutenberg.org/ files/42515/42515-h/42515-h.htm#page_085.

de Bry, Theodor. *Collectiones peregrinatiorum in Indiam orientalem et Indiam occidentalem, XIII partibus comprehenso a Theodoro, Joan-Theodoro de Bry, et a Matheo Merian publicatae.* Frankfurt, 1590–1634.

Buchanan, George. *Georgii Buchanani Opera omnia: historica, chronologica, juridica, politica, satyrica & poetica.* Netherlands: Langerak, 1725. https://www.google.com/ books/edition/Georgii_Buchanani_Opera_omnia/dFYJzQEACAAJ?hl=en.

*Calendar of State Papers (CSP).* All citations of *CSP* are to British History Online, http//:www.british-history.ac.uk/cal-state-papers.

*CSP Spain*, vol. 11: *1553–58,* ed. Royall Tyler. London, 1916.

*CSP Spain (Simancas),* vol 1: *1558–67,* ed. Martin Hume. London, 1892. British History Online. http://www.british-history.ac.uk/cal-state-papers/simancas/vol1.

*CSP Venice*, vol. 7: *1558–80,* ed. Rawdon Brown and G. Cavendish Bentinck. London, 1890.

Camden, William. *Annals, or, the historie of the most renovvned and victorious princesse Elizabeth, late queen of England containing all the important and remarkable passages of state both at home and abroad, during her long and prosperous reigne. VVritten in Latin by the learned mr. William Camden. translated into english by R.N. gent. together with divers additions of the authors never before published London.* Printed by Thomas Harper for Benjamin Fisher, 1641. https://eebo.chadwyck.com/.

Castelnau, Michel de. *Mémoires de messire Michel de Castelnau, seigneur de Mauvissière.* Paris: 1823. Volume 2 of Alexandre Teulet, *Relations politiques de la France et de l'Espagne avec l'Écosse.* Paris: Librarie de la Societé Historie, 1862. https://books .google.com/books?id=fPk9AAAAcAAJ&q=Castelnau.

Cavendish, George. *The negotiations of Thomas Woolsey, the great Cardinall of England containing his life and death, viz. (1) the originall of his promotion, (2) the continuance in his magnificence, (3) his fall, death, and buriall / composed by one of his owne servants, being his gentleman-vsher.* London: William Sheares, 1641. Early English books online, eebo.chadwyck.com.

Elizabeth I, Queen of England. *Elizabeth I: The Collected Works*, ed. Leah Marcus, Janel Mueller, and Mary Beth Rose. Chicago: Chicago University Press, 2002.

———. *The Glass of the Synful Soul.* MS Cherry 36. Bodleian Library, Oxford.

———. *British and Irish Women's Letters 1500–1950; Letters of Elizabeth I and James VI of Scotland*, ed. John Bruce. London, 1849. https://bwld-alexanderstreet-com.

*Holingshed's Chronicles. Mary's Guildhall Speech.* https://thehistoryofengland.co.uk /resource/speech-of-mary-i-1554/.

Knox, John. *The Works of John Knox*, ed. David Laing. Woodrow Society, 1846–64.

———. *John Knox: On Rebellion*, ed. Roger A. Mason. Cambridge: Cambridge University Press, 1994.

Kunz, George Frederick. *The Book of the Pearl: The History, Art, Science and Industry of the Queen of Gems.* 1908. Kindle Edition.

Labanoff, Alexandre ed. *Lettres, instructions et mémoires de Marie Stuart.* London: Dolman, 1844. https://catalog.hathitrust.org/Record/000111814.

Mary I of England. *Last Will and Testament.* https://tudorhistory.org/primary/will .html.

Medici, Catherine de'. *Lettres de Catherine de Médicis*, vol. 3, ed. Hector de la Ferrière. Paris: Imprimerie Nationale, 1880–1943.

Melville, James. *The Memoires of Sir James Melvil of Hal-hill, containing an impartial account of the most remarkable affairs of state during the last age, not mention'd by other historians: more particularly relating to the Kingdoms of England and Scotland, under the reigns of Queen Elizabeth, Mary, Queen of Scots, and King James. In all which transactions the author was personally and publicly concerned.* London, 1683. https://play.google.com/books/reader?id=yWpkAAAAMAAJ&hl=en&pg=GBS .PA29.

Michelet, Jules. *L'Histoire de France*, vol. 12. Paris, 1876. Project Gutenberg, https:// www.gutenberg.org/files/39335/39335-h/39335-h.htm.

Parr, Katherine [Catherine], Queen of England. *Katherine Parr: Complete Works and Correspondence*, ed. Janel Mueller. Chicago: Chicago University Press, 2011.

Paulet, Amias. *The letter books of Sir Amias Paulet, Keeper of Mary, Queen of Scots*, ed. John Morris. London, 1874.

Poujoulat, Jean Joseph François. *Nouvelle collection des mémoires pour servir à l'histoire de France.* Paris: Guyot Frères, 1851.

Ronsard, Pierre de. *Elegies, Mascarades et Bergerie (1565). Oeuvres Complètes*, vol. 13, ed. Paul Laumonier. Paris: Didier, 1948.

Shakespeare, William. *All Is True, Henry VIII. The Norton Shakespeare*, ed. Stephen Greenblatt, Walter Cohen, Jean E. Howard, and Katharine Eisaman Maus. New York: W. W. Norton, 1997.

Sidney, Philip. "Sir Philip Sidney to Queen Elizabeth, Anno 1580, Dissuading her from Marrying the Duke of Anjou." http://www.luminarium.org/editions/sidneyeliza.htm.

Starkey, David, ed. *The Inventory of King Henry VIII: The Transcript*. London: Harvey Miller Publishers for the Society of Antiquaries, 1998.

Teulet, Alexandre. *Relations politiques de la France et de l'Espagne avec l'Écosse*. Paris: Librarie de la Société Histoire, 1862.

Valois, Marguerite de. *Memoirs of Marguerite de Valois, Queen of Navarre, Written by Herself: Being Historic Memoirs of the Courts of France and Navarre*. Boston: L. C. Page, 1899.


## SECONDARY SOURCES

Alford, Stephen. *Burghley: William Cecil at the Court of Elizabeth I*. New Haven, CT: Yale University Press, 2008.

Andrews, Angela Magnotti. "A Tale of Two Pearls: Tracing La Peregrina and Mary Tudor's Pearl Through Portraits." N.d. https://eragem.com/news/a-tale-of-two -pearls-tracing-la-peregrina-mary-tudors-pearl-through-portraits/.

Bell, Susan Groag. *The Lost Tapestries of the City of Ladies: Christine de Pizan's Renaissance Legacy*. Berkeley: University of California Press, 2004. http://www.gutenberg .org/files/3841/3841-h/3841-h.htm.

Bertrand, Pascal François. "A New Method of Interpreting the Valois Tapestries, Through a History of Catherine de Médicis." *Studies in the Decorative Arts* 14, no. 1 (2006–7): 27–52. http://www.jstor.org/stable/40663287.

Chamberlin, Frederick. *Elizabeth and Leycester*. New York: Dodd, Mead, 1939. https:// babel.hathitrust.org/cgi/pt?id=inu.32000001826165&view=1up&seq=52&q1=Hang %20a%20dog.

Chéruel, Adolphe. *Marie Stuart et Catherine de Médicis: Étude historique sur les relations de la France et de l'Écosse dans la seconde moitié du 16e siècle*. Paris, 1858.

Cholakian, Patricia. *Rape and Writing in the Heptaméron of Marguerite de Navarre*. Carbondale: Southern Illinois University Press, 1991.

Cleland, Elizabeth, and Marjorie E. Wieseman. *Renaissance Splendor: Catherine de' Medici's Valois Tapestries*. Cleveland Museum of Art, Yale University Press, 2018.

Collins, A. Jefferies, ed. *Jewels and Plate of Queen Elizabeth I: The Inventory of 1574*. London: British Museum, 1955.

Crawford, Katherine. "Catherine de Médicis and the Performance of Political Motherhood." *Sixteenth Century Journal* 31 (2000): 643–73.

———. *Perilous Performances: Gender and Regency in Early Modern France*. Cambridge, MA: Harvard University Press, 2004.

Doran, Susan. "Elizabeth I and Catherine de' Medici." In *"The Contending Kingdoms": France and England 1420–1700*, ed. Glenn Richardson. London: Routledge, 2008. Kindle Edition.

———. *Monarchy and Matrimony: The Courtships of Elizabeth I.* London: Routledge, 2002. Kindle Edition.

Dunn, Jane. *Elizabeth and Mary: Cousins, Rivals, Queens.* New York: Vintage, 2007. Kindle Edition.

Ellis, Margaret. "The Hardwick Wall Hangings: An Unusual Collaboration in English Sixteenth-Century Embroidery." *Renaissance Studies* 10 (1996): 280–300. https://www.jstor.org/stable/24412272?seq=1.

Ferguson, Margaret, Maureen Quilligan, and Nancy Vickers, eds. *Rewriting the Renaissance: The Discourses of Sexual Difference in Early Modern Europe.* Chicago: University of Chicago Press, 1986.

Ffolliott, Sheila. "Catherine de' Medici as Artemisia: Figuring the Powerful Widow." In Margaret Ferguson, Maureen Quilligan, and Nancy Vickers, eds., *Rewriting the Renaissance: The Discourses of Sexual Difference in Early Modern Europe.* Chicago: Chicago University Press, 1986.

Foutakis, Patrice. *De La Dame à La Licorne.* Editions Hartmattan, 2019.

Fraser, Antonia. *Mary, Queen of Scots.* 1969; rpt. London: Weidenfeld and Nicolson, 1993.

Frieda, Leonie. *Catherine de Medici: Renaissance Queen of France.* New York: Fourth Estate, 2003.

Froude, James Anthony. *History of England from the Fall of Wolsey to the Death of Elizabeth*, vol. 8. New York: Scribner and Sons, 1856. https://www.google.com/books/edition/History_of_England_from_the_Fall_of_Wols/AWMNAAAAIAAJ?hl=en._

Frye, Susan. "The Myth of Elizabeth at Tilbury." *Sixteenth Century Journal* 23, no. 1 (1992): 95–114.

———. *Pens and Needles: Women's Textualities in Early Modern England.* Philadelphia: University of Pennsylvania Press, 2010.

Girouard, Mark. *Robert Smythson and the Elizabethan Country House.* New Haven, CT: Yale University Press, 1983.

Goldberg, Jonathan. *James I and the Politics of Literature.* Baltimore: Johns Hopkins University Press, 1983.

Goldstone, Nancy. *Daughters of the Winter Queen: Four Remarkable Sisters, the Crown of Bohemia, and the Enduring Legacy of Mary, Queen of Scots.* New York: Little, Brown, 2018.

———. *The Rival Queens: Catherine de' Medici, Her Daughter Marguerite de Valois, and the Betrayal That Ignited a Kingdom.* Boston: Little, Brown, 2015.

Goody, Jack. *The Development of the Family and Marriage in Europe.* Cambridge: Cambridge University Press, 1983.

Greer, Margaret, Walter Mignolo, and Maureen Quilligan, eds. *Rereading the Black Legend: The Discourses of Religious and Racial Difference in The Renaissance Empires.* Chicago: Chicago University Press, 2007.

Gristwood, Sarah. *Elizabeth and Leicester: Power, Passion, Politics.* London: Penguin Press, 2012.

———. *Game of Queens: The Women Who Made Sixteenth-Century Europe.* New York: Basic Books, 2016.

Gronau, Georg. "Titian's Portraits of the Empress Isabella." *Burlington Magazine* 2 (August 1903): 281–85.

Guy, John. *My Heart Is My Own: The Life of Mary, Queen of Scots.* London: Fourth Estate, 2004. (Also published in US as *Mary, Queen of Scots: The True Life of Mary Stuart.* New York: Houghton Mifflin, 2004.)

Hentschell, Roze. *The Culture of Cloth in Early Modern England.* London: Routledge, 2006.

Howarth, David. *The Voyage of the Armada: The Spanish Story.* New York: Viking, 1981.

Hume, David. *The History of England, under the House of Tudor. Comprehending the reigns of K. Henry VII. K. Henry VIII. K Edward VI. Q. Mary, and Q. Elizabeth.* London, 1759.

Jardine, Lisa, and Jeremy Brotton. *Global Interests: Renaissance Art Between East and West.* Ithaca, NY: Cornell University Press, 2000.

Jones, Ann Rosalind, and Peter Stallybrass. *Renaissance Clothing and the Materials of Memory.* Cambridge: Cambridge University Press, 2000.

Kamen, Henry. *The Escorial: Art and Power in the Renaissance.* New Haven, CT: Yale University Press, 2010.

Katzew, Ilona. *Casta Painting: Images of Race in Eighteenth-Century Mexico.* New Haven, CT: Yale University Press, 2005.

Kociszewska, Ewa. "War and Seduction in Cybele's Garden: Contextualizing the *Ballet des Polonais.*" *Renaissance Quarterly* 65 (2012): 809–63.

———. "Woven Bloodlines: The Valois Tapestries in the Trousseau of Christine de Lorraine, Grand Duchess of Tuscany." *Artibus et Historiae* 73 ( 2016): 335–63.

Lamana, Gonzalo. "Of Books, Popes, and *Huaca.*" In Margaret Greer, Walter Mignolo, and Maureen Quilligan, eds., *Rereading the Black Legend.* Chicago: Chicago University Press, 1986.

Levey, Santina M. *An Elizabethan Inheritance: The Hardwick Hall Textiles.* Swindon, UK: National Trust, 1998.

Lovell, Mary S. *Bess of Hardwick: Empire Builder.* New York: W. W. Norton, 2006.

Mauss, Marcel. *The Gift: The Form and Reason for Exchange in Archaic Societies.* 1925; rpt. New York: W. W. Norton, 2000.

McLaren, A. N. *Political Culture in the Reign of Elizabeth: Queen and Commonwealth 1558–1585.* Cambridge: Cambridge University Press, l998.

Montrose, Louis. *The Subject of Elizabeth: Authority, Gender, and Representation.* Chicago: Chicago University Press, 2006.

Moss, Jean Dietz. "Galileo's Letter to Christina: Some Rhetorical Considerations." *Renaissance Quarterly* 36, no. 4 (Winter 1983): 547–76, http://www.jstor.org/stable /2860733.

Parker, Geoffrey. *Emperor: A New Life of Charles V.* New Haven, CT: Yale University Press, 2019.

———. *Imprudent King: A New Life of Philip II.* New Haven, CT: Yale University Press, 2014.

Phillips, James Emerson. *Images of a Queen: Mary Stuart in Sixteenth-Century Literature.* Berkeley: University of California Press, 1964.

Porter, Linda. *The Myth of "Bloody Mary": A Biography of Queen Mary I of England.* New York: St. Martin's Press, 2009, print and Kindle Edition.

Quilligan, Maureen. "Allegory and Female Agency." In *Thinking Allegory Otherwise*, ed. Brenda Machovsky. Stanford, CA: Stanford University Press, 2009.

———. "Elizabeth's Embroidery." *Shakespeare Studies* 28 (2000): 208–14.

———. *Incest and Agency in Elizabeth's England.* Philadelphia: University of Pennsylvania Press, 2005.

———, ed. "Theodor de Bry's Voyages to Old and New Worlds." *Journal of Medieval and Early Modern Studies* 41 (2011).

Ronald, Susan. *Queen Elizabeth I, Her Pirate Adventurers, and the Dawn of Empire.* New York: HarperCollins, 2019.

Scher, S. K., ed. *The Currency of Fame: Portrait Medals of the Renaissance.* New York: Thames and Hudson, 1994.

Smith, M. C. "Ronsard and Queen Elizabeth I." *Bibliothèque d'Humanisme et Renaissance* 29 (1967): 93–119. https://www.jstor.org/stable/41610251.

Stannard, David E. *American Holocaust: The Conquest of the New World.* Oxford: Oxford University Press, 1993.

Stewart, Alan. *The Cradle King: The Life of James VI and I, the First Monarch of a United Great Britain.* New York: St. Martin's Press, 2003.

Strong, Roy. *Gloriana: The Portraits of Elizabeth I.* New York: Thames and Hudson, 1987.

Sturm-Scott, Virginia, and Sarah Maddox. *Performance, Politics, and Poetry on the Queen's Day.* Farnham, UK: Ashgate, 2007.

Sutherland, N. M. "Catherine de Medici: The Legend of the Wicked Italian Queen." *Sixteenth Century Journal* 9 (1978): 45–56.

Teskey, Gordon. *Allegory and Violence.* Ithaca, NY: Cornell University Press, 1997.

Trotot, Caroline. "The *Memoirs* of Marguerite de Valois: Experience of Knowledge, Knowledge of Experience." Trans. Colin Keaveney. *Arts et Savoirs* 6 (2016). https://journals.openedition.org/aes/728.

Weiner, Annette. *Inalienable Possessions: The Paradox of Keeping-While-Giving.* Berkeley: University of California Press, 1992.

Weir, Alison. *Elizabeth, the Queen.* New York: Vintage, 2009.

———. *Mary Boleyn: The Mistress of Kings.* New York: Random House, 2011. Kindle Edition.

Williams, Kate. *The Betrayal of Mary, Queen of Scots: Elizabeth and Her Greatest Rival.* New York: Hutchinson, 2018. Apple iBooks.

Yates, Frances. *The Valois Tapestries.* London: Courtauld Institute, 1959.

Zarin, Cynthia. "Teen Queen: The Search for Lady Jane Grey." *New Yorker*, October 15, 2007.

# INDEX

❧

# ABOUT THE AUTHOR

꙲

Maureen Quilligan trained as a scholar of Renaissance culture at the University of California, Berkeley, Harvard University, and one year as a fellow at Linacre College, University of Oxford. She is R. Florence Brinkley Professor of English Emerita at Duke University; before Duke, she taught at Yale University and the University of Pennsylvania. After retiring from Duke, she spent a final semester as the M. H. Abrams Distinguished Visiting Professor at Cornell University. She has received a number of grants from such distinguished institutions as Harvard University, Yale University, the Guggenheim Foundation, and the American Council for Learned Societies (ACLS), and has served as judge on a number of prize panels, including the Christian Gauss award, the National Book Award for nonfiction, and the ACLS board. She also served as Chair of the Duke English Department from 2000–2005. She is the author of four monographs, *The Language of Allegory* (1979), *Milton's Spenser* (1983), *The Allegory of Female Authority* (1991), and *Incest and Agency in Elizabeth's England* (2005). She has also been coeditor of three important collections of essays, *Rewriting the Renaissance: the Discourses of Sexual Difference in Early Modern Europe* (1986), *Subject and Object in Renaissance Culture* (1996), and *Rereading the Black Legend: The Discourses of Racial and Religious Differences in the Renaissance Empires* (2008). She has been working on *When Women Ruled the World* since 1984.